IRISH
PEACOCK

SCARLET
MARQUESS

Merlin Holland is Oscar Wilde's grandson. He is a journal-ist and has been researching the life of his grandfather for the last twenty years. Fourth Estate also publish *The Wilde Album* by Merlin Holland and *The Complete Letters of Oscar Wilde*, edited by Merlin Holland and Rupert Hart-Davis.

For more information on Merlin Holland, please visit www.4thestate.com/merlinholland

IRISH PEACOCK & SCARLET MARQUESS

THE REAL TRIAL OF
OSCAR WILDE

MERLIN HOLLAND

FOREWORD BY SIR JOHN MORTIMER

FOURTH ESTATE · *London* and *New York*

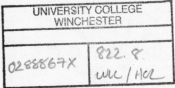
This paperback edition first published in 2004
First published in Great Britain in 2003 by
Fourth Estate
A Division of HarperCollins*Publishers*
77–85 Fulham Palace Road,
London W6 8JB
www.4thestate.com

1 3 5 7 9 10 8 6 4 2

A catalogue record for this book is
available from the British Library

ISBN 0-00-715419-4

Typeset by Rowland Phototypesetting Ltd,
Bury St Edmunds, Suffolk
Printed in Great Britain by
Clays Ltd, St Ives plc

To John in gratitude and affection

CONTENTS

Thursday Morning 4th April

Thursday Afternoon 4th April

Friday Morning 5th April

LIST OF ILLUSTRATIONS

Illustration Credits:
British Library; 8, 10
Pierpont Morgan Library, New York: 7
Public Record Office, Kew: 1
June Radford: 9
The remainder are from the author's own collection

FOREWORD

Libel actions are meant to be cases for re-establishing reputations, confounding malicious gossip and allowing the litigant to emerge in a state of unblemished purity. Anyone contemplating such litigation should be warned that those who start libel actions often emerge with their reputations in tatters and, on three notable occasions, end up in prison. Jonathan Aitken, Jeffrey Archer and, of course, most famous of them all, Oscar Wilde found the entrance to the libel court a direct path to gaol.

Indeed, the steps that led from Wilde's charge against the Marquess of Queensberry to hard labour have a sickening inevitability about them. Wilde's conduct through the three trials that followed seems like a deliberate exercise in self-destruction. The public drama was activated by Queensberry leaving a note at the Albemarle Club addressed to 'Oscar Wilde posing somdomite [sic]'. (It is interesting to see what variations the word gained in these proceedings; Edward Carson, Wilde's cross-examiner, called Huysmans's *À Rebours* a 'sodomitical' book.) The reaction of any sensible man to the note would have been to take the advice of the majority of Wilde's friends, which was to tear it up and forget it. The way to disaster was to start a private prosecution for criminal libel (an antique procedure last notably used by Sir James Goldsmith against *Private Eye*; such prosecutions are usually taken over by the Queen, as happened in Wilde's case). The charge necessarily called for the defence of justification. From then on it was Wilde, and not his enemy the Marquess of Queensberry, who was on trial, and he had laid himself open to every form of attack. There were no Queensberry Rules.

Throughout these ghastly events Oscar's wife, Constance, behaved impeccably. Wilde was a devoted and loving father, although he left his sons, Vyvyan and Cyril Holland, a lifetime of concealment and embarrassment. In a book that adds considerably to our knowledge of his grandfather's trials, Vyvyan's son, Merlin Holland, has filled in the many gaps left in Montgomery Hyde's edition in the 'Notable British Trials' series. We can now live again through the extraordinary drama of the aborted prosecution of Queensberry and watch Oscar, the great dramatist, elegant in a black frock coat, leaning across the rail of the witness box, uttering wonderful but occasionally fatal answers: even as he is earning the audience's applause for his greatest flights of fancy, he is being led inexorably by the dogged persistence of his cross-examiner, Edward Carson, towards the prison gates.

Merlin Holland has published, for the first time, further passages of the cross-examination. We now know what Carson thought of Huysmans' 'sodomitical' book, and we get a full account of the fascinating exchange. We also have a full text of the evidence in the magistrate's court and Carson's excellent opening speech for the defence. As a full record of these tragic judicial proceedings, it will not only be of use to future historians and scholars but to all of us who love, admire and are fascinated by this extraordinarily brilliant, lovable and self-destructive genius.

The Criminal Law Amendment Act that forbade indecent conduct, short of penetration between men, under which Wilde was finally convicted, had only been passed some ten years earlier and was rightly known as a 'Blackmailer's Charter'. At his subsequent trials Wilde was faced with the evidence collected by Queensberry's defence team for the first trial. This was mostly about limited sexual activity with various consenting rent boys, and a heavy cloud of blackmail hung around the proceedings. (It is now revealed that one significant blackmailing letter was, unwisely, put in evidence by Wilde's prosecuting counsel, although the defence knew nothing of it). The amount of evidence against Wilde was overwhelming, as he must have known when he first told his solicitor that there was no truth in Queensberry's claims.

That he, on that fatal afternoon, as he admitted later, sat lying to a lawyer, was a fact he tended to blame on Bosie, who had longed for a fight to the death against his savage and eccentric father. As Merlin Holland says, the question we would all have liked to ask Oscar was, 'Why on earth did you do it?' Was it another case of the destruction of an older man by an obsession with a young lover? Did he somehow feel that his huge success had become unbearable and want to destroy it? Was he attracted by the danger of lying and thought he could get away with it it? Or was he, as I believe, a confused and kindly man who did not think, as we would not think nowadays, that he had done anything wrong and that he could rely on his irresistible charm, and his talent for finding clever answers to tricky questions to see him through? If this was so, he was horribly mistaken.

There is a story about Oscar Wilde that, I think, should always be remembered. His friend Helena Sickert's father had died and her mother, grief stricken and inconsolable, had shut herself away in her room and vowed that she would see no one. Wilde called and, insisting on seeing the mother, he got her to open her door to him. An hour, two hours passed and Helena waited for the inevitable tears and demands to be left alone. Then she heard an unbelievable sound; her mother was laughing. Wilde had entertained her, had pleased her, had made her feel that life was still worth living. He showed, in that and many other cases, that charm works wonders.

It did not, in the end, work down at the Old Bailey. Perhaps it caused the jury in his first criminal trial to disagree; but then, when any merciful prosecutor or Home Secretary might have decided that he had suffered enough, it let him down badly and he was finally convicted.

Passing the ridiculous sentence of two years' hard labour, Mr Justice Wills said that men who could do as Oscar Wilde did were 'dead to all sense of shame'. This judge, who had presided over cases of murder and rape, seriously maintained that Wilde's offence was 'the worst I have ever tried'.

When the verdict and sentence were announced the prostitutes danced in the streets round the Old Bailey, celebrating this triumph for heterosexuality. The truth had been exposed, but it was still a shameful day for British justice.

John Mortimer
November 2002

1. The Marquess's visiting card which goaded Wilde into action and the Albemarle Club envelope, exhibits 'A' and 'B' in the trial.

INTRODUCTION

As a boy of fifteen at the end of the 1950s, I remember finding in a cupboard what was clearly intended to be a secret file full of press cuttings. My father, Vyvyan, had written on it in Cyrillic characters, a quirky habit he had, especially to prevent people reading notes he made in public, but in this instance it had quite the opposite effect to what was intended. My curiosity aroused, I went through the contents and discovered that the clippings all had a common theme – homosexuality. There were the notorious prosecutions of John Gielgud, Lord Montagu and Peter Wildeblood; there was the Wolfenden Report and the homophobic editorials in the tabloid press warning that any relaxing of the laws would lead to an epidemic of this 'vice'; and, inevitably, poor Oscar got dragged into the discussion amidst all the moralising. In retrospect, I think that the Cyrillic was less a feeble attempt at concealment and more Vyvyan's denial to himself that he was interested in the subject; it was, after all, Oscar's homosexuality which had turned my father's childhood upside down, so his interest was more of a melancholy fascination with something which had, to some degree, affected much of his life. He died in 1967 and it is a sobering thought that the legislation under which his father, Oscar Wilde, was sent to prison was only repealed three months before my own father's death.

I kept that file going through the next thirty years, adding cuttings that dealt with prejudice rather than imprisonment, as well as another element which seemed just as relevant – high-profile libel cases. Looking back through it recently, it came as no surprise to see how little has changed over a century whenever fame, sex, pride and libel are shaken up into their intoxicating cocktail of human weakness. The outcome is as predictably fascinating for the onlookers, as it is invariably disastrous for the participants.

Oscar Wilde started to concoct his own version of this heady mixture in 1891 when he made the acquaintance of Lord Alfred Douglas.[1] 'Bosie' Douglas, the third son of the Marquess of Queensberry, was a twenty-one-year-old undergraduate at Magdalen, Wilde's old Oxford college. They had been introduced at Wilde's London home in Tite Street by their friend, Lionel Johnson, who had been at Winchester with Douglas and was now at Oxford. All three shared a common interest in poetry and Douglas, having read *The Picture of Dorian Gray* some months before, was curious to meet the author who was already a controversial and very public figure in the literary world. The visit, as he later described it, 'was just the ordinary interchange of courtesies. Wilde was very agreeable and talked a great deal, I was very much impressed, and, before I left, Wilde had asked me to dinner or lunch at his club, and I had accepted his invitation.'[2]

It was an introduction which Johnson was to regret bitterly, as Oscar and Bosie obviously took to each other at once and Johnson soon felt that his relationship with Oscar, while never intense and physical, was distinctly cooling. This was hardly surprising. Bosie was an attractive, even beautiful young man, already no mean poet and the son of a marquess, which gave him added appeal. At their second meeting a few days later in the Albemarle Club, Oscar gave him a special large-paper copy of *Dorian Gray* inscribed 'Alfred Douglas from his friend who wrote this book. Oscar. July, 1891'. At this point their accounts vary of how the friendship developed. Bosie maintained that they met frequently and that Oscar 'laid siege' to him, which he resisted for six months before finally giving in to his advances;[3] Oscar, by contrast, said that for eighteen months after they first met he only saw Bosie four times and that their relationship began to flourish after Bosie had appealed to him for help in paying off some blackmailers. This he arranged through his long-standing friend, the solicitor Sir George Lewis.[4] Whatever the truth, from about May 1892, Oscar's affection for Bosie turned rapidly into an infatuation with little concern for public discretion. Bosie in turn became captivated by Wilde's charm and the magical quality of his conversation, and within a short time they were inseparable. The fact that Wilde had enjoyed his first theatrical success, *Lady Windermere's Fan*, in February that year meant that he was earning quite considerable sums of money in royalties (about £70 a week or £4000–5000 at today's values) and a very large proportion of it went on his extravagant entertaining of the young aristocrat. The truth of it was brought home starkly enough when he was in prison and made bankrupt in 1895. Forced to detail his income and expenditure by the Official Receiver, he realised that between the autumn of 1892 and the date of his imprisonment, he and Douglas had spent more than £5000.

What Constance, Oscar's wife, made of this 'friendship' one can only conjecture. Like many Victorian husbands, Oscar was in the habit of passing a good deal of time in male company, which in his case included that of good-looking young men with a passion for the arts and poetry in particular. Constance would have seen little to concern her; indeed, may even have been vicariously flattered by what she saw as the attention paid to her successful spouse. It probably would not even have occurred to her that he might be committing infidelities of a homosexual nature. In the autumn of 1892, while she was with her two children in Torquay, Oscar and Bosie spent ten days at Cromer in Norfolk. During that time Bosie fell ill and Constance wrote to her husband asking if he wanted her to come up and help nurse him.[5] Bosie also dined regularly at Tite Street and said that about a year after he and Oscar had first met, Constance said that she liked him the best of all Oscar's friends. He later gave a movingly accurate portrait of her in his autobiography.[6]

The open relationship between Bosie and a man sixteen years his senior did not please his father, the 'screaming, scarlet Marquess', as Oscar termed him. He had written to his son to express his disapproval not long after the relationship started, though in a concerned and kindly rather than an abusive tone.

Douglas replied begging him not to interfere. Then, in November 1892, all three met by chance at the Café Royal and lunched together, during which, predictably, Oscar won over the Marquess to the point that he wrote to his son two days later to say how charming and clever he had found Wilde and was not surprised that Bosie was so fond of him.[7]

This state of affairs did not last long. Rumours about Wilde's private life, combined with the fact that Queensberry had heard of the blackmailing incident from Sir George Lewis, set him on the offensive again. He now began to object in the strongest possible terms to his son's association with Wilde and threatened to cut off Bosie's allowance if it did not cease immediately. When Bosie refused, Queensberry flew into a frenzy and followed the two of them around the various hotels and restaurants that they frequented in London, threatening to cause a public scandal if he found them together. Matters were made worse in the summer of 1893 when Queensberry started to suspect his eldest son, Lord Drumlanrig, of conducting a homosexual affair with the Foreign Secretary, Lord Rosebery.

Towards the end of 1893 the intensity of Wilde's and Douglas's relationship was even beginning to take its toll on Wilde himself. Douglas had left Oxford in July without taking a degree, had spent August translating Wilde's play *Salomé* into English (a gesture on Wilde's part that had more to do with keeping the young man occupied than his confidence in Bosie's ability as a translator) and was leading an 'aimless, unhappy and absurd' life.[8] Wilde wrote to Lady Queensberry and persuaded her to send her son abroad to Egypt for four months. On his return at the end of March 1894, he and Oscar were once more lunching at the Café Royal when the Marquess came in. As before, he was persuaded to join them and they parted on friendly terms. It was a short-lived truce. On 1 April Queensberry wrote to Bosie more or less accusing Wilde of sodomy (see page 214) and the flurry of letters and telegrams that followed meant, in terms that the author of the Queensberry rules would have understood all too well, that the gloves were now off. At the end of June Queensberry turned up at Wilde's

Tite Street house, bringing with him a prizefighter and although he did not accuse Wilde directly of engaging in improper conduct with his son, he said, 'You look it and you pose as it, which is just as bad', and swore that he would thrash Wilde if ever he found him again in a public restaurant with his son. Wilde's famous reply to this threat did not betray the slightest fear: 'I do not know what the Queensberry rules are,' he said, 'but the Oscar Wilde rule is to shoot on sight.' He showed Queensberry to the door, and instructed his manservant never to allow the Marquess to enter his home again. He also consulted Sir George Lewis about possible action to prevent any further threatening behaviour by Queensberry, but discovered to his alarm that Queensberry had already retained Lewis's services for himself.

Then, four months later, on 18 October, Queensberry's heir, Drumlanrig, was killed in what was reported as a shooting accident, but believed by those in the know to have been suicide. There was a suspicion that he was being blackmailed for his relationship with Rosebery, who by now had become Prime Minister. Queensberry, having lost one son to what he saw as the evils of homosexuality, was determined not to let the matter of Oscar and Bosie rest, and planned to create a disturbance with a grotesque bouquet of vegetables at the St James's Theatre on 14 February 1895, the opening night of *The Importance of Being Earnest.* Wilde, tipped off by a friend, alerted the police and the Marquess was denied entry. A few days after, on 18 February, Queensberry left his abusive card at Wilde's club: 'For Oscar Wilde posing somdomite [*sic*].'

It was not until ten days later that Wilde called at the Albemarle and was given the card by the hall porter. He immediately wrote to his close friend Robert Ross from the Avondale Hotel where he was staying,

> Dearest Bobbie, Since I saw you something has happened. Bosie's father has left a card at my club with hideous words on it. I don't see anything now but a criminal prosecution. My whole life seems ruined by this man. The tower of ivory is assailed by the foul thing. On the sand is my life spilt. I don't know what to do. If

you could come here at 11.30 please do so tonight. I mar your life by trespassing ever on your love and kindness. I have asked Bosie to come tomorrow.[9]

At this point some of the many 'what ifs' in this unfurling tragedy begin to emerge. Ross had almost certainly been Wilde's first homosexual lover back in about 1887 and although, at several removes, he had been supplanted in Oscar's affections by Bosie Douglas, he had remained an intimate friend and confidant. Wilde's appeal in the first instance to Ross rather than to Douglas is significant. He knew that even if he did not take Ross's advice, he could rely on his judgement and, had they been able to discuss the situation calmly together, they might have concluded that the best thing to do with Queensberry's card would have been to tear it up. However, by the time Ross arrived, Douglas was already at the hotel. It is not difficult to imagine, therefore, with Douglas spoiling for a fight, what attitude he would have taken to this latest act of aggression from his father – the 'booby trap' as Queensberry later referred to it.

The previous summer, since Lewis was already acting for Queensberry, Robbie Ross had introduced Oscar to his own solicitor, Charles Humphreys, and it was to Humphreys that Oscar had turned after the incident at the theatre with a view to obtaining some sort of restraining order on the Marquess. There was little risk in this course of action, but Humphreys could not persuade the staff of the theatre to give the necessary evidence and wrote to Wilde on the very day he had been given the card at the club,

We regret that we are unable to carry out your instructions to prosecute the Marquis of Queensberry for his threats and insulting conduct towards you on the 14th instant at the St James's Theatre inasmuch as upon investigating the case we have met with every obstruction from Mr George Alexander, the manager, and his staff at the theatre, who decline to give us any statements or to render any assistance to you in your desire to prosecute Lord Queensberry and without whose evidence and assistance we cannot advise you to venture upon a prosecution. You personally would of course be unable to give evidence of that which occurred behind your back as to which you have no personal knowledge beyond information from others who apprised you of the insulting threats and conduct of his Lordship.

Had Lord Queensberry been permitted to carry out his threats you would have had ample ground for instituting a prosecution against him, but the only consolation we can offer to you now is that such a persistent persecutor as Lord Queensberry will probably give you another opportunity sooner or later of seeking the protection of the Law, in which event we shall be happy to render you every assistance in our power to bring him to justice and thus secure to you future peace at his hands.

We are, dear sir, yours faithfully
C. O. Humphreys, Son, & Kershaw[10]

To bind Queensberry over to keep the peace was one thing, but to sue him now for criminal libel was quite another, and it seems unlikely that the normally cautious Robbie would have suggested it.[11] Bosie, on the other hand, whatever else he denied in later life, always accepted some of the responsibility for the action they now took. Indeed, in an article which he wrote for the *Mercure de France* in August 1895, but which at Oscar's request remained unpublished, he admits that he encouraged Oscar to sue.[12]

Another irony is given to the story according to Wilde, who should have left London on 28 February. He was already deeply in debt (he had been served with writs for £400 earlier in the month) and had been unable to pay his hotel bill.

On that fatal Friday [1 March] instead of being in Humphreys's office weakly consenting to my own ruin, I would have been happy and free in France, away from you and your father, unconscious of his loathsome card, and indifferent to your letters, if I had been able to leave the Avondale Hotel. But the hotel people absolutely refused to allow me to go. You had been staying with me for ten days: indeed you had ultimately, to my great and, you will admit, rightful indignation, brought a companion of yours to stay with me also: my bill for the ten days was nearly £140. The proprietor said he could not allow my luggage to be removed from the hotel till I had paid the account in full. That is what kept me in London.

Had it not been for the hotel bill I would have gone to Paris on Thursday morning.[13]

The morning after receiving the card, Wilde went to see Humphreys with Ross and Douglas. The solicitor asked Wilde whether there was any truth in the allegation of sodomy to which Wilde replied there was not, but that he did not have the money to finance the huge expenditure of a court case. Douglas intervened to say that his family would be only too happy to pay the necessary costs as they had all suffered for too long from his father's irrational and abusive behaviour. Humphreys then accompanied Wilde to the magistrates' court at Great Marlborough Street to apply for a warrant and Queensberry was arrested the following morning.

The Marquess was represented in court by Sir George Lewis who asked for a week's adjournment, partly to consult his client and consider the matter, but also to prevent him from having to appear against Wilde, a friend of fifteen years' standing. The instructions were passed on to the young Charles Russell, who on the advice of his father, the Lord Chief Justice, decided to brief Edward Carson. Carson, who had been a contemporary of Wilde's at Trinity College, Dublin, was unhappy about taking the case and initially turned it down. The subject matter was distasteful; Queensberry's only line of defence was based on a single letter from Wilde to Douglas and hearsay about Wilde's private life; and the case was a delicate one as, in establishing his client's justification, he was likely to ruin the young life that Queensberry was nominally trying to protect.

In the meantime private detectives employed by Russell and Queensberry had started to scratch the surface of London's homosexual underworld and were following rumours which, if true, would show that Wilde was not merely a 'posing' but a practising sodomite. With new instructions Russell returned to Carson, who was shocked at what was alleged against Wilde and, still undecided, consulted Lord Halsbury, the former Lord Chancellor. Halsbury's advice was simple: 'The great thing is to arrive at justice, and it is you, I believe, who can best do it.' Carson took the brief and appeared for Queensberry at the adjourned magistrates' court hearing on 9 March. It is said that until the last minute he was considering whether to advise his client to plead guilty but changed his mind on hearing that Russell had discovered the existence of Charles Parker, one of the rent boys whose evidence was to be crucial in all three trials that followed.[14]

The magistrates' court was packed to capacity with an exclusively male crowd including at least thirty journalists. All the available standing room was filled as Wilde, stylishly dressed in a long, dark-blue Chesterfield overcoat trimmed with velvet and sporting a white buttonhole, drove up in a carriage and pair, complete with coachman and footman. With him were Alfred Douglas and his elder brother Percy. As soon as the magistrate had taken his seat on the bench, he noticed Douglas and ordered him to leave the Court. Bosie touched Oscar's arm as though appealing for him to intervene but Oscar made no sign and Bosie was escorted from the Court by an usher. Queensberry was called to the dock; but the magistrate at once instructed him to be given a chair in a less humiliating position at his solicitor's table; and the proceedings began.

The verbatim account of what took place at the committal hearing is reproduced here before the text of the full Old Bailey trial, as four significant incidents occurred during the course of it. Wilde started his examination with a wisecrack and was sharply rebuked by the magistrate. Humphreys tried to introduce some of Queensberry's letters to other family members as further evidence of libel, hinting that 'exalted personages' (including Rosebery) were mentioned in them. Shortly afterwards the magistrate invited Humphreys and Carson to leave the court for a private conference, during which it must be assumed that the content of these letters was discussed and there was no further mention of them. Carson, well aware as an experienced QC that he could not cross-examine Wilde in this lower court as to the truth of the libel, nevertheless attempted to question him on his relationship with Douglas to show the reasons behind Queensberry's action. The magistrate quickly intervened, but the point had been made and was, of course, noted by the press. The hearing ended with Queensberry being committed for trial at the next Old Bailey sessions.

Charles Russell now set about following up the leads he had on Wilde's private life. He had been employing the services of an ex-police detective, Mr Littlechild, who had been having limited success until he was put in touch with a prostitute by Charles Brookfield. Brookfield, an actor and playwright, had for some time been nursing a growing envy of Wilde's theatrical success and was currently playing a small part in *An Ideal Husband.* He had parodied *Lady Windermere's Fan* with a 'musical travesty' of his own in 1892, *The Poet and the Puppets* which, to Brookfield's annoyance, Wilde had accepted with amused tolerance. The prostitute gave Littlechild the address of Alfred Taylor who had been introducing Wilde to young men, and although Taylor had moved some time before, he had ill-advisedly left behind a box of papers which his landlady now gave the detective.[15] In it was enough evidence to enable Queensberry's solicitors to start building up a formidable defence and they tracked down and took statements from Fred Atkins, Alfred Wood, Sydney Mavor and Ernest Scarfe in London, as well as Charles Parker at the Royal Artillery barracks in Dover. By reconstructing what was known of Wilde's life from the summer of 1893 they were able to question the manager of a hotel where Wilde and Douglas stayed before taking The Cottage at Goring that year, the governess of Wilde's children and even a pageboy from the Savoy who had since moved to Calais.[16] They also caught up with the blackmailers Allen and Cliburn who were in hiding at Broadstairs.

Oscar and Bosie, by contrast, decided to treat themselves to a week in Monte Carlo. The mood, on Douglas's side at least, was euphoric. 'I saw Humphreys today,' he wrote to his brother Percy on 11 March, the day before they left. 'He says everything is splendid and we are going to walk over.'[17] It was an act of lunacy at a time when Wilde, as he later said in *De Profundis*, 'should have been in London taking wise counsel, and calmly considering the hideous trap in which I had allowed myself to be caught', and it may even have led Russell's agents to the Savoy pageboy whom Oscar and Bosie saw on their way to the south of France. Quite apart from the misuse of their time, the money spent on the trip and at the gaming tables in the Casino should have been put towards the mounting legal costs. On the morning of Queensberry's arrest, according to Douglas he gave Wilde all the money in his bank, some £360, and his mother and brother Percy had offered to underwrite the lawyers' fees. Wilde had already paid Humphreys 150 guineas and on his return from Monte Carlo he was asked for more on account before Humphreys would brief his counsel. Oscar, according to Bosie, had even had to raise £800 by selling various possessions to prevent his creditors' bailiffs entering his house.[18]

The counsel briefed was a former Solicitor-General, Sir Edward Clarke, whose reputation in high-profile cases of the time was second to none, especially in the 'Baccarat' slander case when he had fearlessly cross-examined the Prince of Wales. Clarke, a man of the highest integrity, asked Wilde the same question as Humphreys, namely that there was not, nor ever had been any foundation for the charges made against him by Queensberry. Once again Wilde declared that they were absolutely false and groundless. Douglas, who had accompanied Wilde to the barrister's chambers and who by this time was regarding the prosecution as 'our case', always maintained that he had extracted a promise from Clarke to put him in the witness box to testify against his father's character, a fact which Clarke denied to the end of his life.[19] Douglas had also persuaded his brother Percy to appear for the prosecution, but had recently heard that Percy's solicitor was strongly against such a move. Their evidence, as Clarke would have known well enough, would anyway have been irrelevant – indeed, inadmissible – in refuting the libel.

As the date for the trial drew near, Wilde's friends were increasingly concerned about what they saw as the total folly of suing Queensberry. Frank Harris recalled a visit from Wilde during which he was asked if he would give evidence that *Dorian Gray* was not an immoral book. Harris agreed but warned that no jury in England would give a verdict against a father trying to protect his son, and told Wilde to go away and sleep on it. They met again the following day at the Café Royal. Harris had been lunching with Bernard Shaw who expressed the same opinion, which they repeated a little later when Douglas arrived to join them. 'Such advice shows you are no friend of Oscar's,' cried Bosie and stormed out, followed shortly by Oscar saying weakly, 'No, Frank, it is not friendly.'[20] George Alexander asked Wilde why he did not withdraw from the case and go abroad. 'Everybody wants me to go abroad,' came the reply. 'I have just been abroad. And now I have come home again. One can't keep on going abroad, unless one is a missionary, or, what comes to the same thing, a commercial traveller.'[21] A day or two before the trial the reality of the situation was forcibly brought home to Wilde when he was confronted with Queensberry's plea of justification (see Appendix A). In it he was accused of immorality and sodomitical tendencies in his published work, especially *The Picture of Dorian Gray*, but there were also fourteen counts of gross indecency with young men, which, if proved, would not only lead to Queensberry's acquittal but, almost inevitably, to his own arrest.

On the morning of 3 April 1895 Wilde set off from his home in Tite Street to the Central Criminal Court. He travelled there and back in a hired carriage and pair, and it cost him £2 5s 6d for what the bill afterwards described, with unconscious irony, as 'a long day'. The proceedings were scheduled to start at 10.30 but the Court already had been packed to capacity by ten o'clock:

> The barristers came first. They wore their wigs and gowns without exception, partly as a tribute to the importance of the occasion, partly perhaps to secure themselves against the inconvenient possibility of being denied admittance. They came not [as] single spies, but whole battalions. And, so far as they were permitted, they took possession of every seat which seemed capable of accommodating their persons. They sat in the barristers' seats; they sat in the solicitors' seats; they sat in the witnesses' seats; they sat in the ushers' seats; and, excepting the Bench, they sat in all the other seats which they could capture. And when the seats were

all used up, they stood, a serried mass of voluble, grey-wigged, black-gowned humanity, in the gangways and approaches of the court. The only serious rivals to the barristers were the reporters. All the seats that were not occupied by briefless barristers contained reporters . . . What few remaining places were not occupied by the reporters were filled by an eager, struggling crowd of lookers-on, who had succeeded, in ways on which it were rash to speculate, in prevailing upon the janitors to grant them entrance. Up above, the public proper looked down on the battling crowd beneath.[22]

Queensberry was the first to arrive wearing a Cambridge-blue hunting stock instead of a collar and tie. With his red mutton-chop whiskers and pendulous lower lip he looked anything but aristocratic. A few minutes later Wilde appeared, forced his way through the crowd to the solicitors' table and started to talk animatedly to Sir Edward Clarke. He was serious and showed none of the tendency to flippancy that had been so evident at his magistrates' court appearance. A wing collar and black tie fastened with a diamond-and-sapphire pin and the noticeable absence of a flower in the buttonhole of his frock-coat emphasised his gravity. Queensberry, until he was called, stood just a yard or two from Wilde, his shiny new tan gloves in aesthetic contrast to the elegant grey suede ones of his opponent. 'His lordship looked old, thin and drawn; Mr Wilde was big, loose and picturesque,' noted the *Sun*.

Sir Edward Clarke opened the proceedings by describing Wilde's career, his family life and his literary success. In an attempt to anticipate and defuse a possible line of attack by Carson, Sir Edward then introduced one of Wilde's more compromising letters to Douglas, which had been the subject of a blackmailing attempt, and of which he assumed Carson would have knowledge. As it turned out Carson had not known about the letter at all (a fact revealed in this text for the first time – see p. 262); it was the first of several tactical errors Clarke would make. The examination-in-chief, lasting an hour and five minutes, passed off satisfactorily. Wilde's manner, according to the *Evening News*, as he 'almost lolled in the witness-box' was confident and he allowed himself the odd touch of humour, recounting events in the style of dinner-table anecdotes, though the *Morning* noted 'his affected manner meant that his replies were rather difficult to catch'. The Marquess, who had refused a chair, stood in the dock, his arms crossed, his lower lip moving ceaselessly over the upper one, and regarded Wilde with an expression of supreme contempt, supplemented occasionally by angry mutterings.

Carson, who was suffering from a bad cold, then cross-examined.

> Mr Wilde folded his arms across the rail of the witness-box, his gloves drooped gracefully from his graceful hand and he faced Lord Queensberry's counsel with a smile. A man might as well have smiled at the rack. 'You stated that your age was thirty-nine. I suggest that you are over forty.' It was blunt; it was almost brutal; it was indicative of the style of what was to follow. It was a duel of thrilling interest. Mr Carson's wig throws his white, thin, clever face into sharp relief. When he is angry it assumes the immovability of a death mask. He is deliberate in the extreme but on the other hand, when he has a good point to make, he bursts out with it in irresistible interruption. When he has not the answer he expects, he pauses; he looks at the bar; he looks at the jury; he looks at the spectators. Then he raises his voice in an 'I ask you, Sir,—.' When, on the contrary, he thinks he has scored, he smiles an exceedingly grim smile to his junior; he glances at the judge and he glances at his client. His self-possession is absolute ... Against him a witness, however good his case, is, while the cross-examination lasts, as a lath against iron. To the spectator, knowing nothing of the merits of a case, he appears to have the witness as a boy has a cockchafer upon a pin.[23]

It was an inauspicious start to have lied about one's age, but, to Wilde's delight, Carson turned to his relationship with Douglas. There was nothing to defend; the evidence was merely circumstantial. Next, Carson questioned Wilde about the epigrams which he had contributed to an issue of *The Chameleon*, an Oxford undergraduate magazine. In the same issue there was a story, 'The

Priest and the Acolyte', much more compromising than anything Wilde had written, but Wilde condemned it as disgusting and Carson was unable to establish guilt by association. As they moved on to *Dorian Gray*, Wilde was in his element defending his views on art and morality. Carson took the first version published in an American magazine, for he called the book 'the purged edition', and found the very sentence that Wilde had judged it prudent to omit from the book. 'Have you ever felt that feeling of adoring madly a beautiful male person many years younger than yourself?' asked Carson. 'I have never given adoration to anybody except myself,' quipped the witness. An uncomfortable moment, but Wilde was soon back playing to the gallery, treating the Court like a theatre and he ended the first day full of confidence.

The curtain went up on Act Two the next morning and Carson started to question Wilde on his private life. Charles Russell's investigations while Oscar and Bosie had been holidaying in Monte Carlo were appalling in their revelations, but still Wilde held the audience in his hand. 'Was it a favourite drink – iced champagne?' – 'Yes, strongly against my doctor's orders.' – 'Never mind your doctor's orders!' – 'I don't. It has all the more flavour if you discard the doctor's orders.' More questions about Douglas and the servant, Walter Grainger, at his lodgings in Oxford. 'Did you ever kiss him?' – 'Oh, no, never in my life. He was a peculiarly plain boy.' And before long it was all over. By giving Wilde a day to defend himself and his art, Edward Carson caught him superbly off his guard. One fatal witticism too many and Oscar had effectively talked himself into prison.

Wilde, on the advice of his counsel, withdrew from the prosecution the following day, halfway through Carson's immensely powerful opening speech for the defence. Sir Edward made a weak attempt to get the Court to agree a verdict of 'Not Guilty' to the libel of 'posing as', based on Wilde's published work alone, but Carson would have none of it, insisting that every element of Queensberry's plea be accepted. The jury conferred for a few minutes before declaring that the libel was true, that it was published for the public benefit and that the accused was not guilty.

Loud applause and cheering broke out in court, which neither the judge not the officials made any serious attempt to suppress and later that day Mr Justice Collins penned a note to Carson: 'Dear Carson, I never heard a more powerful speech nor a more searching crossXam. I congratulate you on having escaped most of the filth. Yrs ever, R. Henn Collins.'

Wilde, who had been at the Old Bailey that morning but not in the courtroom itself, left hurriedly and drove to the Holborn Viaduct Hotel where he was joined for lunch by the two Douglas brothers and Robert Ross. A reporter from the *Sun* tried to interview him but had to speak instead to Percy, who said that he and Bosie had been anxious to go into the witness box, but had been prevented by Wilde.

> I, and every member of our family, excepting my father, disbelieve absolutely and entirely the allegations of the defence. It is, in my opinion, simply a part of the persecution which my father has carried on against us ever since I can remember. I think Mr Wilde and his counsel to blame for not showing, as they could have done, that was the fact.[24]

He added that 'with Mr Wilde's full authority he could state that Mr Wilde had no thoughts of immediately leaving London, and would stay to face whatever might be the result of the proceedings'. In much the same vein Oscar wrote to the *Evening News*,

> It would have been impossible for me to have proved my case without putting Lord Alfred Douglas in the witness-box against his father. Lord Alfred Douglas was extremely anxious to go into the box, but I would not let him do so. Rather than put him in so painful a position I determined to retire from the case, and to bear on my own shoulders whatever ignominy and shame might result from my prosecuting Lord Queensberry.

After lunch they called in on Sir George Lewis who said, 'What's the use of coming to me now? I am powerless to do anything. If you had had the sense to bring Lord Queensberry's card to me in the first place, I would have torn it up and thrown it in the fire and told you not to make a fool of yourself.'[25] They then made their way via Fleet Street and the Bank to the Cadogan Hotel where Bosie was staying.

Meanwhile the agents of the law had moved with surprising swiftness. The moment the trial was over, the Marquess instructed Charles Russell to send his files to the Director of Public Prosecutions at the Treasury. An hour later Russell was summoned by the Public Prosecutor, Hamilton Cuffe, who considered that the information was of such a serious nature that it required immediate action. Cuffe sent one of his staff shortly after 2 p.m. to the House of Commons to consult the two senior law officers, the Attorney-General and the Solicitor-General, as well as the Home Secretary, Herbert Asquith. Asquith gave instructions that an arrest warrant should be applied for at once and Wilde stopped wherever he might be. At 3.30 p.m. a Treasury official and a detective-inspector from Scotland Yard presented themselves at Bow Street where the Magistrate, Sir John Bridge, considered the matter important enough to adjourn his court and accompany them to the Public Prosecutor's office. There he examined the witness statements which Russell had taken but which Carson had not had to use, returned to his court and by five o'clock had issued the warrant. By providing the Crown with evidence of Wilde's criminal behaviour, Queensberry undoubtedly hastened his arrest. It has often been said that the issue of the warrant was delayed until after the departure of the last boat-train for the Continent, allowing Wilde time to escape if he chose, but this is absurd; Wilde was arrested at 6.20 p.m. and, according to *Bradshaw's Railway Guide*, there were four more cross-Channel departures until 9.45 that evening. Alfred Taylor, whose name had figured prominently in the trial, was arrested the next morning and they were both charged under Section 11 of the 1885 Criminal Law Amendment Act for 'committing acts of gross indecency with other male persons'. To his lasting credit Taylor was offered the chance of turning 'Queen's Evidence' against Wilde and refused. No bail was allowed, which was surprising as the offence was classified merely as a misdemeanour.

The press coverage of the trial varied enormously with most

daily newspapers giving long accounts of each day's proceedings. (Incidentally, the *Pall Mall Gazette* printed a review of a newly published book on the very afternoon that Carson was examining Wilde on *Dorian Gray*: its title was *Books Fatal to their Authors*.) The trial was also covered by papers in Paris and New York, the French in particular showing a certain amount of surprise and distaste at what they saw as the English hypocrisy of professing to be shocked and yet reporting as much prurient detail as they could about the case. The *St James's Gazette* took a sanctimonious stand after the first day and refused to publish anything until the verdict and then accompanied it with two self-congratulatory columns of correspondence from readers on its action. Others indulged in vitriolic tirades in their editorials, in particular the *Daily Telegraph*. They were taken to task by a small weekly publication, the *London Figaro*:

> The hideous accusations against Mr Oscar Wilde – perhaps the wittiest man in England, certainly the most brilliant playwright – take one's breath away. It is hardly possible to do more than hold up one's hands in horror and amazement. It is possible, however, to protest most vehemently against the action of the *Telegraph* and other papers in condemning Mr Wilde before he has been tried. No one denies that the evidence against him is appallingly strong, but until he has been convicted he is innocent in law, and it is a dastardly and indecent thing for that section of the press which has never lost a chance of reviling Mr Wilde, to take the present opportunity of venting their spite upon him . . . it will be almost impossible for Mr Wilde to receive a fair trial . . . A giant among pigmies, Mr Wilde has naturally been cordially hated by all the mean and little people, and they now think to increase their own size and importance by belittling his. Men of more wisdom and understanding have laughed at his absurdities, but have admired his undoubted genius. Come the worst, it will not be the first time that a consummate artist has been also a consummate rascal.[26]

Constance, meanwhile, judged it prudent to bring Cyril and Vyvyan home from their boarding schools and sent Cyril off to relations in Ireland. Sixty years later my father recalled that period in his life:

> On my return from school, I remained in London for the time being, and my main recollection is of my mother, in tears, poring over masses of press cuttings, mostly from Continental news-papers. I was, of course, not allowed to see them, though I could not help seeing the name OSCAR WILDE in large headlines: but I had no inkling of the true state of affairs.[27]

Shortly afterwards the two boys were sent off to Switzerland to stay with Constance's brother and never saw their father again.

Wilde's first trial against the Crown took place three weeks after the collapse of his libel action and finished with a hung jury. The Crown made extensive use of the evidence collected by Charles Russell's detectives and produced the witnesses in court. They consisted mostly of rent boys and blackmailers together with their landladies, as well as staff at the Savoy and the furnished chambers that Wilde had used. One of the blackmailers, Fred Atkins, was summarily dismissed by the judge for perjuring him-self. On 24 April, two days before the trial started, the whole contents of Wilde's family home in Tite Street were sold at public auction to pay his debts. His books had largely been withdrawn from sale and although his two plays continued to run in the West End for a few weeks, the author's name was removed from the programmes and pasted over on the billboards. The Lyceum Theatre in New York took the same action over its production of *An Ideal Husband*.

The matter could have ended there, with Wilde sufficiently disgraced in the public eye; the Law was not bound to continue the prosecution. But it did and wheeled in none other than the Solicitor-General himself, Sir Frank Lockwood, to conduct the final trial. Edward Carson is said to have appealed to Lockwood to let up on Wilde but received the reply, 'I would but we cannot: we dare not: it would at once be said both in England and abroad, that owing to the names mentioned in Queensberry's letters we were forced to abandon it.'[28] Had Queensberry written to Rosebery in the meantime, threatening to expose him over his relationship with his late son unless he secured Wilde's conviction? We shall probably never know. He was certainly capable of doing so to judge from his other correspondence. More to the point was that the government needed to show that it could bite as well as just bark at this unmentionable vice, especially after the Cleveland Street fiasco of 1889.[29] Wilde was eventually granted bail on 7 May, one of his sureties being Percy Douglas, whose father saw this as the last act in a series of filial impieties and had a public punch-up with his son on 21 May in Piccadilly. After the public auction at Tite Street, Constance, with courageous and touching loyalty, remained in London offering Oscar what support she could. She stayed with friends at first and then moved to a lodging house near Bayswater. She finally left the country and joined her sons abroad a week after her husband was finally convicted of gross indecency on 25 May 1895 and sentenced to two years' hard labour. He was released on 19 May 1897 and immediately went abroad, never to return to England again. He died in Paris on 30 November 1900 aged forty-six.

If I could ask my grandfather a single question, it would have to be, 'Why on earth did you do it?' That one answer would hold the key to so much in his life that is not satisfactorily explained. Oscar, as he later said in his long apologia, *De Profundis*, lost his head when he sued for criminal libel. 'I ceased to Lord over myself. I was no longer the Captain of my Soul and did not know it. I allowed you to dominate me and your father to frighten me ... In your hideous game of hate together, you had both thrown dice for my soul, and you happened to have lost. That was all.' But there is no simple explanation for his conduct. Arrogance born of social and literary success, and the belief that he was in some way immune from the law unquestionably played a part, as did a desire to please young Douglas. I am certain, too, that there was a perverse element of wanting to play out in court a theatrical piece whose prologue he felt he had 'written', but whose outcome was known only to the Fates: 'The danger,' as he later said of his *demi-monde* life, 'the danger was half the excitement.' When he had been in Algiers with Bosie earlier in the year, they had met André Gide to whom Oscar admitted that Queensberry was hounding him. Gide advised him to be careful. 'Careful!' exclaimed Oscar. 'But how can I be careful? That would be going backwards. I have to go as far as possible. I cannot go any further. Something is bound to happen ... something else.'[30]

If Queensberry's initial 'booby trap' was merely a crude provocation, the inclusion in his plea of justification of the two counts of immorality in Wilde's writings was a far more subtle challenge by the lawyers. They were intended to justify the allegation of 'posing', but it was also poisoned bait. If Wilde had been faced solely with a catalogue of offences with young men, then, they may have reasoned, he might have withdrawn from the case. This would have defeated the Marquess's object, which was to enable him to humiliate Wilde in public. If his work as an artist were to be attacked, however, given his spirited defence of *Dorian Gray* on its first publication, he was more likely to stay and fight. Wilde, though it is improbable that the lawyers' reasoning went so far, was well-acquainted with the trials for obscenity and immorality in 1857 of two of his best-loved French authors: Flaubert for *Madame Bovary* and Baudelaire for *Les Fleurs du mal*. The charge against Flaubert had been that his work was 'an outrage to public and religious morals and to morality' and against Baudelaire the court's verdict stated that *Les Fleurs du mal* contained 'obscene and immoral passages and expressions'. In the event Flaubert was acquitted and Baudelaire fined 300 francs with six of his most cherished poems suppressed. By comparison with what happened to Wilde, they got off lightly. There are some uncomfortably familiar parallels, too, in both authors' views at the time of their trials. Baudelaire wrote to his mother shortly before seizure of the book, 'You know that I have always considered that literature and the arts pursue an aim independent of morality.' And Flaubert, exasperated by the caution of his publisher, Maxime Du Camp, is reported to have said, 'I don't care; if my novel exasperates the bourgeoisie, I don't care; if they take us to trial, I don't care.' There is little Wilde would have relished more than to stand in the witness box and defend his art. The British legal system, though, had an additional attraction, for while the Frenchmen had been obliged to plead through their lawyers, Wilde knew he would be allowed to 'perform' to the court himself.

Was Oscar Wilde, as some modern writers have ventured to suggest, a conscious and willing early martyr to the homosexual cause? Not initially, at least. He loved life too much to throw all away on some absurd squabble with an irascible aristocrat. As he later wrote to Douglas in *De Profundis*:

> Don't you realise now that you should have seen it, and come forward and said that you would not have my Art, at any rate, ruined for your sake? You knew what my Art was to me, the great primal note by which I had revealed, first myself to myself, and then myself to the world; the real passion of my life; the love to which all other loves were as marsh-water to red wine.[31]

But when he appeared for a second time in court, defending himself against the Crown and aware that his case was being fatally weakened with each new witness that the prosecution produced, one cannot help feeling that he had already begun to cast himself in the role of tragic hero. His impassioned and eloquent defence under cross-examination of 'the love that dare not speak its name' was a moment as pivotal in this trial as his flippancy about not kissing Walter Grainger had been in the libel action. Later, after prison, he would write openly and unrepentantly about his sexuality to his friends. 'Yes, I have no doubt we shall win, but the road is long and red with monstrous martyrdoms,' he wrote to George Ives in March 1898. 'Nothing but the repeal of the Criminal Law Amendment Act would do any good. That is the essential. It is not so much public opinion as public officials that need educating.'[32] And to Robbie Ross: 'To have altered my life would have been to have admitted that Uranian [i.e. homosexual] love is ignoble. I hold it to be noble – more noble than other forms.'[33] It was the tragic fulfilment of a wish he had once uttered at school that there was nothing he would like better in afterlife than to be the hero of a *cause célèbre* and go down to posterity as the defendant in a case *'Regina* versus *Wilde'*.[34]

There are questions, too, which need to be asked about the legal aspects of the case. If Wilde was indeed guilty of the offences of which he was accused, however cruel and unfair Section 11 of the Criminal Law Amendment Act may seem to us now, on the face of it, he was justly convicted at the time. The Bill, incidentally, which introduced the law was largely intended to increase the age of consent for girls, to prevent the coercion of women into prostitution and to suppress the ever-increasing number of brothels. Section 11 was added almost as an afterthought by the MP Henry Labouchere, whom Wilde knew socially. But was he convicted on tainted evidence and unsafe procedures?

Russell, in obtaining the witness statements for the Queensberry trial, presumably made it clear to those who had allegedly committed the offences with Wilde that if they refused to co-operate they could equally be liable to prosecution. As a lawyer with no official Crown standing, he would have had no power to grant them any sort of protection from the law. Edward Shelley, it is said, was paid £20 (the equivalent of half a year's salary) to be in attendance at the Queensberry trial, which, if true, amounted more to bribery than witness expenses.[35] The others, also waiting to give evidence, one may reasonably assume had been 'persuaded' to do so with a similar combination of pressure and payment. C. H. Norman, the socialist historian and court shorthand writer, related on good authority many years later that a senior policeman, at the time of Wilde's prosecution by the Crown, had been extremely indignant to hear that the witnesses had been paid £5 a week each from the day of Wilde's arrest to the day of his conviction – a sum also incommensurate with mere expenses.[36] Stuart Mason cites the publication in a morning newspaper between the second and the third trials of an analysis of the voting in the hung jury deliberations, showing that the majority found Wilde guilty, an act which today would be seen as contempt of court and probably lead to abandoning the prosecution.[37] Finally one must question the safety of empanelling a jury for the last trial, half of whom came from the same small London area as those for the Queensberry trial, and two of whom were close neighbours in the same streets. Social intercourse between those who had taken part in the first case and those in the last, high-profile cases as they were, cannot be ruled out and, consequently, the real risk of prejudice.[38]

As soon as the Queensberry case was abandoned, Sir Edward Clarke offered his services to defend Wilde without fee, an offer which was accepted 'with deepest gratitude'. It has often been said that Clarke was quite the wrong man to have been briefed in the first place, which given his high moral principles, may well have been so. But it is undeniable that Wilde grossly misled him from the start and all the more remarkable that Clarke should have been prepared to continue their association. Towards the end of Wilde's sentence Robert Ross wrote to Clarke asking if he could enquire with the Home Secretary about the possibility of applying for Wilde's early release. Clarke's reply was that there would be no point in such an application and added, 'It is impossible for me to forget that, before I undertook the most painful case which I have ever been engaged in, he gave me his word of honour as a gentleman that there was no foundation whatever for the charges which were afterwards so completely proved.' Significantly there is no mention of Wilde at all in Sir Edward's autobiography of 1918.

There are several possible reasons why Clarke decided to abandon the prosecution for libel, the main one being that if Carson had started to introduce the witnesses, Wilde's arrest would then have been inevitable. While plausible, this seems a weak argument since Wilde had already compromised himself to a great extent in open court and, the case having become a very public one, the Public Prosecutor would probably have been forced to act sooner or later. Had Clarke continued and had he had the same tenacity in dealing with the defence witnesses as Carson had shown with Wilde, although the stakes were appallingly high, he might have been able to discredit their evidence as he did, in part, during the next trial. C. H. Norman said that he discussed the matter with Clarke:

> He said that it was anticipated that the case, if fought to a finish, would last at least another three or four days and the expense could not be met. The Queensberry side were in the same dilemma. He and leading counsel for Queensberry had a private discussion the upshot of which was that if the case was dropped nothing more would be heard of the matter. That gentlemen's agreement was not kept ... Clarke admitted to me that a mistake had been made in withdrawing the case against Queensberry.

This, if true, would go some way towards explaining Sir Edward Clarke's generosity in representing Wilde up to his conviction.

Several editions of the Wilde trials have been published since 1895. The first appears to have been in 1896 *Der Fall Wilde und das Problem der Homosexualität* by the Verlag Max Spohr in Leipzig, a publisher well known for issuing books with a homosexual connection. It was a severely condensed account taken from the newspaper reports of all three trials. It was followed in 1906 by *The Trial of Oscar Wilde*, privately printed in Paris by Charles Carrington, purporting to have been made from the shorthand reports, but, again, very much condensed and containing only five pages on the Queensberry libel trial. In 1912 Christopher Millard (Stuart Mason), a close friend of Robert Ross and later Wilde's first bibliographer, published anonymously *Oscar Wilde: Three Times Tried*. It was a noble attempt to dispel, as he put it, 'the vague fog of obscenity in which truths, already sufficiently repulsive, have been covered by inventions even more hateful'. Millard did not state what his sources were, but judging from the text he must have had access to one of the court reports and supplemented it with accounts from the newspapers of the period. Unfortunately the volume was quite heavily edited, so some of the court exchanges, and especially the opening addresses by prosecution and defence, were reproduced in indirect speech. Millard's intention had been simply to reproduce the facts, which, sadly, rendered the sharpness of the duel between Wilde and Carson somewhat two-dimensional. He did, however, include much background information about the atmosphere in the Court, as well as all the proceedings in the magistrates' courts before each of the trials. It was not until 1948 that another edition appeared, edited for the 'Notable British Trials' series by H. Montgomery Hyde. This had an admirable introduction, setting the trials in their proper context, and included a memoir by Travers Humphreys, Wilde's junior counsel and the only surviving member of the legal teams. It also drew on Sir Edward Clarke's unpublished papers, which have since disappeared. The basis for Hyde's edition was Millard's work from 1912 with yet more material from the newspapers and some of the indirect speech now rendered artificially direct through Hyde's imaginative reconstruction. The 1962 popular edition of Hyde's work, containing further conjectures and descriptions of the action in court, while eminently readable as a dramatic text at its time, should now be regarded as a much abbreviated and inaccurate rendering of the Queensberry trial.

In 2000, as I was assisting the British Library to prepare its centenary celebration on Oscar Wilde, a longhand manuscript of the complete Queensberry trial was brought into the Library to be exhibited. Its authenticity was not to be doubted and for the first time I looked in astonishment at the *ipsissima verba* of what had transpired in that courtroom. It is those words which are here reproduced. There are at least eight hands represented in the MS, understandable since a shorthand writer would have been hard put to take down the proceedings for more than about twenty minutes at a time. His shorthand would then have had to be rendered back into longhand and each writer would have transcribed his own notes. The margin for error is therefore considerable: mishearings of the proceedings and misreadings of their own notes by eight different scribes. The consistency was, however, remarkable, though I have made minor editorial interventions. The text has been laid out as a play with proper names for ease of reading, though in the MS the 'characters' are generally designated 'Q' or 'A'. Punctuation has been added and regularised throughout to make sense of some excessively long unpunctuated sentences. Misspelled names have been altered according to official records. And where the sense of the MS has been obscure, a consensus of opinion has been taken from Millard, Hyde and the newspaper reports, and the fact noted.

The present text, with the proceedings of the committal hearings at Great Marlborough Street Court, runs to some 85,000 words. Hyde's text of 1948, the longest so far published, is less than 30,000. Although it would be impossible here to detail all the differences, it may be helpful to note one or two of the significant ones. Edward Carson's opening speech for the defence, described by all who heard it as one of the most powerful pieces of legal oratory they had ever witnessed, can now be read in full. It is three times the length of anything previously published. Carson's cross-examination of Wilde on his view of Huysmans' novel *À Rebours*, supposedly a source for *Dorian Gray*, was ignored by Millard/Hyde and rendered by both as five lines in square brackets. The first part of the cross-examination about Wilde's relationship with Edward Shelley, equally abbreviated to some 160 words, now runs to more than 1700. At the end of both exchanges Wilde, severely rattled, appeals angrily to his counsel and the Bench at Carson's persistent questioning. The full exchange between Carson and Wilde over the latter's flippant remark about not kissing Walter Grainger now has a dramatic poignancy as the turning point in the trial, which it never before had. Wilde states that he 'loved' Lord Alfred Douglas, rendered by Millard/Hyde, probably reticent about the implications, merely as 'liked', and the words 'sodomy' and 'sodomitical' are seen to have been used in court, rather than the Millard/Hyde circumlocutions of 'unnatural practices'. Overall Wilde comes across as rather sharper and perhaps less arrogant, and the difference in forensic ability between the two leading counsels is more marked than ever.

Curiously, the official records of the trial are almost non-existent. The Central Criminal Court Sessions Papers noted the case with its legal teams and simply declared, 'The details of the case are unfit for publication.' The court records, apart from the official indictment, the plea of justification, the jury books and the documents relating to the two magistrates' court hearings, have disappeared. Queensberry's card, together with a small number of receipts for documents returned to the solicitors, are all that has been preserved. This may be partly due to the unusual nature of the trial, which was a private prosecution. It does not explain the complete absence of records for the two trials in which the Crown prosecuted Wilde. Cock-up or conspiracy? I incline to the latter. One file of interest, however, has survived, which indicates how seriously officialdom took the scandal. It is the opinion of Charles Gill, the Senior Treasury Counsel, to Hamilton Cuffe, the Director of Public Prosecutions, on whether or not to prosecute Lord Alfred Douglas (reproduced here as Appendix B). The most interesting reading is between the lines. The evidence against Douglas, though broadly similar to that against Wilde, is considered unsafe and uncorroborated. A case could doubtless have been built with more police investigation, but the fear implicit in Gill's last sentence is that if Douglas were acquitted it might affect their chances of convicting Wilde. Cuffe's argument about Douglas's lesser moral guilt seems at best specious since he was equally guilty of breaking the law with the rent boys, and his concern about a conviction on unreliable evidence could just as well have applied to Wilde.

When they sent my grandfather to prison for breaking the law, they also rid society of a rebel; not just any old political rebel, but one who called into question something much more dangerous – the hypocrisy of those social, sexual and literary values upon which Victorian society was so firmly based. He cast a rainbow of forbidden colours over that drab age of industrial power and empire building; he pushed his subversive ideas and his subversive behaviour to the limits of what they could tolerate – and then just that little bit further, which they could not. So when the Irish Peacock took the Scarlet Marquess to court, he took on the British Establishment and passed, as he said, 'from an eternity of fame to an eternity of infamy'. I hope that publishing this accurate account of his last public appearance as a free man will show that his fight, although insanely quixotic, was fought with all that style and conviction which we have come to expect from Oscar Wilde.

MERLIN HOLLAND
London, October 2002

2. Oscar Wilde in 1892, much as he would have looked at the Old Bailey in 1895, according to the newspaper reports, though in court, significantly, without the buttonhole.

MAGISTRATES' COURT PROCEEDINGS
GREAT MARLBOROUGH STREET

Regina
(on the prosecution of Oscar Wilde)
v.
John Douglas
(Marquess of Queensberry)

BEFORE R. M. NEWTON ESQ. (MAGISTRATE)
2ND MARCH 1895

DEPOSITIONS
BY
SIDNEY WRIGHT,
HALL PORTER OF THE ALBEMARLE CLUB
THOMAS GREET
DETECTIVE-INSPECTOR OF 'C' DIVISION OF POLICE

MR C. O. HUMPHREYS FOR THE PROSECUTION
SIR GEORGE LEWIS FOR THE MARQUESS OF QUEENSBERRY

[FROM THE SHORTHAND NOTES OF MESSRS CHERER, BENNETT AND DAVIS,
8 NEW COURT, CAREY STREET, WC]

3. Lord Queensberry pictured in *Cycling World Illustrated*, 13 May 1896, doubtless more proficient than in May 1895, when he was twice 'confined to his room having met with an accident while cycling'.

On Saturday 2 March, at nine o'clock in the morning, the Marquess of Queensberry was arrested at Carter's Hotel on a warrant which Oscar Wilde and his solicitor, Charles Humphreys, had obtained the day before. The Marquess was taken to Vine Street police station and from there to Great Marlborough Street magistrates' court and charged. The presiding magistrate was Robert Milnes Newton.[39]

CHARLES HUMPHREYS[40] opened the case by saying that Mr Oscar Wilde was a married man living on the most affectionate terms with his wife and family of two sons. He had been the object of a most cruel persecution at the hands of Lord Queensberry. Ten months ago his client had consulted him on the matter, and in consequence of the domestic affairs of the Queensberry family, Mr Wilde was very unwilling to take any steps of a criminal nature; but he had been so fearfully persecuted by that gentleman that he was compelled to take the step he had now taken for protection and peace of mind. The last act in this most terrible and melancholy drama was performed on the 18th of February, although it had only come to the notice of Mr Oscar Wilde the night before last. Mr Wilde was a member of the Albemarle Club, where both ladies and gentlemen were admitted. Mrs Wilde was also a member of the club. On the previous Thursday night, the 28th of February, between five and six o'clock, Mr Wilde went to this club, and the hall porter presented him with a card enclosed in an envelope addressed to 'Oscar Wilde Esq.'. He explained that a gentleman had called and requested that the card should be handed to Mr Oscar Wilde. The porter, being astonished at what was written on the card, considered it of sufficient importance to add the date and hour when the card was left, and he wrote on it '4.30, 18th February 1895'. MR HUMPHREYS said that he could not conceive a more frightful, serious or abominable libel for one man to publish about another. He proposed to go into other cases which had occurred before the 18th of February, and after they had been investigated he would ask the magistrate to commit the defendant for trial.

SIR GEORGE LEWIS asked that before any evidence was taken, the case should be adjourned so that he might consult with his client and have more time to consider the matter.

MR HUMPHREYS said that he only proposed now calling two witnesses, whose evidence would be very short and the whole matter could be gone into next week.

SIDNEY WRIGHT, *hall porter of the Albemarle Club, and* THOMAS GREET, *the detective-inspector who arrested Queensberry, are then examined and give their evidence.*

SIDNEY WRIGHT: I am the hall porter at the Albemarle Club, 13 Albemarle Street, Piccadilly. On the 18th of February last, the defendant came to the club and spoke to me. He handed me the card produced marked 'A' on which he had written in my presence: 'For Oscar Wilde ponce and somdomite'. (QUEENSBERRY *interposes and states the words are 'posing as sodomite'.*)[41] On the card was printed 'Marquis of Queensberry'.[42] He said, 'Give this card to Oscar Wilde.' On the back of the card I wrote the time and date on which the card was handed to me. I put the card in the envelope produced, marked 'B', and addressed it to 'Oscar Wilde Esq.'. I did not seal the envelope. I left it on my desk. On the 28th of February Mr Oscar Wilde called at the club. I knew him and also Mrs Wilde as members of the club. When he called I handed to him the envelope containing the card, saying, 'Lord Queensberry left this for you.'

WRIGHT *is then cross-examined by* SIR GEORGE LEWIS.

SYDNEY WRIGHT: The defendant gave me to understand that I was to deliver the card to Mr Wilde. I knew nothing of the circumstances preceding the delivery of the card.

WRIGHT *then signs his deposition.*

THOMAS GREET: I am a detective-inspector of the 'C' Division of Police. Yesterday I received the warrant produced from this court. About nine o'clock this morning I saw the defendant at Carter's Hotel, Albemarle Street. I said, 'Are you the Marquess of Queensberry?' He said, 'I am.' I said, 'I am a police officer and hold a warrant signed by R. M. Newton Esq. of Marlborough Street police court for your arrest.' I then read the warrant to him.[43] He said, 'In these cases I always thought proceedings were taken by summons but I suppose it's all right.' I said, 'Yes.' He said, 'What's the date?' I said, 'The eighteenth.'[44] He said, 'Yes – I have been trying to find Mr Oscar Wilde for eight or ten days. This thing has been going on for over two years.' I took him to Vine Street police station where he was charged and made no reply.

SIR GEORGE LEWIS:[45] Let me say one word, sir. I venture to say that when the circumstances of this case are more fully known, you will find that Lord Queensberry acted as he did under feelings of great indignation and—

MAGISTRATE (*interrupting*): I cannot go into that now.

SIR GEORGE LEWIS: I do not wish this case to be adjourned without it being known that there is nothing against the honour of Lord Queensberry.

MAGISTRATE: You mean to say that you have a perfect answer to the charge.

SIR GEORGE LEWIS: I ask you, sir, to allow his lordship to be at large on his entering into his own recognizances in the sum of £1000.

CHARLES HUMPHREYS: I should like to have a surety.

SIR GEORGE LEWIS: Lord Queensberry is not going to run away.

MAGISTRATE: The case will be adjourned for a week, and the defendant will have to find one surety in the sum of £500 and enter into his own recognizances in the sum of £1000.

MR WILLIAM TYSER, *merchant, of 13 Gloucester Square W,*[46] *offers the necessary bail and the* MARQUESS OF QUEENSBERRY *leaves the court with his friends.*

4. Edward Carson QC MP, counsel for Lord Queensberry, as caricatured by Liberio Prosperi for *Vanity Fair*, 9 November 1893.

MAGISTRATES' COURT PROCEEDINGS
GREAT MARLBOROUGH STREET

Regina
(on the prosecution of Oscar Wilde)
v.
John Douglas
(Marquess of Queensberry)

BEFORE R. M. NEWTON ESQ. (MAGISTRATE)
9TH MARCH 1895
(ADJOURNED HEARING)

DEPOSITIONS
BY
OSCAR WILDE
THE MARQUESS OF QUEENSBERRY

MR. C. O. HUMPHREYS FOR THE PROSECUTION
MR E. H. CARSON QC MP AND MR C. F. GILL FOR THE MARQUESS OF
QUEENSBERRY

[FROM THE SHORTHAND NOTES OF MESSRS CHERER, BENNETT AND DAVIS,
8 NEW COURT, CAREY STREET, WC]

5. Sir Edward Clarke QC, counsel for Oscar Wilde, by Leslie Ward
for *Vanity Fair*, 11 June 1903.

OSCAR WILDE *is sworn and is examined by* CHARLES HUMPHREYS.

CHARLES HUMPHREYS: Mr Oscar Fingal O'fflahertie Wills Wilde – those are your names?

OSCAR WILDE: Yes.

HUMPHREYS: Are you a dramatist and author?

WILDE (*loftily*): I believe I am well-known as a dramatist and author.

MAGISTRATE (*sharply*): Will you answer the question if you please.

WILDE: Yes.

HUMPHREYS: I believe you have taken a great interest in matters of art?

WILDE: Yes.

HUMPHREYS: And you reside at No. 16 Tite Street, SW?[47]

WILDE: Yes.

HUMPHREYS: Are you acquainted with the defendant and with many members of his family?

WILDE: Yes.

HUMPHREYS: About when did you first become acquainted with the defendant?

WILDE: I think about the year 1893.

HUMPHREYS: Had you not known him before then – when you left Oxford, when did you leave Oxford?

WILDE: I left Oxford in 1879.

HUMPHREYS: How long after you left Oxford was it that you became acquainted with Lord Queensberry?

WILDE: I was reminded by Lord Queensberry when I was introduced to him in 1893 that he had met me once before. I had forgotten the circumstance.

CLERK OF THE COURT:[48] You first became acquainted with the defendant in 1893?

WILDE: To my knowledge, but I was reminded about the other.

9

HUMPHREYS: Do you remember on one occasion you were lunching with Lord Alfred Douglas, his son, at the Café Royal?[49]

WILDE: Yes.

HUMPHREYS: When about was that when you saw the defendant there?

WILDE: My impression was it was in the month of October 1893.

HUMPHREYS: 1893 or 1892?

CLERK: He says 1893.

WILDE: 1892.

CLERK: What is that — you remember lunching with him?

HUMPHREYS: He remembers one occasion when he was lunching with Lord Alfred Douglas at the Café Royal. (*To* WILDE.) Did the defendant come into the room where you were lunching?

WILDE: Yes.

HUMPHREYS: And did Lord Queensberry come up to the same table at which you and Lord Alfred were lunching?

WILDE: Yes.

HUMPHREYS: By invitation or not?

WILDE: By the invitation of his son.

HUMPHREYS: Did he shake hands with either or both of you on that occasion?

WILDE: With both of us.

HUMPHREYS: Did he sit down and lunch at the same table at which you were?

WILDE: Yes.

HUMPHREYS: How long afterwards was it before you saw him again?

WILDE: I don't think I saw Lord Queensberry then till the early part, I should think, of March 1894.

HUMPHREYS: Was that on an occasion when you and Lord Alfred Douglas were lunching together at the Café Royal?

WILDE: Yes.

HUMPHREYS: I believe his lordship entered the room while you were lunching?

WILDE: Yes.

HUMPHREYS: Did he come to the same table?

WILDE: Yes.

HUMPHREYS: Did he receive any invitation to come to the same table or not?

WILDE: No, he came up and shook hands with his son and then with me and we invited him to join us.

CLERK: You personally? Did you say 'I invited him'?

WILDE: A mutual invitation.

CLERK: 'We invited him to join us'?

WILDE: Yes.

HUMPHREYS: Was that shortly after Lord Alfred had returned from Egypt?[50]

WILDE: Just after.

HUMPHREYS: There was a general conversation between the three of you?

WILDE: Yes.

HUMPHREYS: Principally about Egypt, I believe?

WILDE: Yes.

HUMPHREYS: Shortly after that did Lord Alfred Douglas hand to you a letter? Just look at that letter which is dated the 1st of April. (*Proceeding to hand it to* WILDE.)[51]

WILDE: Yes, he handed it to me.

MAGISTRATE: Just wait. I never like to stop any evidence if I can help it. Tell me what you propose to do with that.

HUMPHREYS: I propose to ask the witness whether Lord Alfred Douglas handed to him that letter or showed to him that letter.

MAGISTRATE: Suppose he did – what then?

EDWARD CARSON:[52] I may say, on behalf of Lord Queensberry, I myself would call for these letters on cross-examination. I am very anxious that they should be produced.

MAGISTRATE: The objection I make is that it is evidence of another state of facts. I am enquiring whether this card is a libel or not.

HUMPHREYS: Yes, I propose to put in other libels besides that card and this is one of them.

MAGISTRATE: I cannot stop you.

HUMPHREYS: I have fully considered the matter.

MAGISTRATE: I should have suggested you should not have done so.

HUMPHREYS: Well, sir, your suggestions are always exceedingly valuable.

MAGISTRATE: Looking ahead, I should say that you had much better have stopped.

CARSON: I really hope that the letter will be put in. You see, sir—

MAGISTRATE: I know your point. It is a question for me.

CARSON: My point is that Lord Queensberry was acting in the interests of his son and I am very anxious to have the letter which introduces the whole matter.

MAGISTRATE: Very likely, but, pardon me, you cannot go into that here.

CARSON: I am quite aware of that. I think it affects the truth. I shall do it elsewhere.

MAGISTRATE: I am pointing out that Mr Humphreys is opening a door for something which will not take place in this court but elsewhere.

CARSON: At all events I must say that I make no objection.

HUMPHREYS: I don't see how you could make any objection if I insist upon it.

CARSON: I think I could.

HUMPHREYS: I don't think you could. The only course which I have turned over in my mind has been this – unless the documents are produced here and attached to the depositions, other libels than that which you have had already evidence of cannot be brought before the court above, and no indictment could be preferred upon those documents as other libels.

MAGISTRATE: Surely you could give the defendant notice of your intention to produce other libels at the trial?

HUMPHREYS: I can adopt that course.

MAGISTRATE: Surely that would be competent for you to do?

HUMPHREYS: But unless there is a committal on those other libels I don't think I could indict for those libels.

MAGISTRATE: No, you cannot, it is very true, but you can give them notice that you are going to put in other libels.

HUMPHREYS: Very well, sir, I will adopt your suggestion.

MAGISTRATE: Mr Carson, there will be no objection to that?

CARSON: Well, I should prefer—

MAGISTRATE: You cannot enter onto a cross-examination on the contents of those letters in this court, therefore it would be useless to let Mr Humphreys go on in the course he suggests.

CARSON: I understand Mr Humphreys's view – he means to indict for libels besides the particular postcard.[53]

MAGISTRATE: Yes.

CARSON: If he intends to do that, under the Vexatious Indictments Act[54] there must be a committal upon it, and of course I should take an objection at the trial if there was an indictment on a charge not enquired into here. I am not in the slightest degree intending to infringe the rules, and I am quite aware that I am not to go into the truth of the libel here, because with that you have nothing to do; but at the same time, sir, I would be entitled to do this: to go into the question of the privilege of Lord Queensberry giving advice to his own son and if the ultimate charge arose out of that, it being a mere question of privilege, that surely is a matter I could raise before you here.

HUMPHREYS: You don't know that letter contains any advice to his own son.

CARSON: Don't I? I happen to have a copy.

MAGISTRATE: You are just opening the door to let in something about which there may be a great difficulty hereafter.

HUMPHREYS: Very well, then, I will bow to your superior judgement and adopt your suggestion, which I have already told you is so valuable very often.

MAGISTRATE: What you had better do is this: you had better say that you have received libels from Lord Queensberry and mention the dates.

CARSON: Well, sir, I should, with very great respect, object to that course, unless they are produced, because to have a general statement that there are libels from Lord Queensberry is really begging the question.

MAGISTRATE: You can have the dates.

CARSON: Even with dates I should ask to have the documents put in, in fairness to Lord Queensberry, if they are to be gone into at all. Of course, my friend can confine himself to the postcard, which was the matter on which the warrant was granted him, but if the other matters are to be gone into, I ask to have the documents produced and the fullest investigation of them.

HUMPHREYS: It was never my intention to read them in the first instance, and I intended, supposing these letters were produced, to ask you to read them, and my friends on the other side to read them, but that they should not be read in public, and for this reason: with reference to one particular letter the names of exalted persons are used and I don't think it would be right to them that their names should be called in question in matters of this description, and if the letter were used publicly, of course, those names must.[55]

MAGISTRATE: Is that not a reason the more why my suggestion should be adopted?

HUMPHREYS: Perhaps it is, sir. Very well, then I shall adopt your suggestion.

CLERK: The last I have got is, 'There was a general conversation between the three of us, principally about Egypt.'

HUMPHREYS: I propose to ask this question and I will be governed by your decision upon it, sir. (*To* WILDE.) Have you ever been handed letters by Lord Alfred Douglas written by Lord Queensberry in which your name is mentioned or referred to?

CARSON: I object without the production of the documents. That is giving evidence of the contents of the letter to a certain extent.

MAGISTRATE: You are justified in doing that.

CARSON: I am quite satisfied with one course or the other; either drop them out altogether or put them in. That is all I ask.

MAGISTRATE: Yes.

HUMPHREYS: Very well. (*To* WILDE.) Now, on Thursday the 28th of last month about five o'clock in the afternoon did you drive up to the Albemarle Club?[56]

WILDE: Yes.

HUMPHREYS: There is just one thing I should like to ask before that.

CLERK: Well, it is down now.

HUMPHREYS: Very well then, I can take the other later. (*To* WILDE.) In Albemarle Street number 13, I think?

WILDE: Yes.

HUMPHREYS: Had you recently returned from Algiers?[57]

WILDE: Yes.

HUMPHREYS: And this was the first visit you paid to the club after your return from Algiers?

WILDE: Yes.

HUMPHREYS: On entering the club did you see and speak to the hall porter or the hall porter speak to you – a person of the name of Sidney Wright?

WILDE: I spoke first. I asked the hall porter for a blank cheque.

HUMPHREYS: I cannot go into that.

MAGISTRATE: Be good enough to answer the question.

WILDE: I beg your pardon, I didn't quite understand.

MAGISTRATE: It is an easy question. It is better to wait before you answer. Will you repeat your question.

HUMPHREYS: My question was this. Did you speak to the hall porter or did he speak to you first?

WILDE: I spoke to him.

HUMPHREYS: And did the hall porter hand you the envelope which is produced – that envelope—(*Handing an envelope marked 'B'.*)

WILDE: Yes.

HUMPHREYS: It speaks for itself. Your name is written on the back of that envelope?

WILDE: Yes.

HUMPHREYS: And in handing you that envelope did the hall porter say anything to you?

WILDE: He said—

HUMPHREYS: One moment, he said something to you, did he?

WILDE: Yes.

HUMPHREYS: Was that something a message, which he stated he had been directed to give you from some other person?

WILDE: Yes.

HUMPHREYS: I propose now, sir, inasmuch as this was a direct message from Lord Queensberry through the porter to Mr Oscar Wilde, to ask what that message was. It was given by the direction of the defendant.

CARSON: Is that proved?

CLERK: He said something he said was a message from the defendant.

CARSON: Was it proved by the porter?

HUMPHREYS: Yes.

CARSON: That he got a message?

HUMPHREYS: Yes.

CARSON: Then, I do not object.

HUMPHREYS (*to* WILDE): What did the porter say to you? – the message only from Lord Queensberry.

WILDE: 'Lord Queensberry desired me, sir, to hand this to you when you came to the club.'

HUMPHREYS: And what did he hand to you?

WILDE: He handed me that envelope.

HUMPHREYS: And anything else?

WILDE: Yes, a card contained in it.

HUMPHREYS: Was the card inside the envelope?

WILDE: Inside.

HUMPHREYS: And did he take the card out and hand the card to you?

WILDE: No, he handed me the envelope. He said, 'Lord Queensberry desired me to hand this to you when you came in to the club.' If he said 'this' or 'these' I don't know. The envelope was an open envelope.

HUMPHREYS: Did you thereupon open the envelope?

WILDE: Yes.

HUMPHREYS: You found the card contained therein?

WILDE: Yes.

HUMPHREYS: Which has been produced marked 'A'?

WILDE: Yes.

HUMPHREYS: On the back of the envelope, if you will just look at it please, there is a date I think – four thirty?

WILDE: Yes.

HUMPHREYS: Will you read what it is?

WILDE: 'Four thirty, 18/2/95.'

HUMPHREYS: Did you make any remark to the hall porter about that or he to you?

WILDE: Yes.

HUMPHREYS: What did he say?

CARSON: I do not think this can be evidence.

HUMPHREYS: It has already been given. It is part of the transaction.

MAGISTRATE: Does anything turn upon this? The witness says, 'I got the letter from the porter,' the letter is produced here and the porter says, 'I have got a letter from Lord Queensberry.'

HUMPHREYS: 'To hand to you.'

MAGISTRATE: What does it signify? He has already said that.

HUMPHREYS: Yes, the porter has proved it. (*To* WILDE.) Did you read what was on the card as well as you could?

WILDE: Yes.

HUMPHREYS: Did you immediately communicate with your solicitor and have an interview with him on the following day, the 1st of March?

WILDE: Yes.

HUMPHREYS: And on the same day, the 1st of March, did you apply with your solicitor at this court for a warrant?

WILDE: Yes.

HUMPHREYS: For Lord Queensberry's apprehension?

WILDE: Yes.

HUMPHREYS: That is all I ask this witness.

MAGISTRATE (*after conferring with the* CLERK): Mr Humphreys I suggest that you should accompany me and Mr Carson into the other room and have a word together.

HUMPHREYS: Certainly, sir.

HUMPHREYS *and* CARSON *then retire with the* MAGISTRATE *and return into the Court after an interval of six minutes.* WILDE *in the meantime has been given a seat.*

HUMPHREYS: That is all I propose to ask Mr Wilde.

WILDE *is then cross-examined by* CARSON.

CARSON: How long have you known Lord Alfred Douglas?

MAGISTRATE: Are you entitled to cross-examine in this court?

CARSON: Surely to cross-examine – not to cross-examine as to justification—

MAGISTRATE: How far will your cross-examination go, then?

CARSON: My cross-examination will go to show that the step taken by Lord Queensberry in the present case was with a hope of putting an end to the acquaintance between Mr Wilde and his son.

MAGISTRATE: That is a quasi-justification.

CARSON: All I propose to ask Mr Wilde at present is whether in consequence of the intimacy Lord Queensberry had not forbidden the acquaintance between him and his son.

MAGISTRATE: That would be a quasi-justification.

CARSON: I think not, with great respect. I think that is a question on the privilege of the father in protecting his own son.

HUMPHREYS: I wish to refer you, sir, to the case of *The Queen v. Sir Robert Carden*, which is reported in the Law Reports 5 Queens Bench Division. There the application was made on behalf of the defendant and the writ of *mandamus* asked for was in substance to the following effect: namely to hear evidence in cross-examination by the defendant of the complainant and the complainant's witnesses and that case entirely overruled any such proposition. That was in the Court of Appeal and Lord Chief Justice Cockburn, Mr Justice Lush and Mr Justice Manisty all unanimously decided that the rule must be discharged.[58]

CARSON: I will only say this in reference to that case: I am perfectly well aware of the decision. I read it very recently for the purposes of this case, and it only goes to this: that you should not cross-examine with reference to the plea of justification. It goes no further. It does not take away the ordinary right to cross-examine upon the question of guilty or not guilty. This somewhat peculiar criminal jurisdiction in libel is a matter of very much discretion in the magistrate. He has to find out whether it is probable that a jury, upon the case as presented when he has heard the whole facts, would convict and would hold it a libel because apart altogether from the question of justification it is always for a jury to say under the whole circumstances of the case whether it is or is not a libel and ought to be criminally punished and, sir, I do not propose now to ask any question upon the plea of justification. That is a plea that Lord Queensberry, with the full responsibility of its effect, will raise if this matter is sent for trial, but I do propose to ask certain questions to show how it was that Lord Queensberry came to write this card, his object in writing the card being connected with his previous letters and his previous visits to Mr Wilde and Lord Queensberry's assertion that he was entitled, if he thought it in the interests of the morality of his own son, to do everything in his power to put a stop to the connection of his son with Mr Oscar Wilde. I propose it solely in that view. I am quite prepared to submit most respectfully to any ruling you give on the subject, but it does occur to me it would be going very much beyond the case of *The Queen v. Carden* if I am not allowed to cross-examine on matters which, I submit, do not go to justification.

MAGISTRATE: My objection is this, that the question you put would be this. Was not Lord Queensberry justified in writing this card, having told his son not to make the acquaintance of Mr Wilde? 'If you make the acquaintance of Mr Wilde you must take the consequence.' I object to your question accordingly.

CARSON: I submit to your ruling. It is a case of some difficulty.

HUMPHREYS: There is another case on the point.

MAGISTRATE: I have given my opinion. Mr Carson will abide by it.

CARSON: Certainly I will abide by it. I will only say I am somewhat astonished that Mr Humphreys should persist in it.

HUMPHREYS: I am governed by the rules of evidence in decided cases. It is not a question of my insisting upon it. That is the case, sir.

The CLERK *proceeds to read over* WILDE's *deposition.*

HUMPHREYS (*interposing*): That might be misleading – the envelope was open as a fact; it was never fastened up.

MAGISTRATE: It was unfastened.

CLERK (*to* WILDE): I will put, 'The envelope was unfastened when handed to you by the porter.'

WILDE: Yes.

CARSON: The porter proved that also.

HUMPHREYS: Yes, he proved it.

CLERK (*continuing to read the deposition*): Is that right?

WILDE: I think there is one correction. What the hall porter said to me was, 'Lord Queensberry desired me to hand this card to you.' He then handed me the card.

CLERK: 'Lord Queensberry desired me, sir, to hand this to you when you came into the club.'

WILDE: 'This card.'

CLERK: 'This card to you'?

WILDE: Yes.

CARSON: Might I ask, sir, that it should appear upon the deposition that I put a question which was overruled as I should like it to be known that I was prepared to cross-examine Mr Wilde.

MAGISTRATE: Will you repeat that question.

CARSON: Yes, the question I asked was how long he had known Lord Alfred Douglas.

MAGISTRATE (*to the* CLERK): 'Cross-examined, question objected to.'

CLERK: 'The question "How long had you known Lord Alfred Douglas?" was put on cross-examination and overruled by the Magistrate.'

MAGISTRATE: Yes.

The deposition is handed to WILDE *to sign.*

WILDE: I should like to be allowed to look at a date. There is the date of a year with regard to the first time that I met Lord Queensberry. I should like to see exactly whether that date is correct. I should like to be allowed to see exactly whether I made a mistake or not.

MAGISTRATE (*sternly*): If you would just attend, if you please, this would not have happened.

CLERK: You say, Mr Wilde, 'I am acquainted with the defendant and many members of his family. I first became acquainted with the defendant to my knowledge in 1893.'

WILDE: I believe it to be 1892.

HUMPHREYS: He corrected it afterwards and said 1892.

WILDE: Yes, I think I did.

HUMPHREYS: You will find that.

CLERK: 'I remember lunching on one occasion with Lord Alfred Douglas at the Café Royal, it was in 1893.' It is 1892. Am I to put that down?

WILDE: Yes, 1892.

CLERK: Then, the sentence reads, 'I first became acquainted with the defendant to my knowledge in 1892.'

WILDE *then signs his deposition.*[59]

MAGISTRATE: Is that your case?

HUMPHREYS: I think the inspector's evidence was not read over.

CLERK: The hall porter's was read and signed.

THOMAS GREET *is sworn.*

CLERK: This evidence was taken on the 2nd of March. (*Proceeds to read his deposition.*) Is that right?

GREET: Yes.

GREET *then signs his deposition.*

HUMPHREYS: Then, that is the case, sir, upon which I ask you to commit the defendant for trial.

MAGISTRATE: Just let the defendant stand up. (*Addressing the defendant.*) John Douglas, Marquess of Queensberry, having heard the evidence, now is the time to make an answer to the charge, but recollect that whatever you say will be taken down in writing and may be used in evidence against you at your trial. Have you anything to say?

QUEENSBERRY: I have simply to say this, your worship, that I wrote that card simply with the intention of bringing matters to a head, having been unable to meet Mr Wilde otherwise, and to save my son, and I abide by what I wrote.

CLERK: Lord Queensberry, this is what I have taken down: 'I have simply to say this, that I wrote that card simply with the intention of bringing matters to a head, having been unable to meet Mr Wilde otherwise, and to save my son, and I abide by what I wrote.'

QUEENSBERRY: Yes.

QUEENSBERRY *then signs his deposition.*

MAGISTRATE: Do you call any witnesses, Mr Carson?

CARSON: Not here.

MAGISTRATE: The defendant is committed to take his trial at the next sessions of the Central Criminal Court and the witnesses are bound over in a sum of £40 to attend and prosecute.

CARSON: I suppose the same bail as the last?

MAGISTRATE: Is the gentleman here who bailed the defendant out on the last occasion?[60]

CARSON: Yes.

MAGISTRATE: The same bail.

CARSON: In order that there may be no misapprehension as to witnesses they would come under the same ruling in the *The Queen v. Carden* as to cross-examination?

MAGISTRATE: Yes.

CARSON: Therefore I could not call them.

6. Sir Richard Henn Collins, the judge in the libel trial, as seen by
John Page Mellor for *Vanity Fair* 14 January 1893.

CENTRAL CRIMINAL COURT PROCEEDINGS
THE OLD BAILEY

Regina
(on the prosecution of Oscar Wilde)
v.
John Douglas
(Marquess of Queensberry)

BEFORE
MR JUSTICE COLLINS AND A JURY
3RD APRIL—5TH APRIL 1895

SIR EDWARD CLARKE QC MP, MR CHARLES WILLIE MATHEWS AND MR
TRAVERS HUMPHREYS FOR THE PROSECUTION

MR E. H. CARSON QC MP, MR C. F. GILL AND MR A. E. GILL FOR THE
DEFENDANT

MR EDWARD BESLEY QC AND MR JOHN LIONEL MONCKTON HELD WATCHING
BRIEFS ON THE CASE ON BEHALF OF LORD ALFRED DOUGLAS AND LORD
DOUGLAS OF HAWICK

[FROM THE SHORTHAND NOTES OF MESSRS CHERER, BENNETT AND DAVIS,
8 NEW COURT, CAREY STREET, WC]

FIRST DAY MORNING

SIR EDWARD CLARKE[61] *opens the case for the prosecution.*

SIR EDWARD CLARKE: May it please your lordship,[62] gentlemen of the jury, you have heard that the charge against the defendant is that he published a malicious libel with regard to Mr Oscar Wilde. That libel was published in the form of a card which was left by Lord Queensberry at the club to which Mr Oscar Wilde belongs. It was a visiting card of Lord Queensberry with his name printed upon it and had written upon it the words 'to Oscar Wilde posing as sodomite', and in respect of the libel so published on that card this charge is brought against the defendant.

Now, gentlemen, of course it is a matter of serious moment that such a word as Lord Queensberry had written on that card should in any way be connected with the name of a gentleman who has borne a high reputation in this country. It is not an accusation of that, the gravest of all offences – 'posing as sodomite' indeed appears to suggest there is no guilt of the actual offence – but that in some way or another the person of whom those words are written has appeared to be – nay, desired to appear to be – a person guilty of or inclined to the commission of that gravest of all offences; and the publication of such a statement, the leaving of such a card with the porter of a club, of course, is an act most serious, likely gravely to affect the reputation and the position of the person as to whom that injurious suggestion is made. If we had here to deal only with that publication, simply with the question of whether that libel was published and the further question – not for you, but for my lord – what amount of blame as for a criminal action should be thrown upon the defendant in respect of that matter, there would be many considerations, some of which probably – many of which – may be brought to your notice before this case concludes, which would not have justified such an action, of course, for such action could not be justified unless the statement were true, but would at all events, in regard to a person in the position of the defendant and with such characteristics as the evidence in this case will probably show that he himself has, might have gone to some extent to extenuate the gravity of the offence. But the matter here for consideration today does not stop with the question of whether that card was delivered, and whether the defendant could be in any way excused by strong feeling – mistaken feeling, but strong feeling – for having made that statement. By the plea which the defendant has put before the Court today a much graver issue is raised. He says that that statement is true and that it was for the public benefit that that statement was made. He says that it is true, giving particulars in the plea of matters which, as he alleges, show that statement to be true with regard to Mr Oscar Wilde. The plea has not in full been read to you, but I will state to you this: there is no allegation in the plea that Mr Oscar Wilde has been guilty of the offence of which I have spoken, but there are a series of accusations, mentioning the names of certain persons – many persons – and it is said in regard to all those persons that Mr Oscar Wilde has solicited them to commit with him the grave offence and that he has been guilty with each and all of them of indecent practices.[63] I think it will occur to you as somewhat strange that whereas this plea and the statements which are contained in this plea refer to a very considerable period of time, one would gather from the plea that during all that time Mr Oscar Wilde had been unsuccessfully soliciting those persons to commit this offence with him. I can myself understand how it is that the statement is put in this form for they who may at some time in this case be called before you to sustain, if they can, these serious charges are persons who, although they will necessarily have to admit much in cross-examination if they come to give such evidence, I suppose are not prepared to admit that they themselves have been guilty of the gravest of offences;

but it is notable that these accusations state that Mr Oscar Wilde solicited the commission of the offence and that although that offence is not alleged to have been committed, he was guilty of indecent practices. I shall have to refer before I close specifically to two counts in the plea which has been put upon the record, but with regard to those earlier ones which deal with names and dates and places, of course, I do not propose at this moment to trouble you. It is for those who have taken the very grave responsibility of putting into the plea those allegations to satisfy you if they can, by credible witnesses whose evidence you will consider worthy of consideration and entitled to belief that those charges are true.

Mr Oscar Wilde is a gentleman of thirty-eight years of age at this time. He is the son of Sir William Wilde, a very distinguished Irishman, a surgeon and oculist, and a gentleman who did great public service as chairman of a Census Commission in Ireland.[64] The father died some years ago. Mr Wilde's mother Lady Wilde is now living. He went in the first instance to Trinity College, Dublin and at Trinity College, Dublin greatly distinguished himself – greatly distinguished himself for classical knowledge and earned some conspicuous rewards which are given to the students at that brilliant university – and so distinguished himself there that his father wished him to go to Oxford and he passed to Magdalen College, Oxford.[65] There again he distinguished himself; he took a first class in 'Mods', a first class in 'Greats'; he had a classical scholarship and he attained what was indicative of his future course and future reputation, the Newdigate Prize for English poetry.[66] Leaving the university after a brilliant career, he devoted himself to literature and literature in its artistic side. He published as long ago as 1882 a volume of poems.[67] He wrote essays upon artistic and aesthetic[68] subjects and you may possibly know that many years ago Mr Oscar Wilde became a very public person indeed, laughed at by some, appreciated by many but at all events representing a special and particular aspect of artistic literature, which commended itself greatly to many of those of the foremost minds and most cultivated people of our time. In the year 1884 he had the happy fortune to marry the daughter of late Mr Horace Lloyd, Queen's Counsel, and from that date in 1884 until now he has lived with his wife, and latterly with the two sons of whom he is the father, at Tite Street in Chelsea, and from the date of that marriage to the present time at that home in Tite Street he has been in the habit of receiving with his wife the friends who visited him there. His wife is a member of the Albemarle Club to which he himself belongs and to the porter of which club this offensive card was delivered. Among the friends whom he saw at Tite Street was a gentleman whose name I mention – it is necessary I should mention – Lord Alfred Douglas,[69] and in the year 1891 Lord Alfred Douglas came to Tite Street one afternoon, was introduced by a friend of Mr Wilde and a friend of Lord Alfred's[70] and from that time until now Mr Oscar Wilde has been the friend not only of Lord Alfred Douglas but of Lord Alfred Douglas's brothers and Lord Alfred Douglas's mother Lady Queensberry, who was the wife of the defendant, but who some years ago obtained a release from the marriage tie in consequence of the defendant's conduct.[71] During all this time, as I say, Mr Wilde has been the friend of the sons of the family and of the mother and he has again and again been a guest in her house at Wokingham and at Salisbury,[72] invited to be her guest at a time more than once when a family party has been gathered at that house. On the other hand Lord Alfred Douglas has been the accepted and welcome friend in Mr Oscar Wilde's own home. Of course, they have seen much of each other in London and at theatres and so on from time to time, but on more than one occasion Lord Alfred Douglas has been the guest at the home at which Mr Oscar Wilde and his wife and sons were, at Cromer on one occasion and I think at Goring on another and at Worthing – where Mr and Mrs Wilde and their sons were staying – at either places Lord Alfred Douglas was a guest and a welcome guest in that household.[73] Until the early part of the year 1893 Mr Oscar Wilde did not know the defendant at all, with the exception that they seem to have met once a good many years ago somewhere about 1880 or 1881, an incident of which Lord Queensberry reminded Mr Wilde on the occasion when they met at luncheon in the circumstances which I am now going to mention. In November 1892 Mr Wilde and Lord Alfred Douglas were lunching at the Café Royal in Regent Street and Lord Queensberry came into the room. Mr Wilde was aware that owing to circumstances, with which he had nothing what-ever to do, owing to unhappy family troubles, which I only mention in a sentence because it is absolutely necessary, there had been some strained feelings between Lord Alfred Douglas and his father and he suggested to Lord Alfred that it was a good opportunity for him to go and speak to his father and have a friendly interview. Lord Alfred acted upon that suggestion and went across to Lord Queensberry, shook hands with him, had a little talk with him and brought him to the table at which Mr Wilde and he had sat themselves for lunch. Lord Queensberry was introduced to and shook hands with Mr Wilde and it was Lord Queensberry who recalled to Mr Wilde's recollection that which time had effaced from it, the fact that some eleven or twelve years before they had met at another house of a friend of both of them. On that occasion Lord Queensberry sat down at their table, joined them, had lunch with them. Lord Alfred was obliged to leave about half past two or something of that kind. Lord Queensberry remained chatting with Mr Wilde. Mr Wilde said he and his family were going down to Torquay to stay.[74] It happened this way. Lord Queensberry at that time was about to give some lectures and suggested to Mr Wilde he should come. Mr Wilde explained he was going with his family to Torquay. Lord Queensberry then said that he also was going to Torquay or expected to be going there and he hoped they would see something of each other at Torquay if they were going down there together. As it happened, although Mr Wilde and his family went to Torquay, Lord Queensberry did not at that time come down to that place and a note from Lord Queensberry told Mr Wilde of that fact and just explained how it was that he did not see him at Torquay. That was in the month of November 1892 and of Lord Queensberry Mr Wilde saw nothing whatever until the early part of the year 1894. He did not see him personally during that time; he did become aware – and I confine myself at the moment to that form of a statement – that some statements were made affecting his character – I do not mean by Lord Queensberry – but he became aware of it in this way. There was a man named Wood whom he had once or twice seen, but whom he knew very little indeed, who had been given some clothes by Lord Alfred Douglas and who said that he had found in the pocket of a coat that was given to him four letters that had been written by Mr Wilde to Lord Alfred Douglas.[75] Whether Wood found them in the pocket of the coat or whether Wood had stolen them is a matter upon which at this moment we can only speculate. I do not know whether in the course of the case it will be necessary to investigate that matter or not, but at all events there were some letters of Mr Wilde to Lord Alfred Douglas which were by way of being handed about, and Wood came to Mr Oscar Wilde early in the year 1893 and had with him some letters written by Mr Wilde to Lord Alfred Douglas and wanted Mr Wilde to give him something for the letters. He represented himself as being in some distress and trouble and as wanting to go to America, and Mr Wilde gave him fifteen pounds or twenty pounds in order to pay his passage to America and Wood handed to Mr Wilde three somewhat ordinary letters which had been written by him to Lord Alfred Douglas. I do not think any importance attaches to those letters because you will see that, as is generally the case where people think that they have got letters which are of some importance, the letters which are of no importance are given up and the letter which is supposed to be of importance is retained. That was the case in this instance. We may find out something before this case is over about the set of people – Wood and a man named Allen and a man named Cliburn[76] – who were taking part in this transaction. But at this time in 1893 a play which Mr Oscar Wilde had written and which some of you will remember was a great success at the Haymarket Theatre – *A Woman of No Importance* – was being prepared and of course Mr Wilde was from time to time and very frequently seeing Mr Beerbohm Tree, the actor and manager,[77] and there came into his hands through Mr Beerbohm Tree this paper, which purports to be and to some extent is a copy of a letter, which had been retained by these persons or some of them when the others were handed over to Mr Oscar Wilde. This is a very curious document. It has a note 'To Mr Tree. Mr Tree kindly give this to Mr Wilde and oblige yours' and I cannot quite read that and 'E', I suppose or something of that kind. Then, the letter which is supposed to be a copy of that which was written by Mr Oscar Wilde has got two headings, one Babbacombe Cliff Torquay and the other 16 Tite Street Chelsea SW and Mr Tree naturally handed that document to Mr Wilde. Well, it purports to be a copy of a letter written by Mr Oscar Wilde. Shortly after this date a man named Allen called upon Mr Wilde and said that he had the letter of which that was a copy and wanted Mr Wilde to give him something for it. Mr Wilde absolutely and peremptorily refused, refused in terms which you will hear, but refused on this ground: he said, 'I have got a copy of that letter; now the original is no use to me. I look upon it as a work of art, that letter. I should have desired to possess a copy. Now you have been good enough to send me a copy I do not want the original' (*laughter*) and he sent Allen away with the letter, did not get the letter, would not buy it from Allen, gave him a sovereign, I think, or something of that kind for himself and sent him away with the letter. Almost immediately afterwards a man named Cliburn came in and said that Allen so appreciated Mr Wilde's kindness to him that he had sent him the letter, and Cliburn came and brought the letter and gave it to Mr Wilde, getting no money for it at all. Mr Wilde, I think, gave him a sovereign for his trouble but there the letter was. Well, gentlemen, Mr Wilde was somewhat sensitive upon two matters with regard to this, one was that this letter had been suggested to be a letter of an incriminating character and someone had thought it was worthwhile to copy, not with accuracy, but with some mistakes, this letter and to put it about by sending it, for instance, to Mr Tree as he might have sent it to other persons for the purpose of damaging Mr Wilde. Having once got the original letter in his possession Mr Wilde kept it. The original letter is in my hands now. There was another reason in respect of which Mr Wilde had been interested about this letter. He said to Allen and he says now that he looks upon this letter as being a sort of prose sonnet and he told Allen when Allen came to see him that at some time or other this letter would probably appear in sonnet form. It did so appear. I hold in my hand a copy of a publication which was issued on the 4th of May 1893 called *'The Spirit Lamp.* An aesthetic and literary and critical magazine edited by Lord Alfred Douglas'[78] and on the first page of it there is a French poem, a sonnet, which is thus headed 'A letter written in prose poetry by Mr Oscar Wilde to a friend and translated into rhymed poetry by a poet of no importance'. It is in French.[79] It is signed Pierre Louÿs and it is not a reproduction exactly but a paraphrase of the letter which was written by Mr Oscar Wilde and here is the letter. There is no trace upon the letter itself but it was written to Lord Alfred Douglas. 'My own boy, your sonnet[80] is quite lovely, and it is a marvel that those red, rose-leaf lips of yours should be made no less for music of song than for madness of kissing.[81] Your slim gilt soul walks between passion and poetry. I know Hyacinthus, whom Apollo loved so madly, was you in Greek days. Why are you alone in London and when do you go to Salisbury?' Salisbury was where Lord Alfred Douglas's mother lived. 'Do go there and cool your hands in the grey twilight of Gothic things and come here whenever you like. It is a lovely place: it only lacks you; but go to Salisbury first. Always with undying love, yours Oscar.' Now, gentlemen, the words of that letter appear extravagant to those who are in the habit of writing commercial correspondence or those ordinary letters which the necessities of life force upon one every day (*laughter in which* WILDE *also joins*), but that, Mr

Oscar Wilde said to Allen and says now – that is a sort of prose sonnet, an answer written to a piece of poetry written to Lord Alfred Douglas, a piece of poetry which is transcribed and paraphrased in the sonnet printed in this *Spirit Lamp* which I now hold in my hand. He preserved this letter and preserved it until today and produces it now saying to you it is a letter of which he was and is in *no* way ashamed; that it is a letter he was prepared to produce anywhere, a letter with regard to any imputation connected with which he was absolutely indifferent, a letter with regard to which he says that as an artist and a poet that letter is an expression of poetical feeling and has no relation whatever to the hateful suggestions – hateful to him as to all of you – which are made with regard to him in the plea in this case.

JUROR: May we trouble you for the date of that letter?

CLARKE: There is no date to it. The sonnet is the 4th of May 1893.

JUROR: Yes, I wanted the date of the letter and I have the date of the sonnet.

CLARKE: The letter bears no date.

CARSON: It must be anterior to that.

CLARKE: Of course, it was before that, but it was not, I think, very long before that that it had been got back by Mr Wilde and it was immediately put into that sonnet form and published and I will just hand to my lord the magazine. (*Handing it to the* JUDGE.) I am told that the letter had been written in December 1892. Now, that took place in the early part of the year 1893 as I told you – about the month of April 1893, and there is nothing with which I need trouble you with regard to the remainder of that year, nor indeed need I mention any incident until one comes to the early part of 1894 when Lord Alfred Douglas who had been to Cairo and had returned to this country in, I think, February 1894, again lunched at the Café Royal in the public room of the Café and they again met Lord Queensberry.[82] On that occasion Lord Queensberry came across, shook hands with them and was very friendly and a conversation of a most friendly character took place. Shortly after that

Mr Oscar Wilde became aware that Lord Queensberry was writing letters which affected his character and contained suggestions injurious to him. I do not say in the same sense but having relation to the same sort of matter as that which is suggested now. You may well understand the reason why Mr Oscar Wilde would be extremely reluctant – not for his own sake for he had no question or no reason to hesitate at all with regard to that, but for the sake of others – the natural hesitation which he would have in bringing to public notice the hideous and frightful suggestions which we are now forced in this court to discuss, and although he might reasonably, and would perhaps if he had been alone and if his own interests only were concerned, have brought these to some public notice, he abstained from doing so for reasons which I am not entitled to state, which I do not state, but which I am quite sure will be obvious to all of you before we have gone very far in the conduct of this case; and so the latter part of the year 1894 passed. I should tell you – I will not go into details about it – that there was an interview between Lord Queensberry and Mr Wilde about the middle of the year 1894. The details of that interview I need not tell you, except that Mr Oscar Wilde absolutely repudiated suggestions which he understood Lord Queensberry was making and called upon Lord Queensberry to leave his house and insisted that he should do so, and gave in Lord Queensberry's hearing directions that he should never again be admitted to that house. So the year 1894 passed and then we come to the early part of the year 1895.

Mr Wilde, as you know, has written many plays – *Lady Windermere's Fan*, *A Woman of No Importance*, *The Importance of Being Earnest* and *An Ideal Husband* are the four which have been already produced in this country and he has also written a play which Madame Sarah Bernhardt is going to appear in – a French play called *Salomé* in French, but these four have been produced and on the 14th of February 1895, the play called *The Importance of Being Earnest* was about to be produced at the St James's Theatre. In the course of the day some information was given to the manager of that theatre and to other persons with regard to certain intentions on the part of Lord Queensberry. It is a matter of public dramatic history that on one occasion when a play of the late Poet Laureate was produced, *The Promise of May*, Lord Queensberry made observations in public in the theatre and made some sort of disturbance by commenting—[83]

CARSON: My lord, I do not see how that is evidence against a man being tried on a criminal charge or how you can go into antecedent matters. It has nothing to say to this case.

JUDGE: It may be relevant as explaining the subsequent action of Mr Oscar Wilde towards Lord Queensberry on this particular occasion.

CLARKE: It does, my lord. I was saying that it is known that on a previous occasion Lord Queensberry at the production of a play called *The Promise of May*, which was written by the late Poet Laureate, had got up in the theatre and had made objection to the play and in his character as an agnostic had objected to the representation which was then put on the stage of agnosticism in a character which was presented by Mr Hermann Vezin, and, of course, a disturbance or trouble of that kind in the theatre on the night of a new play would be at all times a great injury to a play and the management of the theatre, but it would be still more serious if there were a possibility of Lord Queensberry appearing in the theatre and his there interrupting the course of the performance by any observations. It would be much more serious if there was a probability of that interruption and possibly the nature of the observations made might seriously affect Mr Oscar Wilde's character and must seriously affect the prospects of the theatre and play. Precautions were taken. Lord Queensberry, I believe, had paid for his seat in the theatre; his money was returned to him; the police were on duty and Lord Queensberry made his appearance at the box office in the course of the evening and brought with him a large bouquet made of vegetables. (*Laughter.*) What the intention of Lord Queensberry was if he could have obtained admission to the theatre with this thing in his hand I do not know, but he could not obtain admission to the theatre; and he handed it in at the box office with a message for Mr Oscar Wilde.[84] I can hardly complain seriously as I feel at this moment the importance of the matter with which we are dealing that the mention of that circumstance should have moved others to laughter, but gentlemen, it is by no means unimportant when you will have to consider in this case, as you will have to consider, the way in which Lord Queensberry, if he had any reason whatever for attacking the character of Mr Oscar Wilde, departed from the course which any gentleman would have taken in such circumstances, and condescended to such a pantomimic expedient as that to which I have just referred. Whether Lord Queensberry is at all times responsible for his actions is a matter upon which you, I think, may possibly have your doubts at some time before this case ends, and further, instead of doing what I think it would have come to the mind of a gentleman to do in respect, for instance, of writing to the committee of one of Mr Oscar Wilde's clubs stating what he had to say against the character of the member of that club, asking them, as gentlemen desirous of keeping their club honourable and pure, to make enquiry into the matter – instead of that he gets a bunch of vegetables and goes down to the theatre on the first night of Mr Wilde's play. Well, he was refused admission; his money was given back to him; no notice was taken of this insult or intended insult. He made his way up the gallery stairs and tried to get into the gallery, but there the police had received notice and were on duty, and he was unable to get into the theatre and he went away. It was not until some time after that that Mr Oscar Wilde had occasion to go to the Albemarle Club. It was not until the 25th of February or the 28th of February, I think, that he called at that club and when he went in the club the porter handed him an envelope, in which the porter, a very sensible man, had put the card which had been received from Lord Queensberry as long before as the 18th of February. It had been ten days at the club, but Mr Wilde had not happened to call. That card was then handed to

Mr Wilde and then Mr Wilde felt it incumbent upon himself to take some proceeding in the matter because here for the first time there was the publication by Lord Queensberry of the accusation – anything which could properly be called a publication by Lord Queensberry of the accusation – which he was making against Mr Wilde. I have told you that that accusation, if not made in terms, was at all events hinted in the communications which had been made – letters written by Lord Queensberry before, but those letters were not written to Mr Wilde, they were written to members of Lord Queensberry's family and although Mr Wilde had become aware of them and could, if he so chose, have taken action in the matter, that action could only have been taken by bringing into immediate prominence the relations between Lord Queensberry and members of his own family. That Mr Wilde did not do and will not do so far as he is able to avoid it in this case. The insult that was intended at the opening of the play on the 14th of February might possibly have been made – indeed, I think the question was considered – the subject of complaint against Lord Queensberry, but it was obvious that that was too trivial an incident to form the ground of so serious an accusation as this.[85] It was too trivial to take notice of, but when this card was delivered to the porter of the club, this suggestion was for the first time published in a way which enabled Mr Wilde to take notice without directly bringing into public consideration the relation of different members of the Queensberry family and immediately that notice was taken. It was on the 28th of February that he received that card. On the 1st of March an application was made for a warrant against Lord Queensberry. He was arrested on the morning of the 2nd of March and on that day the investigation took place which has led to this committal. Gentlemen, I have concluded the story so far as it is necessary for me to tell it to you on my part with regard to Mr Wilde's history during this period. I have just a word or two to say with regard to the pleas which are here put upon the record. I told you that there were a certain number of names mentioned in this plea. I should not refer in detail to the accusations that are there made, nor indeed shall I even mention the names of the persons who are mentioned in that plea. I cannot but believe that those names have been, some of them at all events, hostilely put upon the proceedings. I do not believe that with regard to all the names that are there mentioned, there will be any suggestion adverse to Mr Oscar Wilde and nothing that I do in the course of this case shall ever be referred to as having extended its trouble beyond the range of the enquiry here. But at the end of this plea there are two counts – I should call them two allegations – which are extremely curious, to which I wish to direct your attention. It is said at the end of the plea 'that in the month of July 1890, Mr Wilde did write and publish, and cause and procure to be printed and published, with his name upon the title page, a certain immoral and obscene work in the form of the narrative entitled *The Picture of Dorian Gray*, which work was designed and intended by Mr Wilde, and was understood by the readers thereof, to describe the relations, intimacies and passions of certain persons of sodomitical and unnatural habits, tastes and practices.'

'And that in the month of December in the year 1894, was published a certain other immoral and obscene work in the form of a magazine entitled *The Chameleon*, which contained divers obscene matters and things relating to the practices and passions of persons of sodomitical and unnatural habits and tastes, and that Mr Wilde joined in procuring the publication of this work, and that he published his name on the contents sheet of the magazine as its first and principal contributor, and published in it certain immoral maxims as an introduction to the same under the title of "Phrases and Philosophies for the Use of the Young".' That concludes the allegation with regard to this literature. Gentlemen, these are two very curious allegations. Why they are added to this statement I can hardly imagine, unless it be that my learned friends are so conscious of the character of the persons upon whom they must be relying to support their other parts of the plea, that they desire to have something to fall back upon with regard to which no controversy can exist as to its credibility, and intend to suggest that even if all the other evidence should break down, if they have got any, Mr Wilde ought to be branded by you as a person inclined to sodomitical practices because he joined in publishing *The Chameleon* and because he did publish a volume called *Dorian Gray*. Both those books are lying before me. This is *The Chameleon*, which it is said that Mr Oscar Wilde procured to be published. It is called 'A bazaar of dangerous and' what looks like 'smiling chances'.[86] It is volume 1, number 1. Three numbers were to be published in the year – published by Gay and Bird of 5 Chandos Street, Strand and only one hundred copies were to be printed as has become rather the fashion with regard to certain books, large-paper books and so on – only a certain number of copies printed.[87] It is believed when that is the case that these copies, of course, will be eagerly subscribed for because, of course, they may become scarce. This is a paper, a magazine with regard to which it is true that Mr Oscar Wilde contributed 'Phrases and Philosophies for the Use of the Young', and on the first three pages of that magazine there are a certain number of epigrammatic statements – epigrams such as those which many of us have enjoyed when being interchanged in dialogue by the characters in such a play as *A Woman of No Importance*. They give brilliancy and effect to dialogue and often – if one could say 'always' Mr Oscar Wilde would be the happiest of men – they are often wisdom in a witty form. I do not say that they are always so in plays or in the magazine, but I shall be amazed if my learned friend is able to get from these 'Phrases and Philosophies' anything that in the most remote degree supports a suggestion hostile to the moral character of Mr Wilde in respect to such matters as we are discussing here. For the rest of the magazine Mr Oscar Wilde was no more responsible than any one of you gentlemen sitting in that box. A young Oxford man was the editor of the magazine.[88] He asked Mr Wilde, whose name, of course, was well-known and whose name upon the title page would undoubtedly attract purchasers for the magazine, to contribute something and Mr Wilde was good enough to give him a selection, I suppose, from epigrams which Mr Wilde has made and noted, but with regard to the contents of the magazine Mr Wilde knew nothing. Directly he saw that magazine, he saw that in it there was an article or a story called 'The Priest and the Acolyte' which is a disgrace to literature – which is amazing that anybody wrote and still more amazing that any decent publishers allowed to be issued under their name. Directly Mr Wilde saw that, he saw the editor or wrote to the editor of that magazine and it was upon Mr Wilde's insistence that the editor withdrew, so far as he could withdraw, that magazine from circulation. He had no knowledge that the article had ever been written or was going to appear; he knew nothing of it until he saw it in print and then expressed his opinion about it, expressed his opinion, I think, that it was badly written, not worthy to be published, not proper to be published and insisted upon this being withdrawn. That is the only connection Mr Wilde had at any time with the publication of *The Chameleon*. It is strange indeed to him and to those who represent him to find that publication put upon the particulars here as justifying the terrible imputation which is here made against him. Now, gentlemen, the other thing is this, a volume published by him with his name upon the title page called *'The Picture of Dorian Gray* by Oscar Wilde', a book published by him as they say. I wonder when they said in that plea 'with his name upon the title page' they did not see that to attack a man for being guilty of describing and encouraging sodomitical practices on the ground that he had written a book which for five years 'with his name upon the title page' has been upon the bookstalls and at bookshops and in libraries was a very extraordinary method of attack.[89] Now, gentlemen, there is always the difficulty; of course, when upon a plea of this kind a statement is made referring to a particular book, because it puts one into the difficulty of considering what that book is. All I need say about it is this. *The Picture of Dorian Gray* is an actual picture which is the subject of the story. It is the story of a young man of good birth, of great wealth and of much personal beauty. His friend, a distinguished painter, paints a portrait of him, a portrait which represents him in all the brightness and brilliancy of his youthful beauty. Dorian Gray desires to possess the portrait and it is given him and Dorian Gray expresses the strange wish that it might happen that as life goes on he might be allowed to continue to possess the undiminished personal beauty which belonged to his youth, while upon the painted figure there should fall any scars of experience or of trouble or of wrong which the years might bring with them through his conduct, and the strange wish is granted. He soon knows that upon the picture and not upon his own features his conduct in life will be leaving its trace and its record, for at the beginning of the book he dismisses with cruelty and hardness a girl in humble life whom he has promised to marry and she commits suicide, and when next he looks at the picture he notes that on the lips of the portrait there has come a change and there is a hard and cruel line about the mouth, and so the story goes on. He plunges into dissipation, is guilty of murder and, as his life goes on, this portrait, which he has locked up in an unused room that no eye but his own should ever fall upon it, gradually changes and all evil that he is doing in life which leaves his face in undisturbed beauty records itself upon the picture. At last he can stand it no longer: he takes a knife and strikes at the picture. As he strikes he falls dead himself and those who come into the room find the picture once more a record of youthful beauty and find lying upon the floor an almost unrecognisable, hideous old man. That is the story of the book and it describes – I will not say describes – it hints at and suggests, for it does not describe, vices and weaknesses of which Dorian Gray is guilty, but to attack Mr Oscar Wilde as being a person showing himself to be addicted to this sort of offence, because in the book he states that the person in the book is a vicious creature in all ways, is surely the most strange inference. I have read the book for the purpose of this case and with care to see upon what my learned friend can build. Here is the thing with Mr Oscar Wilde's name upon the title page and I shall be surprised if my learned friend can point to any passage within those covers which does more than describe as a novelist may or a dramatist may – nay, must – describe the passions and the vices of life if he desires to produce any work of art which, while idealising reality, may be artistic in the sense of harmony and beauty and truth.[90] Now, gentlemen, that is all I have to say with regard to this matter. My learned friend and I will call before you the witnesses who will prove the publication of the libel in question. My learned friend has the task upon him, if he really proposes to address himself to that, of endeavouring to satisfy you by evidence that the accusations that they have made are true.

SIDNEY WRIGHT *is sworn and examined by* WILLIE MATHEWS.

MATHEWS: You are the hall porter of the Albemarle Club?

WRIGHT: Yes.

MATHEWS: Which is situate at number 13 Albemarle Street?

WRIGHT: Yes.

MATHEWS: And of which both Mr and Mrs Oscar Wilde are members?

WRIGHT: Yes.

MATHEWS: On the 18th of February last did the defendant, the Marquess of Queensberry, call at the club and speak to you?

WRIGHT: Yes.

MATHEWS: And did he at that time hand to you a card which I now hand to you? (*It is handed to the witness.*)

WRIGHT: Yes.

MATHEWS: And prior to handing that card to you, in your presence had Lord Queensberry written some words upon it?

WRIGHT: Yes.

MATHEWS: The words are there, they must be read at some time, they had better be read now. They run, do they not, 'For Oscar Wilde posing as sodomite', whilst upon the other side of the card is either printed or lithographed the name and title of the Marquess of Queensberry?

WRIGHT: Yes.

CLERK OF THE COURT: On the same side?

MATHEWS: What did Lord Queensberry say to you when he handed you the card?

WRIGHT: He wished me to give that to Oscar Wilde.

MATHEWS: Did you look at it and see what was written upon it?

WRIGHT: I looked at the card but I could not understand what was written upon it.

MATHEWS: And did you at that time make an entry of the date upon which it was given to you?

WRIGHT: Yes.

MATHEWS: And the hour?

WRIGHT: Yes.

MATHEWS: Is that upon the back of the card?

WRIGHT: Yes.

MATHEWS: Your entry being the 18th of the second month, '95, four thirty p.m.?

WRIGHT: Yes.

MATHEWS: Lord Queensberry left, I presume, after he had given you the card?

WRIGHT: Yes, he left the club at once.

MATHEWS: And did you put it into an envelope?

WRIGHT: I placed it in an envelope.

MATHEWS: The envelope in which it is now or was a short time ago?

WRIGHT: Yes.

MATHEWS: And wrote upon the envelope Mr Oscar Wilde's name?

WRIGHT: Yes.

MATHEWS: And kept it in your custody until the 28th of February, which was the first date after the 18th when Mr Wilde came to the club?

WRIGHT: Yes.

MATHEWS: And on seeing Mr Wilde on the 28th did you hand the envelope with the card in it to Mr Wilde?

WRIGHT: I did.

MATHEWS: Giving him the message from Lord Queensberry to the effect that Lord Queensberry had left it for him?

WRIGHT: Yes.

CARSON: My lord, I do not ask this witness any questions.

OSCAR FINGAL O'FFLAHERTIE WILLS WILDE *is sworn and examined by* SIR EDWARD CLARKE.

CLARKE: You are the prosecutor in this case?

WILDE: Yes.

CLARKE: I think you are thirty-eight years of age?

WILDE: I am thirty-nine years of age.

CLARKE: Was your father the late Sir William Wilde a surgeon in Dublin?

WILDE: Yes.

CLARKE: Chairman of the Census Commission?

WILDE: Yes.

CLARKE: He died, I think, some years ago?

WILDE: He died when I was at Oxford.

CLARKE: Were you a student at Trinity College, Dublin?

WILDE: Yes.

CLARKE: And at that University or College did you obtain a classical scholarship and the Gold Medal for Greek?[91]

WILDE: Yes.

CLARKE: Then, I believe, you went to Magdalen College, Oxford?

WILDE: Yes.

CLARKE: You there had a classical scholarship?

WILDE: Yes.

CLARKE: You took a first in Mods and a first in Greats?

WILDE: Yes.

CLARKE: And obtained the Newdigate Prize for English Verse?

WILDE: Yes.

CLARKE: In what year did you leave Oxford?

WILDE: I took my degree in 1878.

CLARKE: Did you come down at once after taking your degree?

WILDE: Yes, at once.

CLARKE: From that time have you devoted yourself to art and literature?

WILDE: Yes.

CLARKE: I believe as early as 1882 you published a volume of poems?[92]

WILDE: I did.

CLARKE: Did you afterwards make a lecture tour in America?[93]

WILDE: Yes.

CLARKE: And have lectured also in England, I think?

WILDE: Yes.

CLARKE: Have you since that time written many essays of different kinds?

WILDE: I have.

CLARKE: For publication. During the last few years you have devoted yourself specially to dramatic literature?

WILDE: I have.

CLARKE: I think I am right in mentioning *Lady Windermere's Fan*, *A Woman of No Importance*, *The Importance of Being Earnest* and *An Ideal Husband* as the four plays of yours which have been interpreted on the stage in this country?

WILDE: Yes.

CLARKE: And all of them successful?

WILDE: They have all, I am glad to say, been successful.

CLARKE: Is it the fact that all those four plays were produced between February of 1892 and February of 1895?

WILDE: Yes.

CLARKE: During the same period did you write the French play of *Salomé*?

WILDE: Yes.

CLARKE: Is that in rehearsal now?[94]

WILDE: I don't know that it is actually in rehearsal, Madame Sarah Bernhardt promised to produce it before the middle of May. It would probably take about three—

CLARKE: But you had occasion to go to Paris more than once with regard to the production of that piece?

WILDE: With regard to the publication, twice, and with regard to the production, once.

CLARKE: And besides during these three years having had to deal with this dramatic literature, have you also written articles on different subjects?

WILDE: Yes – let me see, I must think of that.

CLARKE: And you have written other plays, I think, which have not yet been produced?

WILDE: Yes, two other plays – yes, I think I have written articles, I forget.[95]

CLARKE: In the year 1884 you married Miss Lloyd?

WILDE: Yes.

CLARKE: And from the date of that marriage up to now you have been residing with her at Tite Street, Chelsea?

WILDE: Yes.

CLARKE: You have two sons?

WILDE: I have two sons.

CLARKE: Of what age?

WILDE: The eldest will be ten in June and the youngest will be nine in November.[96]

CLARKE: And from the date of your marriage until now have you resided with your wife at Tite Street, Chelsea and have you resided at other places at Worthing, Cromer and Goring with her?

WILDE: Yes.

CLARKE: And at Torquay?[97]

WILDE: Yes. At certain times.

CLARKE: In the year 1891 did you make the acquaintance of Lord Alfred Douglas?

WILDE: I did.

CLARKE: Was he brought by a mutual friend to your house at Tite Street?

WILDE: Yes, by a friend of Lady Queensberry and of my own, and also a friend of Lord Alfred's too.[98]

CLARKE: I don't know whether before 1891 you had been acquainted with Lady Queensberry herself?

WILDE: No, I had not.

CLARKE: But since the year 1891 have you been acquainted with Lady Queensberry?

WILDE: Yes.

CLARKE: Have you been a guest in her house more than once?

WILDE: Yes, many times.

CLARKE: At 'The Hut' at Wokingham?

WILDE: Yes.

CLARKE: And also at a house which she had at Salisbury, I think?

WILDE: Yes.

CLARKE: And have you stayed in that house on one occasion, at all events, when there was a family party assembled there?

WILDE: Yes.

CLARKE: Has your friendship with Lady Queensberry continued up to the present time?

WILDE: Yes.

CLARKE: Besides your acquaintance with Lord Alfred Douglas, have you been on friendly terms with his brother Lord Douglas of Hawick?[99]

WILDE: Yes.

CLARKE: And are so up to now?

WILDE: Yes.

CLARKE: And also with the late Lord Drumlanrig who was the eldest son?[100]

WILDE: Yes.

CLARKE: Since the time of his introduction to you in 1891 has Lord Alfred been from time to time to dine with you at Tite Street?

WILDE: Oh, yes, continually.

CLARKE: With your wife?

WILDE: Oh, yes, certainly.[101]

CLARKE: Also at the Albemarle Club?

WILDE: Yes.

CLARKE: I think Mrs Wilde is a member of that club?

WILDE: Yes.

CLARKE: And has also stayed with you and your family at Cromer?

WILDE: Yes.

CLARKE: At Goring?

WILDE: Yes.

CLARKE: And at Worthing?

WILDE: Yes.

CLARKE: And Torquay?[102]

WILDE: Yes.

CLARKE: Now, I will not go through the details of it, but I will come to the end of the year 1892. Before November 1892 had you to your then recollection known Lord Queensberry at all?

WILDE: Not to my then recollection.

CLARKE: In November 1892 were you lunching with Lord Alfred Douglas at the Café Royal in Regent Street?

WILDE: Yes.

CLARKE: In the public room there?

WILDE: Yes.

CLARKE: Did Lord Queensberry come into the room?

WILDE: Yes.

CLARKE: Just answer me 'yes' or 'no' to this question: were you aware that there had been any estrangement between Lord Queensberry and Lord Alfred Douglas?

WILDE: Yes.

CLARKE: And upon your suggestion did Lord Alfred go across to his father and shake hands with him and talk to him?

WILDE: Yes.

CLARKE: Did Lord Queensberry then come and join you at lunch?

WILDE: Yes.

CLARKE: Do you remember Lord Alfred having to go away early?

WILDE: Yes.

CLARKE: Did Lord Queensberry remain chatting with you after he had left?

WILDE: Yes.

CLARKE: Then I think something was said – I will take this very shortly – about your going to Torquay and about the possibility of Lord Queensberry calling upon you or seeing you there?

WILDE: Yes.

CLARKE: You did go to Torquay, I think?

WILDE: Yes.

CLARKE: Lord Queensberry did not come?

WILDE: No.

CLARKE: But you had a note from him telling you so — telling you that he was not coming?

WILDE: Yes.

CLARKE: On that occasion did Lord Queensberry remind you of having met you some time before at the house of some friend?

WILDE: Yes.

CLARKE: It was, I think, eleven years before that time?

WILDE: Yes. Ten or eleven.

CLARKE: Now, from November 1892 until March 1894 you did not see Lord Queensberry, I think?

WILDE: No, I did not see Lord Queensberry.

CLARKE: But in the year 1893 did you hear that some letters which you had written to Lord Alfred Douglas had come into the possession of some person, whatever the man's name was?

WILDE: Yes.

CLARKE: And did a man named Wood eventually come to see you?

WILDE: No, he didn't come to see me, I met him by appointment.

CLARKE: Where?

WILDE: At the rooms of Mr Taylor.[103]

CLARKE: Had he then some letters written by you in his possession?

WILDE: Yes.

CARSON: My lord, I am anxious that my learned friend should not lead on these questions.[104]

CLARKE: Certainly. Did he give you any account of how they had come into his possession?

WILDE: He said he had found them in a suit of clothes that Lord Alfred Douglas had been kind enough to give him.

CLARKE: Did he ask for anything — what passed — what did he say?

WILDE: Would you repeat that question?

CLARKE: Yes. Did he ask you for anything – for any money?

WILDE: I don't think he made a direct demand, it is very difficult for me to say if I am to tell the story – if I am to reply to your question.

CLARKE: Tell me what he said – tell me what took place.

WILDE: When he entered the room he said, 'I suppose you think very badly of me?'

CLARKE: What did you say?

WILDE: I said, 'I hear you have letters of mine to Lord Alfred Douglas and you certainly should have given them back to him.'

CLARKE: Yes, will you go on and tell us what took place?

WILDE: After I had said that, he took three or four letters out of his pocket and handed them to me and said, 'Here are the letters,' and I read the letters and I said, 'I do not consider these letters of any importance.' He said, 'They were stolen from me the day before yesterday by a man called Allen and I had to employ a detective to get them back as they wished to extort money from you for them.' I said, 'I do not consider that they are of any value at all.' He said, 'I am very much afraid of staying on in London as this man and other men are threatening me. I want to go away to America.' I said, 'What better opening as a clerk could you have in America than in London?' He replied that he was very anxious to get out of London and was afraid of this man who had taken these letters from him. He made a very strong appeal to me to enable him to go to New York as he could find nothing to do in London. I gave him fifteen pounds. The letters had remained in my hand the whole time.

CLARKE: Did that end the interview?

WILDE: That ended the interview – yes.

CLARKE: Was it before or after that, that you had this copy letter from Mr Tree? Let me ask you that.

WILDE: Oh, long after.

CLARKE: Long after that?

WILDE: Yes, it was the morning of the 23rd of April that I was handed by Mr Tree—

CLARKE: 1893?

WILDE: 1893.

CLARKE: That you were handed by Mr Tree the copy letter to which I referred?

WILDE: Yes, the day after the production of my play – that is why I know the date.

CLARKE: I cannot ask you what took place between you and other people but did some man eventually come with this letter, another letter of which that purported to have been a copy?

WILDE: Yes.

CLARKE: What man was that?

WILDE: Do you mean the man who returned me the letter?

CLARKE: Who came and brought you the letter first.

WILDE: The man who called first at my house told me that the letter was not in his possession.

CLARKE: Do you remember the name of the man who called upon you first?

WILDE: Yes.

CLARKE: What was his name?

WILDE: Allen.

CLARKE: He called and spoke of this letter and said that it was not in his possession?

WILDE: Yes.

CLARKE: What did you say? If you will kindly tell us what took place then—

WILDE: If I might tell what took place—

CLARKE: Please – at that interview.

WILDE: I was told by my servant that a Mr Allen wished to see me, or a man wished to see me on particular business, and I went down to the hall. I saw this man there, he was standing in the hall. I at once felt I knew from previous information I had received that he was the man who desired to extort money from me for this letter, that I had known—

CLARKE: Had you ever seen him before?

WILDE: Personally I had never seen him before – no. I said to him, 'I suppose you have come about my beautiful letter to Lord Alfred Douglas.' (*Laughter.*)

CLARKE: Will you go on kindly telling us the tale of what took place?

WILDE: 'If you had not been so foolish as to send a copy of it to Mr Beerbohm Tree, I would gladly have paid you a very large sum of money for the letter as I consider it to be a work of art.' He said, 'A very curious construction could be put upon that letter, Mr Wilde.' I said in reply, 'Art is rarely intelligible to the criminal classes.' He said, 'A man has offered me sixty pounds for it.' I said to him, 'If you take my advice you will go to that man and sell my letter to him for sixty pounds.' (*Laughter.*) I said, 'I myself have never received so large a sum for any prose work of that very small length, but I am glad to find that there is someone in England who considers that a letter of mine is worth sixty pounds.' (*Laughter.*) He was somewhat taken aback at my manner perhaps. He said, 'This man is out of town.' I said, 'But he is sure to come back again. Why not wait?'

CLARKE: Do you mean this man who had offered sixty pounds?

WILDE: He was the man who had offered sixty pounds for my letter and I said to him, 'He is sure to come back.' And I said, 'As far as I am concerned I can only assure you on my word of honour that I will not pay one penny of money to have back that letter to this man who has offered sixty pounds, so if you dislike this man very much you should sell my letter to him for sixty pounds.' I then said to him – it was then about a quarter to eight – 'I cannot discuss the matter any further, I am very sorry. I am going in to dine' – I was dining at home – and I said, 'Take my advice; go to this man who offers sixty pounds. Don't bother me about it.' He then said to me, changing his manner a little, that he hadn't a single penny, that he was very poor and that he had been on many occasions trying to find me in order to talk about this matter. I said that I couldn't guarantee his cab expenses, but that I would gladly give him half a sovereign. He took the half-sovereign and went away.

CLARKE: Let me just ask you this: in the course of that interview, had you said anything about a sonnet that you remember?

WILDE: Yes, I told him – I said, 'This letter which is a prose poem

will shortly be published in sonnet form in a delightful magazine
and I will send you a copy.' (*Laughter.*)

CLARKE: Before I go to the next interview, as a matter of fact
was that letter the basis of the French poem which was published
in *The Spirit Lamp*?

WILDE: Yes. In May 1893.

CLARKE: That is signed 'Pierre Louÿs'?

WILDE: Yes.

CLARKE: Is that a friend of yours or is it a *nom de plume*?

WILDE: Oh, no, it is a young friend of mine, a young French poet
who was visiting England, a poet of great distinction.[105]

CLARKE: This man went away, did he?

WILDE: Yes.

CLARKE: How soon after did someone else come in?

WILDE: About six minutes I should think – five or six minutes.

CLARKE: Who was the person who then came in?

WILDE: Cliburn.

JUDGE: How long after the first do you say?

WILDE: Five or six minutes, my lord.

CLARKE: Now, what took place with him?

WILDE: I was told by my servant, I was then in my library – that
is on the ground floor – my servant came to me and said, 'There
is a man wants to see you.'

CLARKE: Then, you saw him?

WILDE: I felt instinctively—

CLARKE: Never mind.

WILDE: I went out, I saw Cliburn, and I said to Cliburn, 'I cannot
really be bothered any more about this letter. I don't care twopence for the letter.' He produced the letter out of his pocket
and said, 'Allen has asked me to give it back to you.' I did not
take it immediately.

CLARKE: Now, what passed, what was said and what was done?

WILDE: Would you tell me what I said last?

JUDGE: You said, 'Allen asked me to give it back.'

CLARKE: He said Allen had sent the letter and handed it back.

WILDE: I said to him, 'Why does he give me back this letter?' He said, 'Well, he says that you were kind to him and that there is no use trying to rent you.'

JUDGE: Rent?

WILDE: R–e–n–t. A slang term. 'There is no use trying to rent you as you only laugh at us.' I looked at the letter and it was extremely soiled and I said to him, 'I think it quite unpardonable that better care was not taken of an original manuscript of mine.' (*Laughter.*) He said that he was very sorry but it had been in so many hands. I took the letter and then I said, 'Well, I will accept the letter back and you can thank Mr Allen from me for all the anxiety he has shown about the letter.' I gave Cliburn half a sovereign for his trouble in bringing back the letter, and then said to him, 'I am afraid you are leading a wonderfully wicked life.' (*Laughter.*) He said, 'There is good and bad in everyone of us, Mr Wilde.' I told him that he was a born philosopher (*laughter*) – he then left.

CLARKE: The letter then was in your possession and has it remained in your possession ever since?

WILDE: Yes.

CLARKE: And you have produced it here in court today?

WILDE: Yes.

CLARKE: Now, I pass to the end of the year 1893. I think Lord Alfred Douglas went to Cairo about the end of that year – just the beginning of 1894.

WILDE: Lord Alfred Douglas went to Cairo at the end of 1893 – December 1893.

CLARKE: And after his return from Cairo were you lunching with him one day at the Café Royal again and did Lord Queensberry come in?

WILDE: We were lunching together at the Café Royal and Lord Queensberry came in.

CLARKE: Did he join you?

WILDE: Yes.

CLARKE: Did he join you at lunch, I mean?

WILDE: Yes.

CLARKE: Shook hands with you both?

WILDE: Yes.

CLARKE: Was on perfectly friendly terms?

WILDE: Yes.

CLARKE: And you chatted, I suppose, with regard to Egypt and with regard to various subjects?

WILDE: Yes.

CLARKE: Shortly after that meeting at the Café Royal – if you will kindly answer my questions 'yes' or 'no' when you can – did you become aware that Lord Queensberry was making suggestions with regard to your character and behaviour?

WILDE (*after a pause*): Yes.

CLARKE: And were you aware that those suggestions were made in communications with his own family?

CARSON: That could not be the way of proving it; it is really telling communications.

JUDGE: I think not.

CLARKE: Very well, I will be perfectly fair about it. (*To* WILDE.) Will you kindly tell me this: those suggestions, I think, were not contained in letters to you?

WILDE: Oh, no, certainly not.

CLARKE: Now, somewhat later in the year, I think at the end of June, there was an interview between you and Lord Queensberry.

WILDE: Yes.

CLARKE: Where was that?

WILDE: At 16 Tite Street.

CLARKE: About what time in the day was it?

WILDE: About four o'clock.

CLARKE: In the afternoon?

WILDE: Yes.

CLARKE: Did Lord Queensberry come by appointment or not?

WILDE: No, certainly not.

CLARKE: You heard that Lord Queensberry and a gentleman were there?

WILDE: Yes.

CLARKE: Who was the gentleman, do you know, who came with him?

WILDE: He was introduced to me by Lord Queensberry as a Mr Pape; as well as I remember that is the name.

JUDGE: He came with Lord Queensberry?

WILDE: Yes.

CLARKE: The name is not of importance I am told, my lord – I think that is a mistake but, however, the name is not of importance.

CARSON: I have, of course, no objection if there is any real point in the name being mentioned, but it would be convenient as far as possible to eliminate names.

JUDGE: Quite.

CLARKE: I am quite content. (*To* WILDE.) There was a gentleman with Lord Queensberry, a gentleman with whom you were not acquainted?

WILDE: Oh, no, of course not.

CLARKE: What room did this interview take place in?

WILDE: My library on the ground floor.

CLARKE: What passed?

WILDE: I had dressed to go down in the country and on arriving at home my servant said to me—

CLARKE: Never mind, you need not begin quite so early – if you would come to the exact thing.

WILDE: My servant said to me, 'Lord Queensberry and another gentleman are in the library.' I at once went into the library.

CLARKE: And then what took place?

WILDE: Lord Queensberry was standing by the window; I walked over to the fireplace. Lord Queensberry said to me, 'Sit down.' I said, 'I don't allow you to talk like that to me or anyone to talk like that to me in my house or anywhere else.' I said, 'I suppose you have come to apologise for the statement you made about my wife and myself in the letter you wrote to your son.'[106] I said, 'I could have you up any day I chose for criminal libel for writing such a letter.' He said, 'The letter was privileged as it was written to my son.' I said to him, 'How dare you say such things as you do about your son and me?'

JUDGE: 'How dare you say such things about—'?

WILDE: 'Your son and me', my lord. He said, 'You were both kicked out of the Savoy Hotel at a moment's notice for your disgusting conduct.' I said, 'That is a lie.' He said, 'You have taken furnished rooms for him in Piccadilly.' I said, 'Somebody has been telling you an absurd set of lies about your son and me. I haven't done anything of the kind.' He said, 'I hear you were thoroughly well blackmailed last year for a disgusting sodomitic letter that you wrote to my son.' I said to him, 'The letter was a beautiful letter.' – What did I say last?

CLARKE: 'I said, "The letter was a beautiful letter."'

WILDE: I said, 'The letter was a beautiful letter and I never write except for publication.'

CLARKE: 'And I never write—'?

WILDE: Yes, 'and I never write except for publication.' I then said to him, 'Lord Queensberry do you seriously accuse your son and me of sodomy?' He said, 'I don't say that you are it, but you look it (*laughter*) –

JUDGE: I shall have the Court cleared if I hear the slightest disturbance again.

WILDE: – but you look it and you pose as it, which is just as bad.' He said, 'If I catch you and my son together again in any public restaurant, I will thrash you.' I said to him, 'I don't know what the Queensberry rules are, but the Oscar Wilde rule is to shoot at sight.' (*Laughter.*) I then said, 'Lord Queensberry, leave my house.' He said he would not do so. I told him I would have him put out by the police. He said, 'You and my son—'. He repeated his phrase about myself and his son, adding – he said, 'It is a disgusting scandal all over London.' I said, 'If it were – If it is so,' I suppose I said – 'If it is so, you are the author of that scandal and no one else. The letters that you have written about me are infamous and I see that you are merely trying to ruin your son through me.'[107] I then said to him, 'Now you have got to go. I will not have in my house a brute like you.' I went out into the hall followed by Lord Queensberry and the gentleman with Lord Queensberry. I said to my servant, pointing at Lord Queensberry as I spoke, I said, 'This is the Marquess of Queensberry, the most infamous brute in London. You are never to allow him to enter my house again. Should he attempt to come in, you must send for the police.'

CLARKE: Did Lord Queensberry and his friend then leave?

WILDE: Yes, with violent words on both sides.

CLARKE: Was it the fact that you had taken rooms in Piccadilly for his son?

WILDE: No.

CLARKE: Or any of his sons?

WILDE: No, quite untrue.

CLARKE: Was there any foundation whatever for the statement that you, at any time with or without either of his sons, were expelled from or required to leave the Savoy Hotel?

WILDE: Perfectly untrue.

CLARKE: Now, I come to the early part of this year when, on the 14th of February this year, it had been arranged to produce your piece *The Importance of Being Earnest* at the St James's Theatre?

WILDE: Yes.

CLARKE: On that date did certain communications reach you from the theatre and from other persons?

WILDE: Yes.

CLARKE: With regard to Lord Queensberry?

WILDE: Yes.

CLARKE: Were you aware of what had taken place some years ago on the production of *The Promise of May*?

WILDE: Yes.

CLARKE: On the evening of the performance you went to the theatre, I think?

WILDE: Yes.

CLARKE: And was the play successful?

WILDE: A great success, I am glad to say.

CLARKE: And you appeared after the performance, I think, to bow your acknowledgements?

WILDE: Yes.

CLARKE: And are you aware that police were on duty that night at the theatre?

WILDE: Yes.

CLARKE: Lord Queensberry did not in fact get admission.

WILDE: No.

CLARKE: He tried to get in through the gallery, I think, and was refused admission. (*To the* JUDGE.) It is not necessary, my lord, to call another witness, of course, to prove it. (*To* WILDE.) And are you acquainted with the fact that he had handed in a bundle of vegetables?

WILDE: Yes.

CLARKE: At the box office, I believe. In consequence of this matter on the 14th you did consult a solicitor but did not take any proceedings upon that?[108]

WILDE: Yes.

CLARKE: Now, you had been away from England, I think, until a few days before the production of that piece?

WILDE: Until ten days or a fortnight – ten days, I think.

CLARKE: And did you for the first time after your return to England go to the Albemarle Club upon the 28th of February?

WILDE: Yes.

CLARKE: Upon that day did you receive from the porter at the club who has been called as a witness, the card which has been produced here?

WILDE: Yes.

CLARKE: Was that the first time that, except in such letters as have been mentioned – such letters as Lord Queensberry has said were privileged – any statement had been made in writing affecting your character?

WILDE (*doubtfully*): No.

CLARKE: When?

WILDE: I had been shown several communications from Lord Queensberry, not to his son but to a third person.

CLARKE: Yes, but if you follow the question, I said to members of his family – members of his wife's family.

WILDE: Yes, certainly.

CLARKE: Very well, that is the question.

WILDE: Yes, that is the first.

CLARKE: On getting this card on the 28th of February did you at once instruct your solicitor?

WILDE: Yes.

CLARKE: A warrant was issued the next day?

WILDE: Yes.

CLARKE: And executed on the 2nd of March?

WILDE: Yes.

CLARKE: And then you gave evidence?

WILDE: Yes.

CLARKE: Now, there are only two other topics I have to mention. It is suggested here that you are responsible for the publication of a magazine called *The Chameleon* in which certain 'Phrases and Philosophies for the Use of the Young' and certain aphorisms of yours appear on the first three pages.

WILDE: Yes.

CLARKE: Had you anything to do with the ownership or the preparation of or publication of that number of *The Chameleon* except in sending your contribution?

WILDE: Nothing whatsoever, I had nothing to do with it – nothing.

CLARKE: Until you saw this number of *The Chameleon* in type, had you ever seen or did you know anything about the story called 'The Priest and the Acolyte' which is contained in it?

WILDE: Nothing at all.

CLARKE: Upon seeing that in print did you communicate with the editor?

WILDE: I didn't personally communicate with the editor if you mean by writing, but he came to see me at the Café Royal to speak to me about it.

CLARKE: I didn't ask you for the conversation, but did you or did you not express disapproval of that?

CARSON: That is really the same.

CLARKE: I will ask the conversation if my learned friend likes.

CARSON: No, I think that is part of the conversation and you must know that it is not evidence.

CLARKE: If my learned friend objects to the conversation, which I really do not think is necessary for the purpose, I am surely entitled to ask this witness whether he approves or disapproves of that?

JUDGE: That is another matter.

CLARKE: Do you approve or disapprove of 'The Priest and the Acolyte'?

WILDE: I highly disapprove of it. I think it is bad, indecent literature.[109]

CLARKE (*to the* JUDGE): Then, I think I am entitled to ask if he conveyed that disapproval – (*to* WILDE) do not answer the question – (*to the* JUDGE) to the editor. I am entitled to ask if that disapproval was expressed by him to the editor.

JUDGE: Yes, I think you are.

CLARKE (*to* WILDE): Just answer 'yes' or 'no': was that disapproval expressed to the editor?

WILDE: Yes.

CLARKE: The other matter which is mentioned is this book called *The Picture of Dorian Gray* with your name upon the title page.

WILDE: Yes.

CLARKE: Was *Dorian Gray* originally published in serial form as a serial?

WILDE: It was published in *Lippincott's Magazine* of the previous year.

CLARKE: Then, was it with alterations or additions or what – was any change made – when it was published in this country?

WILDE: In book form there were several changes made; two new chapters were added, three chapters, in fact, were added.[110]

CLARKE: Three chapters were added?

WILDE: Yes.

CLARKE: This is the only volume, I think, with your name upon the title page that has been published?[111]

WILDE: Yes.

CLARKE: Of *Dorian Gray*?

WILDE: Yes.

CLARKE: In what year was the volume published about?

WILDE: In 1891, I think, that volume is. I think the original story was published in 1890.

CLARKE: Answer me again please 'yes' or 'no'; was it somewhat widely noticed and reviewed?[112]

WILDE: Yes, very much – very much so indeed.

CLARKE: And has it been in circulation and on sale from that time to this?

WILDE: From that time to this.[113]

CLARKE: Now, I need not trouble you with further questions but I think I may ask you this: I do not want you to endorse any language that I may have used, but in the sketch which I attempted to give of the novel of *Dorian Gray*, was I substantially representing the current of the story of that book?

WILDE: Is that 'yes' or 'no', Sir Edward?

CLARKE: I should have liked you to have been able to say 'yes'.

WILDE: I say, with one slight addition, I thought it a perfect description of what I meant by the book. There is just one omission.

CLARKE: Then, I must ask you to supply it, if you think it material in this case.

WILDE: That the picture as is stated in the last chapter, and often through the book, had become – the change was meant to symbolise, of course, the ruin that he brought on his own soul – that the picture became to him conscience; and in the last chapter the reason he destroys it is that he says, 'This picture mars my pleasure in life. It is conscience to me; I shall kill it; I shall get rid of this visible emblem of conscience,' and by trying to kill his own soul the man directly dies. That is the only small addition I wish to make.

CLARKE: If you please; you are referring to this I think. 'Why had he kept it so long? Once it had given him pleasure to watch it changing and growing old. Of late he had felt no such pleasure. It had kept him awake at night. When he had been away, he had been filled with terror lest other eyes should look upon it. It had brought melancholy across his passions. Its mere memory had marred many moments of joy. It had been like conscience to him. Yes, it had been conscience. He would destroy it.'

WILDE: Yes.

CLARKE: Your attention has been called, I think, to the statements which are made in this plea here?

WILDE: Yes.

CLARKE: Referring to different persons and impugning your conduct with them?

WILDE: Yes.

CLARKE: Is there any truth whatever in either of those accusations?

WILDE: There is no truth whatsoever in any one of them.

WILDE *is cross-examined by* EDWARD CARSON

CARSON: You stated at the commencement of your examination that you were thirty-nine years of age. I think you are over forty, isn't that so?

WILDE: I don't think so. I think I am either thirty-nine or forty – forty my next birthday. If you have my certificate there that settles the matter.

CARSON: You were born, I believe, upon the 16th of October 1854?

WILDE: Yes, I have no intention of posing for a younger man at all. I try to be correct in the date.

CARSON: It makes you somewhat over forty.

WILDE: Very well.

CARSON: May I ask you, do you happen to know what age Lord Alfred Douglas was or is?

WILDE: Lord Alfred Douglas was, I think, twenty-four his last birthday. I think he will be twenty-five his next birthday.

CARSON: May I take it that when you knew him first he was something about twenty or twenty-one?

WILDE: Yes.

CARSON: With reference to your interview with Lord Queensberry, as I understood your evidence, he was friendly with you at any interview you had with him up to the interview in Tite Street?

WILDE: Yes, certainly.

CARSON: And showed, as I understand, no inclination to unfriend-liness in any way?

WILDE: No.

CARSON: Before the interview in Tite Street, had you had a letter from him dated the 3rd of April saying that he did not desire you to continue your acquaintance with his son?

WILDE: No, I received no such letter.[114]

CARSON: Are you quite sure?

WILDE: Quite sure.

CARSON: But you had no doubt whatsoever after the interview in Tite Street that, whether rightly or wrongly, he didn't wish that association to continue?

WILDE: Yes.

CARSON: And for the reasons he gave?

WILDE: Yes.

CARSON: I think I may take it, Mr Wilde, that notwithstanding his protests upon occasion you have continued very intimate with Lord Alfred Douglas down to the present time?

WILDE: Down to the present moment, certainly.

CARSON: Staying with him at many places?

WILDE: Yes.

CARSON: Oxford?

WILDE: Oxford.

CARSON: Brighton?

WILDE: Yes.

CARSON: On several occasions?

WILDE: Yes, several occasions.

CARSON: Worthing?

WILDE: Yes.

CARSON: You never took rooms for him?

WILDE: Never, never.

CARSON: Were you at other places with him?

WILDE: Do you mean in other cities?

CARSON: No, in other places in England?

WILDE: Cromer.

CARSON: Tulbeck Farm?[115]

WILDE: Yes – Torquay.

CARSON: And, I think, at various hotels in London?

WILDE: Yes.

CARSON: Two hotels in Albemarle Street?

WILDE: One in Albemarle Street and one in Dover Street.[116]

CARSON: The Savoy?

WILDE: Yes.

CARSON: Did you ever take rooms yourself, Mr Wilde, in addition to having your house in Tite Street?

WILDE: Yes.

CARSON: Where?

WILDE: In 10 and 11 St James's Place.

CARSON: How long had you these rooms?

WILDE: From October till the beginning of April I fancy.

CARSON: October of what year?

WILDE: From the October of 1893 to, I think, the end of March or beginning of April 1894.

CARSON: Did Lord Alfred Douglas stay in those chambers?

WILDE: He has stopped there.

CARSON: They are not very far from Piccadilly?

WILDE: No.

CARSON: I believe you also went abroad with him?

WILDE: We have been abroad several times.

CARSON: And even lately, I think?

WILDE: Yes.

CARSON: To Monte Carlo?

WILDE: To Monte Carlo, yes.[117]

CARSON: With reference to those books, the last thing my learned friend examined you about – you were staying at Brighton, I think at 26 Kings Road?[118]

WILDE: Yes.

CARSON: Was it at 26 Kings Road that you wrote your article for *The Chameleon*?

WILDE: No. Oh, no.

CARSON: What?

WILDE: That I wrote it?

CARSON: Yes.

WILDE: No. Oh, no, certainly not.

CARSON: My friend objects to my calling it an article.

WILDE: No – I mean my contribution.

CARSON: Your 'Phrases'?

WILDE: No, it was not written there.

CARSON: You understood what I meant. You observed, I suppose, in *The Chameleon* that there were also contributions from Lord Alfred Douglas?

WILDE: Yes.

CARSON: Did he write those while you were staying in Brighton?

WILDE: No.

CARSON: What?

WILDE: No.

CARSON: Are you quite sure of that?

WILDE: Yes, quite certain.

CARSON: Do you know when he wrote them?

WILDE: They were written while he was at Oxford – while he was an undergraduate at Oxford.

CARSON: Did he show them to you before he sent them to *The Chameleon*?

WILDE: No.

CARSON: He didn't show them to you?

WILDE: No.

CARSON: Are you quite sure of that?

WILDE: Yes. Oh, yes, quite certain – yes, he didn't show them to me.

CARSON: You had never seen them?

WILDE: I had seen them – yes.

CARSON: Did you approve of them?

WILDE: I think they are exceedingly beautiful poems, both of them.

CARSON: Exceedingly beautiful poems?

WILDE: Yes.

CARSON: They are the one 'In Praise of Shame'?

WILDE: The one 'In Praise of Shame'.

CARSON: And the other 'Two Loves'?

WILDE: Yes.

CARSON: Two loves were two boys?

WILDE: Yes.

CARSON: One calls his love 'true love'?

WILDE: Yes.

CARSON: The other boy's love is 'shame'?

WILDE: Yes.

CARSON: Did that suggest to you—

WILDE: Are you quoting from the poems?

CARSON: Yes, I have it here:

> 'I am true Love, I fill
> The hearts of boy and girl with mutual flame.'
> Then sighing said the other, 'Have thy will,
> I am the Love that dare not speak its name.'

WILDE: Yes, that is the last line.

CARSON: Do you think that made improper suggestions?

WILDE: No.

CARSON: Nothing whatsoever?

WILDE: Certainly not.

CARSON: You read 'The Priest and the Acolyte'?

WILDE: Yes.

CARSON: You have no doubt whatsoever that that was not an improper contribution?

WILDE: From a literary point of view, I think it highly improper.

CARSON: Do you only disapprove of it from a literary point of view?

WILDE: It is impossible for a man of letters to judge of a piece of writing otherwise than from its fault in literature. By literature, of course, one includes treatment of subject, selection of subject, everything. I mean, I couldn't criticise a book as if it was a piece of actual life. I think the choice was wrong, the subject wrong, the writing perfectly wrong, the whole treatment wrong – wrong!

CARSON: The whole treatment was wrong?

WILDE: And subject wrong. It might have been made beautiful.

CARSON: I think you are of the opinion, Mr Wilde, that there is no such thing as an immoral book?

WILDE: Yes.

CARSON: You are of that opinion?

WILDE: Yes.

CARSON: Then, I suppose I may take it that in your opinion the piece was not immoral?

WILDE: Worse, it is badly written. (*Laughter.*)

CARSON: It is the story, is it not, of a priest having fallen in love with the acolyte, the boy who attended him at the Mass?

WILDE: Yes.

CARSON: Having conceived a passion for him?

WILDE: By the story I understood the passion is not physical – however, you say 'having conceived a passion for him' – a mere detail – yes.

CARSON: Having conceived a passion for him, the acolyte being found in the priest's room by the rector?

WILDE: I am not responsible for this matter.

CLARKE: My lord, I don't want to interpose, but surely, after the witness has expressed his disapproval and says he at once expressed his disapproval, it is a very strange thing that he should be cross-examined as to the contents of a book which he disapproved of.

JUDGE: No, not as to its contents, but as to his view of the contents with a view to seeing what was meant by saying that he disapproved.

CARSON: Yes.

JUDGE: I think it is quite relevant.

CLARKE: We are not dealing here with matters of literary criticism or literary taste.

CARSON: No, we are not. (*To* WILDE.) And the boy is found by the rector in the bedroom and a scandal is created?

WILDE: My impression is that the rector arrives with a statement of the scandal. I am prepared to accept your statement.

CARSON: He comes to that conclusion by finding the boy in his bedroom?

WILDE: I have read it only once. Nothing would induce me to read it again. You cannot cross-examine me as to the details of the story. I don't care about the story.

CARSON: Did you think the story blasphemous?

WILDE: I thought the end, the account of the death, violated every artistic canon of beauty.

CARSON: That is not what I asked.

WILDE: That is the only answer I can give you.

CARSON: Did you think it blasphemous?

WILDE: How do you mean? I thought it wrong, utterly. Let me say so.

CARSON: Did you think it blasphemous, sir?

WILDE: Yes.

CARSON: I want to see what position you pose in.

WILDE: Now, that is not the way to talk to me – 'to pose as'. I am not posing as anything.

CARSON: Yes; I beg your pardon. I want to see exactly what is the position you take up in reference to this line of publication, and I want to know, sir, did you consider that story was blasphemous?

WILDE: The emotion produced in my mind when I read the story—

CARSON: Will you answer 'yes' or 'no'?

WILDE: I will answer the question – was that of dislike and disgust.

CARSON: I have a great deal to ask you. Will you answer 'yes' or 'no'. You are a gentleman who understands a question perfectly. Did you or did you not consider that story of 'The Priest and the Acolyte' a blasphemous production?

WILDE: I did not consider that story a blasphemous production.

CARSON: Very well; I am satisfied with that.

WILDE: I thought it disgusting.

CARSON: When the priest in the story administers poison to the boy, does he use the words of the sacraments of the Church of England?

WILDE: That I entirely forget. You cannot cross-examine me. I

dare say he does. I think it is horrible. The word blasphemous
is not my word. I think it is horrible and disgusting.

CARSON: It isn't blasphemous?

WILDE: It is not the word I used myself, it is a word of yours.

CARSON: Let me for a moment read to you the words as they are:
'He administered the sacred wafer to the child, and then he took
the beautiful gold chalice, set with precious stones, in his hand;
he turned towards him; but when he saw the light in the beautiful face he turned again to the crucifix with a low moan. For
one instant his courage failed him; then he turned to the little
fellow again, and held the chalice to his lips: "The Blood of our
Lord Jesus Christ, which was shed for thee, preserve thy body
and soul unto everlasting life."' Was that blasphemous?

WILDE: I didn't consider that it was so intended by the writer.

CARSON: That is not what I asked.

WILDE: I don't see why you are pinning me down to a word. They
are not my words.

CARSON: We have that perfectly clear, Mr Wilde, I am not in the
slightest degree accusing you of having published it, and I take
it that you expressed your disapproval, but what I wanted to
get at was, what you disapproved of.

WILDE: What I disapproved of was the tone, treatment, subject,
everything; the whole thing from beginning to end.

CARSON: Listen to this: 'Never had the priest beheld such perfect
love, such perfect trust, in those dear eyes as shone from them
now; now, as with face raised upwards, —'

CLARKE: I really think I am bound to interrupt again. There can
be no possible object in reading these extracts out to Mr Wilde
when he has said that this production is a horrible and disgusting production, except for the sake of, in some way or other,
attempting to identify him with this, or to affect his case by the
reading of that, and the reading of a horrible and disgusting
production by somebody else surely cannot be relevant to any
sort of cross-examination.

JUDGE: I think Mr Carson is quite entitled to test the witness's
view of a production of this kind. I think it is germane to the

issues under the consideration of the jury and I do not think, therefore, that I can interfere at this stage.

CARSON: Listen to this, sir. Was it only from a literary point of view that you disapproved of this: 'The instant he had received Ronald fell on his knees beside him and drained the chalice to the last drop. He set it down and threw his arms round the beautiful figure of his dearly loved acolyte. Their lips met in one last kiss of perfect love, and all was over.'

WILDE: I think it disgusting twaddle.

CARSON: Disgusting what?

WILDE: Twaddle.

CARSON: Is that all?

WILDE: I think it is quite enough.

CARSON: I think you would admit, Mr Wilde, that anyone who was connected with or who would allow himself publicly to approve of that article would be posing as a sodomite?

WILDE: No, would you repeat your question?

CARSON: Anyone who would allow himself to be connected with that article or who publicly approved of that article would be, at least, posing as a sodomite.

WILDE: No.

CARSON: You don't think so?

WILDE: No, if you ask me – another contributor to the magazine – it is wrong and I should think it should have been withdrawn.

CARSON: I am asking you, supposing a person had been connected with the production or had approved of it in public, would you say he was posing as a sodomite?

WILDE: I should say he had very bad literary taste.

CARSON: That is all you would say, that he had very bad literary taste?

WILDE: I think the thing horrid. I don't see why I should be cross-examined on a thing I dislike. I object to it.

CARSON: It is no use your objecting to it.

WILDE: I mean to the story. I object to it entirely.

CLARKE: It is to the story he objects.

CARSON: You disapproved of this from a literary point of view?

WILDE: Yes.

CARSON: Did you ever do any public act to inform the public that you disapproved of *The Chameleon*?

WILDE: No, I never did.

CARSON: And notwithstanding the article, a portion of which I have just read, being in a paper to which you yourself had contributed, you did not think it the least necessary to disassociate yourself from it?

WILDE: Do you mean by a public letter?

CARSON: In any public way.

WILDE: It would be beneath my dignity as a man of letters to write to disassociate myself from the work of an Oxford undergraduate.

CARSON: From the work of what?

WILDE: Of an Oxford undergraduate.

CARSON: Was this work meant for distribution amongst Oxford undergraduates?

WILDE: I have not the smallest conception. I don't know.

CARSON: What?

WILDE: I haven't any idea.

CARSON: Do you know it was circulated?

WILDE: No doubt it was.

CARSON: Amongst Oxford undergraduates?

WILDE: I have no doubt it was. I don't know anything about it.

CARSON: Do you agree with these 'Phrases and Philosophies' of yours in the first article in *The Chameleon* – your contribution?

WILDE: Yes.

CARSON: Do you think that they were articles likely to tend – maxims likely to tend – to immorality amongst young men?

WILDE: My work never aims at producing any effect but that of literature.

CARSON: Literature?

WILDE: Yes, literature.

CARSON: May I take it that you are not concerned whether it has a moral or an immoral effect?

WILDE: I don't myself believe that any book or work of art ever produces any effect on conduct at all. I don't believe it.

CARSON: But I am right in saying that you do not consider that when you come to write these things, you do not consider the effect in creating morality or immorality?

WILDE: Certainly not.

CARSON: I think I may take it that so far as your works are concerned you pose as not being concerned about morality or immorality?

WILDE: I don't know whether you use the word 'pose' in any particular sense.

CARSON: 'Pose' is a favourite word of yours, I think?

WILDE: Is it? I have no 'pose' in the matter. I do my own work in writing a plot, a book, anything. I am concerned entirely with literature, that is with Art. The aim is not to do good or to do evil, but to try and make a thing that will have some quality of beauty that is to be attained or in the form of beauty and of wit and of emotion.

CARSON: Listen, sir. Here is one of your 'Phrases and Philosophies for the Use of the Young': 'Wickedness is a myth invented by good people to account for the curious attractiveness of others.' (*Laughter.*)

WILDE: Yes.

CARSON: Do you think that is true?

WILDE: I rarely think that anything I write is true. (*Laughter.*)

CARSON: Did you say 'rarely'?

WILDE: I said 'rarely'. I might have said never.

CARSON: Nothing you ever write is true?

WILDE: Not true in the sense of correspondence to fact; to represent wilful moods of paradox, of fun, nonsense, of anything at all – but not true in the actual sense of correspondence to actual facts of life, certainly not; I should be very sorry to think it.

CARSON: 'Religions die when they are proved to be true'?[119]

WILDE: Yes, I hold that.

CARSON: Is that true?

WILDE: Yes – well, it is a suggestion towards philosophy of the absorption of religion into science. It is too big a question to go into now.[120]

CARSON: I should just like to take your opinion upon this point – do you think that that was a safe axiom to put forward as a 'Phrase and Philosophy for the Use of the Young'?

WILDE: Most stimulating to thought, I should say. (*Laughter.*)

CARSON: 'If one tells the truth one is sure sooner or later to be found out'?[121]

WILDE: Yes, I think that is a very pleasing paradox, but I don't set any high store on that as an axiom. (*Laughter.*)

CARSON: Do you think it was a good educational axiom for youth?

WILDE: Anything that stimulates thought in people of any age is good for them. (*Laughter.*)

CARSON: Anything that stimulates thought?

WILDE: Yes, anything.

CARSON: Whether moral or immoral?

WILDE: Thought is never either one or the other.

CARSON: No such thing as an immoral thought?

WILDE: No, there are immoral emotions, but thought is an intellectual thing, at least that is the way I use the word.

CARSON: Listen to this: 'Pleasure is the only thing one should live for, nothing ages like happiness.'[122] Do you think pleasure is the only thing that one should live for?

WILDE: I think self-realisation – realisation of one's self – is the primal aim of life. I think that to realise one's self through pleasure is finer than to realise one's self through pain. That is the pagan ideal of man realising himself by happiness as opposed to the later and perhaps grander idea of man realising himself by suffering.[123] I was, on that subject, entirely on the side of the ancients – the Greeks, I will say – the philosophers. (*Laughter.*)

CARSON: 'Any preoccupation with ideas of what is right or wrong in conduct shows an arrested intellectual development'?

WILDE: Well, have you asked me a question?

CARSON: I asked you is that your opinion?

WILDE: Oh, no, certainly not.

CARSON: Then, why did you put that down as a 'Phrase and Philosophy for the Young'?

WILDE: Because if you will allow me to answer, it contains a half-truth – just half a truth put deliberately in a very perverse and paradoxical form; it contains half a truth.

CARSON: 'A truth ceases to be true when more than one person believes in it'?

WILDE: Yes.

CARSON: Do you think that is right?

WILDE: Ultimately, I think, yes, that would be my philosophical definition of truth – something so personal that when another person holds the same – that in fact the same truth can never be apprehended by two minds, that is what it means; that to each mind there is its own truth; it is an important physical condition entirely.

CARSON: 'The condition of perfection is idleness'?[124]

WILDE: Oh, yes, I think so, half of that is true.

CARSON: That is true?

WILDE: Half of it is true. I think the life of contemplation is the highest life, and I think so recognised by the philosopher and the saint – the life of contemplation—[125]

CARSON: Listen to this: 'There is something tragic about the enormous number of young men there are in England at the present moment who start life with perfect profiles, and end by adopting some useful profession.'[126] Is that a 'Phrase and Philosophy for the Young'?

WILDE: I should think the young had enough sense of humour to see the beautiful nonsense.

CARSON: You think that is humorous?

WILDE: I think it is an amusing paradox, an amusing play with words.

CARSON: That when people have perfect profiles – that is I suppose young men with good-looking faces—

WILDE: Perfect profiles they must have.

CARSON: That they can adopt a useful profession?

WILDE: What do you say?

CARSON: Now, sir, I ask you this: what would anybody say would be the effect of 'Phrases and Philosophies' like that appearing in conjunction with such an article as 'The Priest and the Acolyte'?

WILDE: It was undoubtedly that – the idea that that might be so taken that made me object so strongly to 'The Priest and the Acolyte' – that I saw at once that maxims that were meant to be perfectly nonsensical, paradoxical, anything one likes – several of them appear in my plays – that they would then be regarded as serious. That is what I was annoyed about.

CARSON: As regards *Dorian Gray*, this other work that has been referred to, I think you told us that you first published that in *Lippincott's Magazine*?

WILDE: Yes.

CARSON: There were a good many criticisms upon it?[127]

WILDE: Yes.

CARSON: And I think that you took notice of one of those yourself?

WILDE: Of several of them.

CARSON: I only know of one. There was one from the *Scots Observer*.

WILDE: That is the one I took notice of.

CARSON: That is the one you took notice of?

WILDE: That is the one I took notice of. The critic said—

CARSON: The critic says, 'The story, which deals with matters only fitted for the Criminal Investigation Department or a hearing *in camera*, is discreditable alike to author and editor.'

WILDE: Yes.

CARSON: 'Mr Wilde has brains and art and style; but if he can write for none but outlawed noblemen and perverted telegraph boys,[128] the sooner he takes to tailoring (or some other decent trade), the better for his own reputation and the public morals.'

WILDE: Yes.

CLARKE: Whose opinion is this?

CARSON: The *Scots Observer* on the 5th of July 1890.[129] (*To* WILDE.) You wrote an answer to that on the 19th of July 1890, and you say this at the end: 'It was necessary, sir, for the dramatic development of this story to surround Dorian Gray with an atmosphere of moral corruption.'

WILDE: Yes.

CARSON: 'Otherwise the story would have had no meaning and the plot no issue. To keep this atmosphere vague and indeterminate and wonderful was the aim of the artist who wrote the story.'

WILDE: Yes.

CARSON: 'I claim, sir, that he has succeeded. Each man sees his own sin in Dorian Gray. What Dorian Gray's sins are, no one knows. He who finds them has brought them.'

WILDE: Yes.

CARSON: Then, you left it open to be inferred, I take it, that the sins of Dorian Gray, some of them, may have been sodomy?

WILDE: That is according to the temper of each one who reads the book; he who has found the sin has brought it.

CARSON: Then, I take it that some people upon reading the book, at all events, might reasonably think that it did deal with sodomy?

WILDE: Some people might think so. Whether it would be reasonable or not—

CARSON: The volume that has been referred to by my learned friend, Sir Edward Clarke was the volume brought out after these criticisms?

WILDE: Yes.

CARSON: And, I think, was modified and purged a good deal?[130]

WILDE: No.

CARSON: In contrast with the original book?

WILDE: No.

CARSON: Do you say 'not at all'?

WILDE: No, I say there were additions made in one case or two – in one case, certainly. It had been pointed out to me not by any newspaper criticism or anything, but by the only critic of this century I set high, Mr Walter Pater, he had pointed out to me that a certain passage was liable to misconstruction.[131]

CARSON: In what respect?

WILDE: In every respect.

CARSON: In what respect?

WILDE: In the respect that it would convey the impression that the sin of Dorian Gray was sodomy.

CARSON: You altered it?

WILDE: I made one addition.

At this point the court is adjourned for luncheon.

WILDE *is further cross-examined by* EDWARD CARSON

CARSON: This is your introduction to *Dorian Gray?*

WILDE: Yes.

CARSON: 'There is no such thing as a moral or an immoral book'?

WILDE: Yes.

CARSON: 'Books are all well written or badly written'?

WILDE: I think 'either well written—'

CARSON: 'Books are all well written.'

WILDE: 'Or badly written.'

CARSON: 'That is all.'

WILDE: Yes.

CARSON: That expresses your view?

WILDE: My view of art, yes.

CARSON: May I take it that no matter how immoral a book was, if it was well written it would be a good book?

WILDE: If it were well written it would produce a sense of beauty, which is the highest feeling that man is capable of. If it was badly written it would produce a sense of disgust.

CARSON: A well written, immoral book would—

WILDE: I beg your pardon – I say if a book is well written, that is if a work of art is beautiful, the impression that it produces is a sense of beauty, which is the very highest sense that I think human beings are capable of. If it is a badly made work of art, whether it be a statue or whether it be a book, it produces a sense of disgust; that is all.

CARSON: A well written book putting forth sodomitical views might be a good book?

WILDE: No work of art ever puts forward views of any kind.

CARSON: What?

WILDE: No work of art ever puts forward views. Views belong to people who are not artists. There are no views in a work of art.

CARSON: We will say a sodomitical novel might be a good book according to you.

WILDE: I don't know what you mean by a sodomitical novel.

CARSON: Don't you?

WILDE: No.

CARSON: I will suggest to you *Dorian Gray.* Is that open to the interpretation of being a sodomitical book?

WILDE: Only to brutes – only to the illiterate; perhaps I should say brutes and the illiterate.

CARSON: An illiterate person reading *Dorian Gray* might consider it a sodomitical book?

WILDE: The views of the Philistine on art could not be counted: they are incalculably stupid. You cannot ask me what misinterpretation of my work the ignorant, the illiterate, the foolish may put on it. It doesn't concern me. What concerns me in my art is my view and my feeling and why I made it; I don't care twopence what other people think about it.

CARSON: The majority of people would come within your definition of Philistines and illiterate, wouldn't they?

WILDE: Oh, I have found wonderful exceptions.

CARSON: But the majority of people, I say. Do you think the majority of people live up to the pose that you are giving us, Mr Wilde, or are educated up to that?

WILDE: I am afraid they are not cultivated enough. (*Laughter.*)

CARSON: Not cultivated enough to draw the distinction that you have done between a good book and a bad book?

WILDE: Oh, certainly not. Nothing to do with art at all.

CARSON: The affection and the love that is pictured of the artist towards Dorian Gray in this book of yours might lead an ordinary individual to believe it had a sodomitical tendency, might it not?

WILDE: I have no knowledge of the ordinary individual.

CARSON: Oh, I see. But you do not prevent the ordinary individual from buying your book.

WILDE: I have never discouraged them. (*Laughter.*)

CARSON: Now listen to this. This is your account of the introduction of the artist.

CLARKE: The plea in this case, as your lordship sees – and, of course, in a case like this it is necessary to be strict – alleges – my learned friend has handed me a copy.

CARSON: Would you just consider this passage.

CLARKE: I am sorry to interrupt my friend. I think I must take exception to this. Your lordship will see that the plea says 'he published in the month of July 1890, published with his name upon the title page thereof, a work in the form of a narrative entitled *The Picture of Dorian Gray*'. I have the work with his name upon the title page. My learned friend hands to me a number of *Lippincott's Monthly Magazine* which is alleged to contain the entire story.[132]

CARSON: The original story.

CLARKE: It contains also articles on cheiromancy and contributions to science, 'A Round Robin', 'Tales of the Powers of the Air' and the like. Of course, it is extremely difficult when one is acquainted once with the contents of the volume described in the plea to enter upon a critical examination of the difference between two books. But I submit that my learned friend by that is confined to a certain book – the work – with the name printed upon the title page. It is this, and this, so far as I know, only.[133]

CARSON: My lord, I submit—

JUDGE: I have not seen the work that you have in your hand. (*A copy is handed to the* JUDGE.)

CLARKE: Your lordship sees how difficult it is to compare—

CARSON: Even if my learned friend's objection were in any wise a good one, that it was the actual volume containing alone this that we referred to, which is not the fact, if that were so, it would certainly be open to me on cross-examination to cross-examine Mr Wilde upon any work which he had contributed.

JUDGE: Yes, I think so certainly.

CLARKE: It is not in support of the plea.

CARSON: As a matter of fact I took great pains to describe this as a narrative and with the date so as to refer to the contribution in *Lippincott* and not to the other volume. I have already asked Mr Wilde whether he did not afterwards – when there were criticisms upon the original – make certain modifications.

JUDGE: This was published in 1891 we are told.

CARSON: There is no year stated.[134]

JUDGE: But we are told it was published in 1891 by Mr Wilde.

CARSON: I have the original edition signed by Mr Wilde himself. It is in 1891.

CLARKE: If your lordship pleases, it will take some time, I am afraid.

CARSON: I shall give you a copy.

JUDGE: I see the name is on the title page.

CLARKE: I am much obliged to my learned friend; my learned friend has given me a copy.

CARSON: I have given a copy which shows all the differences.

JUDGE: *The Picture of Dorian Gray* by Oscar Wilde.

CARSON: That is, as a matter of fact, what we did refer to.

WILDE *steps down from the box in order to speak to his counsel for a few minutes.*

CLARKE: I am sure your lordship will allow me to state the communication made to me by Mr Oscar Wilde. It is a matter of perfect indifference to him, he tells me, with regard to which edition of the book he is challenged. I explained to him it was because I did not know the other and knew this, that the objection was taken, but at his wish I withdraw the objection at once.

CARSON: As a matter of convenience to my learned friend I have given him a book showing him.

CLARKE: I am much obliged.

CARSON: Here is the introduction of the artist to Dorian Gray and the question I am about to found upon that is this: to ask you whether—

CHARLES GILL: Page 8 in the book.

CARSON: And page 6 in *Lippincott* if your lordship has it. Here is the passage. This is the conversation between Lord Henry Wotton and the artist Basil Hallward:

'I want you to explain to me why you won't exhibit Dorian Gray's picture. I want the real reason.'

'I told you the real reason.'

'No, you did not. You said it was because there was too much of yourself in it. Now, that is childish.'

'Harry,' said Basil Hallward looking him straight in the face, 'every portrait that is painted with feeling is a portrait of the artist, not of the sitter. The sitter is merely the accident, the occasion. It is not he who is revealed by the painter; it is rather the painter who, on the coloured canvas, reveals himself. The reason I will not exhibit this picture is that I am afraid that I have shown with it the secret of my own soul.'

Lord Henry laughed. 'And what is that?' he asked.

'I will tell you,' said Hallward; and an expression of perplexity came over his face.

'I am all expectation, Basil,' murmured his companion, looking at him.

'Oh, there is really very little to tell, Harry,' answered the young painter; 'and I am afraid you will hardly understand it. Perhaps you will hardly believe it.'

Lord Henry smiled and, leaning down, plucked a pink-petalled daisy from the grass and examined it. 'I am quite sure I shall understand it,' he replied gazing intently at the little golden white-feathered disc, 'and I can believe anything provided that it is incredible.'

'Well, this is incredible,' repeated Hallward rather bitterly, 'incredible to me at times. I don't know what it means. The story is simply this. Two months ago I went to a crush at Lady Brandon's. You know we poor painters have to show ourselves in society from time to time, just to remind the public that we are not savages. With an evening coat and a white tie, as you told me once, anybody, even a stockbroker, can gain a reputation for being civilised. Well, after I had been in the room about ten minutes, talking to huge overdressed dowagers and tedious academicians, I suddenly became conscious that someone was looking at me. I turned half-way round, and saw Dorian Gray for the first time. When our eyes met, I felt that I was growing pale. A curious instinct of terror came over me. I knew that I had come face to face with someone whose mere personality was so fascinating that, if I allowed it to do so, it would absorb my whole nature, my whole soul, my very art itself. I did not want any external influence in my life. You know yourself, Harry, how independent I am by nature. My father destined me for the army. I insisted on going to Oxford. Then he made me enter my name at the Middle Temple. Before I had eaten half a dozen dinners I gave up the bar, and announced my intention of becoming a painter. I have always been my own master; had at least always been so, till I met Dorian Gray. Then – but I don't know how to explain it to you. Something seemed to tell me that I was on the verge of a terrible crisis in my life. I had a strange feeling that Fate had in store for me exquisite joys and exquisite sorrows. I knew that if I spoke to Dorian I would become absolutely devoted to him and that I ought not to speak to him.[135] I grew afraid and turned to quit the room. It was not conscience that made me do so; it was cowardice. I take no credit to myself for trying to escape.'

Then afterwards he says,

'Our eyes met again. It was mad of me, but I asked Lady Brandon to introduce me to him. Perhaps it was not so mad after all. It was simply inevitable. We would have spoken to each other without any introduction. I am sure of that. Dorian told me so afterwards. He, too, felt that we were destined to know each other.'

Now, I ask you, Mr Wilde, do you consider that that description of the feeling of one man towards a youth, just grown up, was a proper or an improper feeling?

WILDE: I think this is the most perfect description possible of what an artist would feel on meeting a beautiful personality that he felt some way was necessary to his art and life.

CARSON: A beautiful personality?

WILDE: Yes, a beautiful young man.

CARSON: You mean a beautiful person?

WILDE: Yes, I would rather say personality; that he felt instinctively that he and Dorian would be friends.

CARSON: Would be friends?

WILDE: And that his life was going to meet his. But I will take any word you like. I will say a beautiful young man if you choose. I say that I think that is a perfectly beautiful description.

CARSON: You think that is a moral kind of feeling for one man to have towards another much younger than himself?

WILDE: I say it was the feeling of an artist towards a beautiful personality.

CARSON: A beautiful personality?

WILDE: Yes, personality.

CARSON: He had never spoken to this Dorian Gray.

WILDE: I use the word 'personality' on account of the peculiar effect on this artist, this spectre, this appearance of Dorian Gray produced. That is part of the story.

CARSON: Now listen – this, my lord, is at page 56 – listen to the artist's description and to his own confession.

WILDE: Might I have a copy of *Lippincott's Magazine*? It is immensely difficult for me to listen. I dislike it.

CLARKE: I think I had better hand Mr Wilde this copy which my learned friend has been good enough to give me, which shows the interpolation and omissions. I will try and follow it as well as I can.

WILDE: Which chapter?

CARSON: It is chapter 7. It is page 56 in *Lippincott's*.

WILDE: I have got it.

CARSON: It is where he confesses his love to Dorian Gray. I believe this was left out of the purged edition afterwards.

WILDE: I deny the expression 'purged'.

CARSON: You don't call it purged but we will see.

WILDE: We will.

CARSON: Now, here it is. Wait till you hear. This is the artist making his confession to Dorian Gray. It is written in.

WILDE: It is the part written in.

CARSON: It was left out of the second edition.

CLARKE: What page of the English edition does it come in?

WILDE: It is not in the English edition.

CARSON: What page of the English edition is it written in upon?

WILDE: Page 168 if that is the passage that Mr Carson is referring to.

CARSON: Page 56, my lord. It is in the middle of the page. Now listen, Mr Wilde, please. 'Basil,' he said – that was what Dorian Gray said –

coming over quite close and looking him straight in the face, 'we have each of us a secret. Let me know yours and I shall tell you mine. What was your reason for refusing to exhibit my picture?'

Hallward shuddered in spite of himself. 'Dorian, if I told you, you might like me less than you do, and you would certainly laugh at me. I could not bear your doing either of those two things. If you wish me never to look at your picture again I am content. I have always you to look at. If you wish the best work I have ever done to be hidden from the world, I am satisfied. Your friendship is dearer to me than any fame or reputation.'

'No, Basil, you must tell me,' insisted Dorian Gray. 'I think I have a right to know.' His feeling of terror had passed away and curiosity had taken its place. He was determined to find out Basil Hallward's mystery.

'Let us sit down, Dorian,' said Hallward, looking pale and pained. 'Let us sit down. I will sit in the shadow and you shall sit in the sunlight. Our lives are like that. Just answer me one question. Have you noticed in the picture something you did not like, something that probably at first did not strike you, but that revealed itself to you suddenly?'

'Basil!' cried the lad, clutching the arms of his chair with trembling hands, and gazing at him with wild, startled eyes.

'I see you did. Don't speak. Wait till you hear what I have to say. It is quite true that I have worshipped you with far more romance of feeling than a man usually gives to a friend. Somehow, I had never loved a woman. I suppose I never had time. Perhaps, as Harry says, a really *grande passion* is the privilege of those who have nothing to do, and that is the use of the idle classes in a country. Well, from the moment I met you, your personality had the most extraordinary influence over me. I quite admit that I adored you madly, extravagantly, absurdly. I was jealous of every-one to whom you spoke. I wanted to have you all to myself. I

7. A manuscript page from chapter 7 of *The Picture of Dorian Gray* as first published in 1890, showing the 'dangerous' passage which Wilde omitted from the book version in 1891.

was only happy when I was with you. When I was away from you, you were still present in my art. It was all wrong and foolish. It is all wrong and foolish still. Of course I never let you know anything about this. It would have been impossible. You would not have understood it. I did not understand it myself. One day I determined to paint a wonderful portrait of you. It was to have been my masterpiece. It is my masterpiece. But as I worked at it, every flake and film of colour seemed to me to reveal my secret. I grew afraid that the world would know of my idolatry. I felt, Dorian, that I had told too much. Then it was that I resolved never to allow the picture to be exhibited.'

Do you mean to say that that passage describes a natural feeling of one man towards another?

WILDE: It describes the influence produced on an artist by a beautiful personality.

CARSON: You prefer personality?

WILDE: I said Dorian Gray's personality. You can describe him as you like.

CARSON: I want to know what your opinion is. Mine is of little value.

WILDE: I say Dorian Gray is a most remarkable personality.

CARSON: Do you think that that passage is open to the construction that the feeling between these two men was not a natural or a moral feeling?

WILDE: No, I don't think that.

CARSON: Have you yourself ever had that feeling towards a young man?

WILDE: An intense admiration?

CARSON: No, but a feeling that would be properly described by those words that you have used there.

WILDE: Which words?

CARSON: All those words that I have just read. 'I quite admit that I adored you madly, extravagantly, desperately. I was jealous of everyone.'

WILDE: No, I have never been jealous of anyone in my life. No, certainly not.

CARSON: May I take it that you yourself as an artist have never known the feeling towards a younger man that is described there?

WILDE: I don't know whether you wish to pin me down to the actual words.

CARSON: I don't wish to pin you to anything. I only want to know.

WILDE: Then, I shall have to read the passage again. No, I have never allowed any personality to dominate my art, which is the second part of the passage that you read out. I say no, certainly not.

CARSON: Then, you have never known the feeling that you describe?

WILDE: No.

CARSON: What?

WILDE: No, it is a work of fiction I am describing.

CARSON: So far as you personally are concerned, you have no experience of its being a natural feeling from one man towards a younger man?

WILDE: I think it is perfectly natural for any artist to intensely admire and to love a younger man. I think it is an incident in the life of almost every artist. But let us go over the thing phrase by phrase.

CARSON: Is it an incident in your life?

WILDE: Let us go over the thing phrase by phrase.

CARSON: Is it an incident in your life?

WILDE: I will not answer about an entire passage. Pick out each sentence and ask me what I mean.

CARSON: I will. 'I quite admit that I adored you madly.' Have you ever adored a young man, some twenty-one years younger than yourself, madly?

WILDE: No, not madly, not madly.

CARSON: Well, adored him?

WILDE: I have loved one friend in my life.

CARSON: You asked me to take your own phrase 'adored'.

WILDE: I prefer 'loved' – that is higher.

CARSON: 'Adored', sir?

WILDE: And I say 'loved' – it is greater.

CARSON: Never mind going higher. Keep down to the level of your own words.

WILDE: Keep your own words to yourself. Leave me mine. Don't put words to me I haven't said.

CARSON: I beg your pardon. I am putting your own words at your own request.

WILDE: Is it? Where is your passage?

CARSON: 'I quite admit that I adored you madly.' I ask you, sir?

CLARKE: It is written in. It is not in the English.

WILDE: This is what I have in my copy here.

CARSON: I don't ask you that. Now, please keep to the very simple—

WILDE: You are giving me a copy. You must quote from it.

CARSON: I am quoting from *Lippincott's*. I have given you nothing. I will read you these words. It is a very, very simple question, now; and as I go on, when I have to deal with a number of cases in the plea, it will be necessary to go into those matters.

WILDE: Yes.

CARSON: I want an answer to this simple question. Have you ever felt that feeling of adoring madly a beautiful male person many years younger than yourself?

WILDE: I have never given adoration to anybody except myself. (*Loud laughter.*)

CARSON: I am sure you think that is a very smart thing?

WILDE: I don't at all. I object strongly. I have a copy. I object strongly to your not listening to my answers. I object to it most strongly.

CARSON: I will let you have *Lippincott's*.

WILDE: Very well. Why am I given another copy?

CARSON: Now page 57, sir.

WILDE: Do not call me 'sir'.

CARSON: 'I quite admit that I adored you madly.' Have you ever had that experience towards a beautiful male person many years younger than yourself?

WILDE: I have given you my answer. Adoration is a thing I reserve for myself.

CARSON: I ask you 'yes' or 'no', sir, to my question.

WILDE: I have given it to you. I have never adored any young man younger than myself or any person older than myself of any kind. I do not adore them. I either love a person or do not love them.

CARSON: Then, you never had that feeling that you depict there?

WILDE: No, it was borrowed from Shakespeare I regret to say. (*Laughter.*)

CARSON: From Shakespeare?

WILDE: Yes, from Shakespeare's sonnets.

CARSON: 'I adored you madly, extravagantly'?

WILDE: Yes.

CARSON: Have you ever extravagantly adored?

WILDE: Do you mean financially or emotionally?

CARSON: Financially? – do you think we are talking here of finance?

WILDE: I don't know what you are talking about.

CARSON: Don't you?

WILDE: You must ask me a plain question.

CARSON: I hope I will make myself very plain before I am done. 'I was jealous of everyone to whom you spoke.' Have you ever been jealous?

WILDE: Never in my life.

CARSON: Never?

WILDE: Never. What should I be jealous of?

CARSON: 'I wanted to have you all to myself.' Did you ever have that feeling towards—

WILDE: I should consider it an intense bore. I should consider it an intense nuisance. (*Laughter.*)

CARSON: An intense nuisance?

WILDE: Certainly, an intense bore.

CARSON: May I take it, Mr Wilde – because this was really a question I put to you generally and I will take your answer one way or another – may I take it that you yourself have never experienced the sensation which you described there as being the sensation of this artist towards Dorian Gray?

WILDE: No, I varied it from Shakespeare's sonnets. I took it—

CARSON: I believe you have written an article pointing out that Shakespeare's sonnets were practically sodomitical.[136]

WILDE: On the contrary, Mr Carson, I wrote an article to prove that they were not so.

CARSON: You did write an article to prove that they were not sodomitical?

WILDE: Yes, the statement had been made against Shakespeare by Hallam,[137] the historian, and by others. I wrote an article to prove that they were not so, and I consider I have proved it.

CARSON: In your opinion they were not sodomitical?

WILDE: Certainly not.

CARSON: I suppose in that article you dealt fully with the subject?

WILDE: With the Shakespeare sonnets?

CARSON: With the question of sodomy.

WILDE: No, except that I said I object to the shameful perversion put on Shakespeare's sonnets by Hallam and a great many French critics. I was explaining that the love of Shakespeare to the young man to whom he dedicated them, was the love of an artist for a personality which I imagine to be a part of his art.

CARSON: 'I grew afraid that the world would know of my idolatry.' Why should he grow afraid that the world should know of it? Was it anything to be concealed?

WILDE: Yes, because there are people in the world who cannot understand the intense devotion and affection and admiration that an artist can feel for a wonderful and beautiful person, or for a wonderful and beautiful mind. Those are the conditions under which we live. I regret them.

CARSON: And these unfortunate people who have not that high understanding that you have, might put it down to something wrong?

WILDE: Undoubtedly.

CARSON: And sodomitical?

WILDE: Hallam had done it about Shakespeare.

CARSON: And sodomitical?

WILDE: To any point they choose. I am not concerned with the ignorance of others. Don't cross-examine me about the ignorance of other people. It has nothing to do with me at all. (*Laughter.*)

CARSON: You have told me before, you did not limit the circulation of your work to those people who would not draw the natural conclusion, as I say, from the words?

WILDE: I have a great passion to civilise the community.

CARSON: And I suppose these works of yours are with a view of civilising the community?

WILDE: Any work of art, even if it be small or great, is good for people. I think so.

CARSON: You describe further on the gift by Sir Henry Wotton.

WILDE: What chapter?

CARSON: If you look at *Lippincott's* page 63, you describe the gift of a novel.

WILDE: Yes.

CARSON: You had, I suppose, a particular novel in your mind at the time?

WILDE: No, a suggestion.

CARSON: Do you say that you hadn't?

WILDE: Well, if you will allow me to say, there is a French novel which I do not admire very much myself.

CARSON: If you will tell me the name of it, we will see about it.

WILDE: No, I think you had better leave it. I don't mind telling you the name. The novel is called *À Rebours* and the artist is Huysmans.[138] I consider it a badly written book, but it gave me a suggestion that there might be a wonderful—

CARSON: The novel was *À Rebours*?

WILDE: Yes.

CARSON: Now, here is the description of the effect of it upon Dorian:

His eye fell on the yellow book that Lord Henry had sent him. What was it, he wondered. He went towards the little pearl-coloured octagonal stand that had always looked to him like the work of some strange Egyptian bees who wrought in silver, and took the volume up. He flung himself into an armchair, and began to turn over the leaves. After a few minutes, he became absorbed. It was the strangest book that he had ever read. It seemed to him that in exquisite raiment, and to the delicate sound of flutes, the sins of the world were passing in dumb show before him. Things that he had dimly dreamed of were suddenly made real to him. Things of which he had never dreamed were gradually revealed.

It was a novel without a plot, and with only one character, being, indeed, simply a psychological study of a certain young Parisian, who spent his life trying to realise in the nineteenth century all the passions and modes of thought that belonged to every century except his own, and to sum up, as it were, in himself the various moods through which the world-spirit had ever passed, loving for their mere artificiality those renunciations that men have unwisely called virtue, as much as those natural rebellions that wise men still call sin. The style in which it was written was that curious jewelled style, vivid and obscure at once, full of *argot* and of archaisms, of technical expressions and of elaborate paraphrases, that characterises the work of some of the finest artists of the French school of *Décadents*. There were in it metaphors as monstrous as orchids, and as evil in colour.[139] The life of the senses was described in the terms of mystical philosophy. One hardly knew at times whether one was reading the spiritual ecstasies of some mediæval saint or the morbid confessions of a modern sinner. It was a poisonous book. The heavy odour of incense seemed to cling about its pages and to trouble the brain. The mere cadence of the sentences, the subtle monotony of their music, so full as it was of complex refrains and movements elaborately repeated, produced in the mind of the lad, as he passed from chapter to chapter, a form of revery, a malady of dreaming, that made him unconscious of the falling day and the creeping shadows.

Cloudless, and pierced by one solitary star, a copper-green sky gleamed through the windows. He read on by its wan light till he could read no more. Then, after his valet had reminded him several times of the lateness of the hour, he got up and, going into the next room, placed the book on the little Florentine table that always stood at his bedside, and began to dress for dinner.

It was almost nine o'clock before he reached the club, where he found Lord Henry sitting alone, in the morning-room, looking very bored.

'I am so sorry, Harry,' he cried, 'but really it is entirely your fault. That book you sent me so fascinated me that I forgot what the time was.'

'I thought you would like it,' replied his host rising from his chair.

'I didn't say I liked it, Harry. I said it fascinated me. There is a great difference.'

'Ah, if you have discovered that, you have discovered a great deal,' murmured Lord Henry, with his curious smile. 'Come let us go into dinner. It is dreadfully late, and I am afraid the champagne will be much too iced.'

For years, Dorian Gray could not free himself from the memory of this book. Or perhaps it would be more accurate to say that he never sought to free himself from it. He procured from Paris no less than five large-paper copies of the first edition, and had them bound in different colours, so that they might suit his various moods and the changing fancies of a nature over which he seemed, at times, to have almost entirely lost control. The hero, the wonderful young Parisian, in whom the romantic temperament and scientific temperament were so strangely blended, became to him a kind of prefiguring type of himself. And, indeed, the whole book seemed to him to contain the story of his own life, written before he had lived it.

Now, that book that you say you referred to there, *À Rebours*, was that an immoral book?

WILDE: Not very well written, but I would not call it an immoral book. It is not well written.

CARSON: Was it a book, sir, dealing with undisguised sodomy?

WILDE: *À Rebours*?

CARSON: Yes.

WILDE: Most certainly not.

CARSON: Let me read to you.

WILDE: You must remember Mr Carson – I wish distinctly to state that while the suggestion of the book – the thing being a work of fiction – while the suggestion of a young man taking up a book in a yellow cover and having his life influenced by it – while that to a certain degree suggested to me that I might write a book like *À Rebours*, on the other hand when I quote from the book, as I do later on, and allude to passages in the book, those passages do not occur in the book. It was merely what I imagined. I read this book *À Rebours* and I imagined it as being grander than it was.

CARSON: Was *À Rebours* a sodomitical book?

WILDE: *À Rebours*?

CARSON: Yes.

WILDE: No.

CARSON: Now, just take the book in your hand.

WILDE: You must describe to me what you mean by a sodomitical book.

CARSON: You don't know?

WILDE: I don't know.

CLARKE: I really want to see how far this is going. In the book upon which Mr Carson, of course, is most properly cross-examining because it is contained in the plea here, there is a reference to some supposed French novel, not mentioned by name – and – as Mr Wilde says, not representing or purporting to give a specific book. He is asked what book suggested that idea to him, and then he is to be cross-examined as to the contents of that book. I do not know whether your lordship does not think we are going a long way.[140]

CARSON: My lord, I asked him the question as to whether this book *À Rebours* was a book depicting sodomy. My lord, he admits that is the book he referred to there.

WILDE: No, I don't admit that.

CARSON: What?

WILDE: I don't. I say that the idea of the book was suggested by *À Rebours*, but that when I came to quote in the next passage of *Dorian Gray* from this supposed imaginary book, I quote chapters that do not exist in *À Rebours*. It was merely a motive, that is all. There is the difference. When I quote – if you read the next chapter – I say 'in the seventh chapter of this book'. There is no chapter of the character I speak of.

CARSON: But the book you had in your mind was *À Rebours?*

WILDE: No, the book I had in my mind was a book that I should like to have written myself.

CARSON: I ask you, now, was the book you had in your mind as the book sent by Lord Henry Wotton to Dorian Gray, was it *À Rebours* or was it not?

WILDE: It was not.

CARSON: But you told me a moment ago it was.

WILDE: No.

JUDGE: I certainly took it down.

WILDE: What I meant was – if you will allow me to say so – I am not quibbling about the matter – in the book sent to Dorian Gray by Lord Henry Wotton there is an allusion in the next chapter—

CARSON: I do not want to know that.

WILDE: To a particular chapter that does not occur in *À Rebours* and I was particularly anxious not—

CARSON: I will take your answer one way or the other.

WILDE: Will you kindly allow me to say this – that I would not have taken the work of a French man of letters deliberately and said, 'This is a book that has poisoned a young man's life.' I would not have done it. I should consider that dishonourable, untrue and unjust. I would not have done it.

CARSON: I will not take it if you say you did not refer to *À Rebours*, but it was you who mentioned *À Rebours* not myself.

WILDE: But you asked me what gave me the suggestion of the plot of the book that Lord Henry Wotton sent to Dorian Gray, but I would no more say that I meant that Monsieur Huysmans – a man of letters – highly distinguished in Paris – nothing would induce me to say that any book of his put into the hands of Dorian Gray would poison his life – a thing no artist would say about another: it would be an impertinence and a vulgarity.

CARSON: If you say it was not *À Rebours*, I will not pursue the matter further.

WILDE: I say the book sent by Lord Henry Wotton to Dorian Gray was not *À Rebours*. I say the idea of the book that might have been written was suggested to me by *À Rebours* but the book was not *À Rebours*.

CARSON: Then I asked you whether you were plainly thinking at the time you wrote it of *À Rebours* and I asked you then was *À Rebours* a book that dealt with sodomitical incidents. You can look – you have *À Rebours* there – if you like, at that passage I have marked. I will read it to you.[141]

WILDE: It might be the passage or it might not.

CARSON: Here is a translation.

WILDE: It is quite unnecessary. Oh, yes that is, I suppose, Mr Huysmans? I give no opinion on another artist's work, but what Monsieur Huysmans would say, I do not know.

CARSON: What do you think?

WILDE: I don't think you have a right to cross-examine me on the work of another artist. I entirely decline to – I will not give my opinion. You can read it out and do as you like. I don't think it is fair to ask me because to begin with – when you have used the expression—

CARSON: Just let me read a passage to you.

WILDE: No, I beg you not. I would much sooner read the passage myself.

CLARKE: I interpose here to respectfully protest. The exact state of things now is that Mr Wilde has said that in suggesting a book which affected for evil the mind of Dorian Gray, he had in his mind some such book as *À Rebours*. Therefore, it is proposed to read to him a passage from *À Rebours* in precisely the same way as the passage which he had already repudiated as horrible and disgusting out of 'The Priest and the Acolyte', which was read to him an hour or two ago. Now, I submit that while it is perfectly open to my learned friend – and perfectly fair – that upon any language of his own, Mr Wilde should be cross-examined as severely as my learned friend may choose, upon the language of another person – which he has never adopted or repeated in any way whatever – I submit that my learned friend is not entitled to read that in court for whatever purpose he desires so to use it, because it is not relevant and cannot be relevant to any question in this case.

CARSON: My lord, I submit to your lordship that it is a perfectly legitimate question to put upon cross-examination. I have asked this gentleman what work it was that was in his mind when he wrote this particular passage in *Dorian Gray*. He told me it was *À Rebours*. Surely, my lord, where the issue here is whether Mr Wilde was posing as a sodomite, which is the justification pleaded here – I have a right to show when he was publishing that book he had in his mind a novel, which according to the extract that I have was plainly a novel which would lead to and teach sodomitical practices? My lord, surely I ought to be allowed to ask the witness and to test the witness as to whether the book was of that description?

CLARKE: My lord, I submit if my learned friend will find here in Mr Wilde's book a reference to *À Rebours*, anything by which the reader of his book would be induced to the perusal of *À Rebours*, then the contents of *À Rebours* might be relevant to this extent.

JUDGE: I think it is not admissible. Mr Wilde has repudiated that passage from being in his mind at all. He says that all that *À Rebours* did was to suggest the plot which he put into the novel and which appears in the book. Therefore, I do not see that anything in *À Rebours* is subject matter of cross-examination of Mr Wilde.

CARSON: Very well, my lord. Just one more passage I will draw your attention to from *Dorian Gray*. It is at page 79 of *Lippincott's* – a passage which is part of a conversation when Hallward is making his confession to Dorian Gray:

'And now, my dear fellow, I want to speak to you seriously. Don't frown like that. You make it so much more difficult for me.'

'What is it all about?' cried Dorian in his petulant way, flinging himself down on the sofa. 'I hope it is not about myself. I am tired of myself tonight. I should like to be somebody else.'

'It is about yourself,' answered Hallward, in his grave, deep voice, 'and I must say it to you. I shall only keep you half an hour.'

Dorian sighed and lit a cigarette. 'Half an hour!' he murmured.

'It is not much to ask of you, Dorian, and it is entirely for your own sake that I am speaking. I think it right that you should know that the most dreadful things are being said about you in London — things that I could hardly repeat to you.'

'I don't wish to know anything about them. I love scandals about other people, but scandals about myself don't interest me. They have not got the charm of novelty.'

'They must interest you, Dorian. Every gentleman is interested in his good name. You don't want people to talk of you as something vile and degraded. Of course, you have your position, and your wealth, and all that kind of thing. But position and wealth are not everything. Mind you, I don't believe these rumours at all. At least, I can't believe them when I see you. Sin is a thing that writes itself across a man's face. It cannot be concealed. People talk of secret vices. There are no such things as secret vices. If a wretched man has a vice, it shows itself in the lines of his mouth, the droop of his eyelids, the moulding of his hands even. Somebody — I won't mention his name, but you know him — came to me last year to have his portrait done. I had never seen him before, and had never heard anything about him at the time, though I have heard a good deal since. He offered an extravagant price. I refused him. There was something in the shape of his fingers that I hated. I know now that I was quite right in what I fancied about him. His life is dreadful. But you, Dorian, with your pure, bright, innocent face, and your marvellous untroubled youth — I can't believe anything against you. And yet I see you very seldom, and you never come down to the studio now, and when I am away from you, and I hear all these hideous things that people are whispering about you, I don't know what to say. Why is it, Dorian, that a man like the Duke of Berwick leaves the room of a club when you enter it? Why is it that so many gentlemen in London will neither go to your house nor invite you to theirs? You used to be a friend of Lord Cawdor. I met him at dinner last week. Your name happened to come up in conversation, in connection with the miniatures you have lent to the exhibition at the Dudley. Cawdor curled his lip, and said that you might have the most artistic tastes, but that you were a man whom no pure-minded girl should be allowed to know, and whom no chaste woman should sit in the same room with. I reminded him that I was a friend of yours, and asked him what he meant. He told me. He told me right out before everybody. It was horrible! Why is your friendship so fatal to young men? There was that wretched boy in the Guards who committed suicide. You were his great friend. There was Sir Henry Ashton, who had to leave England with a tarnished name. You and he were inseparable. What about Adrian Singleton, and his dreadful end? What about Lord Kent's only son, and his career? I met his father yesterday in St James's Street. He seemed broken with shame and sorrow. What about the young Duke of Perth? What sort of life has he got now? What gentleman would associate with him?'[142]

Do you think that, taken in its natural meaning, would suggest that what they were talking about was a charge of sodomy?

WILDE: The passage you have read describes Dorian Gray as a man of very corrupt influence. There is no statement about what the nature of his bad influence was, nor do I think there is such a thing as a bad influence in the world.

CARSON: Nor do you think what?

WILDE: Nor do I think that, except in fiction; I think such an idea as a bad influence is rather a question for fiction than actual life.

CARSON: Did you say you thought there was no such thing as bad influence in the world?

WILDE: I don't think there is any influence, good or bad, from one person over another. I don't think so.

CARSON: A man never corrupts a youth?

WILDE: I think not.

CARSON: Nothing he could do would corrupt him?

WILDE: Oh, if you are talking of separate ages it is nonsense.

CARSON: No sir, I am talking common sense.

WILDE: Do not talk like that. I say it is a question of bad and good influence: but personally, as a mere philosophical point, I don't think – I am talking of grown human beings – that one person influences another. I don't think so. I don't believe it.

CARSON: You don't think that one man could exercise any influence over another? I may take that as a general statement?

WILDE: As a general statement, yes. I think influence is not a power that can be exercised at will by one person over another: I think it is quite impossible psychologically.

CARSON: You don't think that flattering a young man, telling him of his beauty, making love to him in fact, would be likely to corrupt him?

WILDE: No.

CARSON: Wasn't that the way in your own novel that Lord Henry Wotton corrupted Dorian Gray in the first instance?

WILDE: Lord Henry Wotton – no – in the novel he doesn't corrupt him; you must remember that novels and life are different things.

CARSON: It depends upon what you call corruption.

WILDE: Yes, and what one calls life. In my novel there is a picture of changes. You are not to ask me if I believe they really happened; they are motives in fiction.

CARSON: I want to ask you a few questions about this letter which was brought to you.

WILDE: Yes.

CARSON: This is a letter, as I understand, which you wrote to Lord Alfred Douglas?

WILDE: Yes.

CARSON: Where was he staying when you wrote him that letter?

WILDE: At the Savoy Hotel.

CARSON: Where were you staying?

WILDE: At Babbacombe, Torquay.

CARSON: It was a letter in answer to something that he sent you?

WILDE: Yes, in answer to a poem which he had sent me.

CARSON: Did it go as it is there, by itself in an envelope?

WILDE: Yes, in an envelope – not torn, of course.

CARSON: No, and perhaps not so soiled?

WILDE: And not so soiled.

CARSON: Is that an ordinary letter?

WILDE: Ordinary? I should think not. (*Laughter.*)

CARSON: What!

WILDE: Certainly not an ordinary letter, no.

CARSON: What!

WILDE: No, certainly not an ordinary letter.

CARSON: 'My own boy.'

WILDE: Yes.

CARSON: Was that ordinary?

WILDE: No, I say it is not ordinary.

CARSON: Just wait. I want to see what is extraordinary about it.

WILDE: Yes.

CARSON: 'My own boy.'

WILDE: Yes.

CARSON: That you say was not ordinary?

WILDE: No, I should think not ordinary.

CARSON: You would think, I suppose, Mr Wilde, that a man of your age to address a man nearly twenty years younger as 'My own boy' would be an improper thing?

WILDE: No, not if I was fond of him. I don't think so.

CARSON: Not in the least?

WILDE: If I call people my boy – I say 'My own boy'. I was fond of Lord Alfred Douglas. I had always been.

CARSON: Did you adore him?

WILDE: No, I loved him.

CARSON: 'Your sonnet is quite lovely. It is a marvel that those red rose-leaf lips of yours should be made no less for music of song than for madness of kissing.'[143]

WILDE: Yes.

CARSON: Do you mean to tell me, sir, that that was a natural and proper way to address a young man?

WILDE: I am afraid you are criticising a poem on the ground—

CARSON: I want to see what you say.

WILDE: Yes, I think it was a beautiful letter. If you ask me whether it is proper, you might as well ask me whether *King Lear* is proper, or a sonnet of Shakespeare is proper. It was a beautiful letter. It was not concerned with – the letter was not written – with the object of writing propriety; it was written with the object of making a beautiful thing.

CARSON: But apart from art?

WILDE: Ah! I cannot do that.

CARSON: But apart from art?

WILDE: I cannot answer any question apart from art.

CARSON: Suppose a man, now, who was not an artist had written this letter to a handsome young man, as I believe Lord Alfred Douglas is?

WILDE: Yes.

CARSON: Some twenty years younger than himself – would you say that it was a proper and natural kind of letter to write to him?

WILDE: A man who was not an artist could never have written that letter. (*Laughter.*)

CARSON: Why?

WILDE: Because nobody but an artist could write it.

CARSON: Supposing a man had an unholy and immoral love towards a boy or a young fellow; I believe that has happened?

WILDE: Yes.

CARSON: And he addressed him in the language that would perhaps probably be used in a love letter – he might use that language?

WILDE: He certainly could not use such language as I used unless he was a man of letters and an artist. He could not do it.

CARSON: There is nothing very—

WILDE: I disagree with you, there is everything—

CARSON: I was just going to suggest there is nothing very wonderful in this: 'that those red, rose-leaf lips of yours should be made no less for music of song than for madness of kissing'.

WILDE: Literature depends upon how it is read, Mr Carson. It must be read in a different way.

CARSON: Is there anything wonderful in that?

WILDE: Yes, I think it is a beautiful phrase.

CARSON: A beautiful phrase?

WILDE: Yes, a beautiful phrase.

CARSON: 'Your slim quiet soul—'

WILDE: No, 'gilt'—

CARSON: 'Your slim gilt soul walks between passion and poetry.'

WILDE: Yes.

CARSON: That is a beautiful phrase too?

WILDE: Not when you read it, Mr Carson. When I wrote it, it was beautiful. You read it very badly.

CARSON: I don't profess to be an artist, Mr Wilde.

WILDE: Then, don't read it to me.

CARSON: And if you will allow me to say so, sometimes, when I hear you give evidence I am glad I am not. (*Laughter.*)

WILDE: Yes.

CLARKE: I do not think my friend is entitled to say that.

CARSON: When he assails me as to the way I have read the letter – I have read the letter in a perfectly proper way.

WILDE: Any letter may sound vulgar or ignoble—

CLARKE: Kindly do not find fault with my learned friend's reading again. It disturbs the proceedings.

CARSON: 'I know Hyacinthus, whom Apollo loved so madly, was you in Greek days. Why are you alone in town?' Is that a beautiful phrase?

WILDE: Well, that is the actuality of correspondence.

CARSON: 'And when do you go to Salisbury?'

WILDE: That is an enquiry – nothing particular about that.

CARSON: There is nothing?

WILDE: No. I would not claim much for that.

CARSON: That is not the beauty of the letter?

WILDE: No, I would not rank it with my best work.

CARSON: 'Do go there and cool your hands in the grey twilight of Gothic things, and come here whenever you like. It is a lovely place and only lacks you. But go to Salisbury first. Always with undying love.' So that is a beautiful phrase?

WILDE: Beautiful when it is meant really as it was meant then – beautiful.

CARSON: 'Always with undying love, yours Oscar'?

WILDE: Yes.

CARSON: Now, that was an exceptional letter?

WILDE: Unique, I should think. (*Laughter.*)

CARSON: Unique?

WILDE: Beautiful.

CARSON: Was that the ordinary way in which you carried on your correspondence with Lord Alfred Douglas?

WILDE: One could not write a letter like that every day. It would be like writing a poem every day. You cannot do it.

CARSON: You never wrote him any other letter of a similar description?

WILDE: Oh, I have written him most beautiful letters.

CARSON: Did you ever write any other letter expressing that he was your 'own boy' and your love for him in the same style or way?

WILDE: I have often written to Lord Alfred Douglas 'My own Boy'. He is much younger than myself. I write to him as 'My own Boy', and that I have expressed, and feel great and, I hope, undying love for him as I say I do. He is the greatest friend I have.

CARSON: Do you think that is a proper kind of letter to write?

WILDE: I think it is a beautiful letter.

CARSON: To a young person?

WILDE: I think it is a beautiful letter.

CARSON: Did you write to other persons in the same way?

WILDE: Oh, never.

CARSON: What?

WILDE: Never.

CARSON: To young boys?

WILDE: No.

CARSON: To any other young men?

WILDE: No.

CARSON: But you have written, as I take it, many of these letters to Lord Alfred Douglas?

WILDE: I don't know what you call 'these letters'?

CARSON: Of this particular class.

WILDE: There is no class in that letter. That is a beautiful letter. It is a poem and I have written other beautiful letters to Lord Alfred Douglas.

CARSON: Other beautiful letters? Have you written others in the same style?

WILDE: I don't repeat myself in style. (*Laughter.*)

CARSON: Now here is another letter which I believe you also wrote to Lord Alfred Douglas. Will you just take that in your hand?

WILDE: Yes.

CARSON: Is that a poem – is that your writing?

WILDE: Yes, that is a letter of mine.

CARSON: Now, as I read the last one so badly, will you kindly read that out?

WILDE: No, Mr Carson, it is for you.

CARSON: I must ask you to read it.

WILDE: I decline.

CLARKE: Let an officer of the Court read it.

CARSON: If he objects to read it—

WILDE: I don't object, but I don't see why I should be called upon to read it.

CARSON: 'Savoy Hotel, Victoria Embankment, London WC. Dearest of all Boys, Your letter was delightful.' Have you got that letter?

WILDE: No, I haven't looked at the date of that.

CARSON: This is a letter written by you when you were at the Savoy Hotel.

CLARKE: Read the letter through. Perhaps there is something to show.

CARSON: 'Dearest of all Boys, Your letter was delightful – red and yellow wine to me: but I am sad and out of sorts. Bosie, you must not make scenes with me: they kill me. They wreck

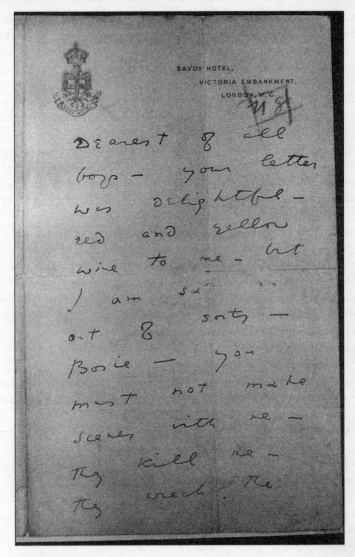

SAVOY HOTEL,
VICTORIA EMBANKMENT,
LONDON, W.C.

Dearest of all
boys — your letter
was delightful —
red and yellow
wine to me — but
I am sad
out of sorts —
Bosie — you
must not make
scenes with me —
they kill me —
they wreck the

8. Oscar Wilde's letter of early March 1893 which was stolen from
Lord Alfred Douglas and used by Edward Carson to support
Queensberry's plea of justification.

the loveliness of life. I cannot see you, so Greek and gracious, distorted by passion – I cannot listen to your curved lips saying hideous things to me. Don't do it. You break my heart. I had sooner—' then there is something I cannot read, but I will ask the witness[144] – 'all day than have you bitter, unjust, horrid. I must see you soon. You are the divine thing I want – the thing of grace and genius, but I don't know how to do it. Shall I go to Salisbury? There are many difficulties. My bill here is forty-nine pounds for a week. (*Laughter.*) I have also got a new sitting room over the Thames. But you – why are you not here, my dear, my wonderful boy? I fear I must leave. No money, no credit, and a heart of lead. Ever your own Oscar.' Is that an extraordinary letter?

WILDE: An extraordinary letter? I think everything I write extraordinary. I think that is an extraordinary letter. Yes, I don't pose as being ordinary – good heavens! – I don't pose as being ordinary. Ask me any questions you like about it.

CARSON: I am afraid I have a good deal to ask you. Isn't that a love letter?

WILDE: It is a letter expressive of love.

CARSON: Is it the kind of letter that one man writes towards another man?

WILDE: It is the kind of letter that I have written to Lord Alfred Douglas. What other men write to other men I know nothing about, nor do I care.

CARSON: Have you got the letter from Lord Alfred Douglas to which that was an answer?

WILDE: I don't think so. I don't know what letter it was at all.

CARSON: 'It was delightful red and yellow wine' to you. Do you recollect that letter?

WILDE: I don't recollect what letter it was at all.

CARSON: You don't recollect what letter it was?

WILDE: No, I don't.

CARSON: It was not a beautiful letter?

WILDE: A beautiful letter? Let me see – let me read the letter – let me see the letter.

CARSON: The letter that Lord Alfred Douglas wrote to you?

WILDE: It might have been. I don't understand what you mean. I don't remember the letter.

CARSON: You don't remember the letter, but you describe it as 'delightful red and yellow wine' to you?

WILDE: Oh, yes, a beautiful letter certainly.

CARSON: Have you got it?

WILDE: No, I don't think I have got it.

CARSON: What would you pay for that beautiful letter?

WILDE: For Lord Alfred's?

CARSON: Yes.

WILDE: I suppose, I couldn't get a copy—

CARSON: How much would you give now, if you could get a copy?

WILDE: I don't know. Why do you taunt me with such questions?

CARSON: You really don't know? Was this letter a beautiful letter, this one of yours?

WILDE: Yes. I think it contains reproaches. It isn't like the other – a prose poem. It is a letter expressive of my great devotion to Lord Alfred Douglas. I can say no more.

CARSON: Were you living at the Savoy then?

WILDE: Yes.

CARSON: For how long?

WILDE: I think I was there for about a month.

CARSON: Had you a house at Tite Street at the same time?

WILDE: Yes.

CARSON: Had you rooms in St James's Place at the same time?

WILDE: No – oh, no.

CARSON: Had Lord Alfred Douglas been staying with you at the Savoy immediately before that?

WILDE: Yes.

CARSON: Now, as to the letter which is described as the sonnet. You told my learned friend, I think, that a man named Wood first came to you about certain letters that he had got in Lord Alfred Douglas's coat.

WILDE: He didn't come to me at the Savoy; he told me.

JUDGE: He met him by appointment at the rooms of a man called Taylor.

CARSON (*to* JUDGE): Yes, he met by appointment. (*To* WILDE.) Who made the appointment?

WILDE: The appointment was made through Mr Alfred Taylor who knew Mr Wood.

CARSON: I may take it, then, that Alfred Taylor was a very intimate friend of yours?

WILDE: 'Intimate' is perhaps not the word. I have known Mr Alfred Taylor for three years. Previous to his seeing me, I hadn't been in town for a long time. I met him first in the month of October and I think I left town in the month of November.

CARSON: Was he an intimate friend?

WILDE: I would not call him an intimate friend. He was a friend of mine.

CARSON: It was he whom you employed to bring about this meeting between you and Alfred Wood?

WILDE: Yes, he called on me, told me he had heard this and I said I should like to see Alfred Wood.

CARSON: When did you last see Taylor?

WILDE: When did I last see Taylor?

CARSON: Yes.

WILDE: Yesterday.

CARSON: Last night?

WILDE: No, not last night – yesterday morning.

CARSON: Yesterday morning?

WILDE: Yes.

CARSON: Was he in Tite Street yesterday evening?

WILDE: No.

CARSON: Are you quite sure?

WILDE: Not to my knowledge. I myself dined out. I didn't go home till half past ten. There was no one there.

CARSON: You are still in communication with Taylor?

WILDE: Yes, I saw him yesterday morning.

CARSON: Before you brought about the appointment through

Taylor with Alfred Wood, had you been to Sir George Lewis?

WILDE: Yes.

CARSON: And had you got Sir George Lewis to write a letter to Wood?

WILDE: Yes.

CARSON: And Wood had refused to go near Sir George Lewis?

WILDE: That I don't know.

CARSON: But he didn't go?

WILDE: He did not go, no.

CARSON: And then you made the appointment through Taylor?

WILDE: Yes.

CARSON: And were you anxious about those letters?

WILDE: About my private correspondence, I should think so.

CARSON: Were you anxious about these letters—

WILDE: I should think so. What gentleman wants his private correspondence published. 'Anxious', yes – there might have been a thousand things—

CARSON: Had you known Wood previously?

WILDE: Yes.

CARSON: How long have you known Wood?

WILDE: I think I met him first at the end of January.

CARSON: That is January 1893?

WILDE: That would be January 1893 – yes, and this particular occurrence happened in March 1893.

CARSON: Where had you met Wood?

WILDE: At the Café Royal.

CARSON: With whom?

WILDE: With no one.

CARSON: With no one?

WILDE: There was no one else.

CARSON: Who introduced you to him?

WILDE: Lord Alfred Douglas had telegraphed to Wood who had written to him asking him to help him with some advance. He wanted to get a position as clerk. Lord Alfred Douglas had received this letter at Salisbury where I was staying with Lady Queensberry. He said to me, 'Will you see Alfred Wood and do what you can for him?' I said, 'Certainly.' He telegraphed then to Alfred Wood to say that I would be probably in the Café Royal that evening. Alfred Wood came in and knowing me by sight, as many people do, came over to my table and produced the telegram and said, 'You are Mr Oscar Wilde? I have received this telegram from Lord Alfred.'

CARSON: Where was he living at that time?

WILDE: That I don't know.

CARSON: Was he living with Taylor?

WILDE: I don't think so.

CARSON: Come, now.

WILDE: You asked me where he was living. I was under the impression that he was living, from what he told me, near Portland Street.

CARSON: Where was Taylor living at that time?

WILDE: I fancy in Chapel Street, Westminster.

CARSON: No, 13 Little College Street, I suggest.

WILDE: 13 Little College Street, yes; not Chapel Street.[145]

CARSON: Used you frequently to go to 13 Little College Street?

WILDE: I have been there on many occasions, yes.

CARSON: Was Wood living there at any time while you were there?

WILDE: No.

CARSON: What?

WILDE: No.

CARSON: Did you say that?

WILDE: Yes.

CARSON: Used you to go there to tea-parties?

WILDE: Yes, I have been there to tea-parties.

CARSON: I think they were all young men who were at the tea-parties?

WILDE: No, not all.

CARSON: They were all men?

WILDE: All, yes.

CARSON: All men?

WILDE: Yes, they were men.

CARSON: Did you dine at the Florence Restaurant in Rupert Street with Wood?[146]

WILDE: No, I never dined with him there. The first night that we met I asked him – it was about nine o'clock – whether he had had any dinner and whether he would take some supper and we went round to the Florence and I ordered some supper for him.

CARSON: What was Wood?

WILDE: Wood was a friend – a young man whom Lord Alfred Douglas had asked me—

CARSON: What was he – I mean his occupation?

WILDE: As far as I can make out he had none and was wanting an occupation. He had none and was looking after a situation.

CARSON: What occupation had he ever had – a clerkship?

WILDE: He told me he had a clerkship, yes.

CARSON: What was his age at that time?

WILDE: I should think about twenty-three or twenty-four – I don't know.

CARSON: Then, am I to understand that the very first day you met Wood you took him round to dinner at the Florence Restaurant in Rupert Street?

WILDE: Yes, I was asked to be kind to him.

CARSON: Was Taylor also present?

WILDE: No.

CARSON: Was anyone else?

WILDE: No.

CARSON: Did you on a subsequent occasion dine with him there?

WILDE: No.

CARSON: When Taylor was present?

WILDE: No.

CARSON: And another gentleman?

WILDE: No.

CARSON: Was that gentleman present on any occasion when you dined with him? (*Handing* WILDE *a paper.*)

WILDE: Not on any occasion.

CARSON: Did you know that gentleman?[147]

WILDE: Certainly.

CARSON: I suggest to you that it was Taylor who introduced you to Wood.

WILDE: It isn't the case.

CARSON: It is not the case?

WILDE: Wood was introduced to me through this telegram.

CARSON: Wood was not a man living in the society you do?

WILDE: No. Oh, no.

CARSON: What?

WILDE: Oh, no, certainly.

CARSON: Did you become intimate with Wood?

WILDE: Oh, no. I only saw him about four times – three times.

CARSON: Did you say that?

WILDE: Yes.

CARSON: Are you quite sure of that?

WILDE: Yes.

CARSON: Did you ask him to your house at Tite Street?

WILDE: Oh, never, not that I would not have, but I never did.

CARSON: Are you quite sure?

WILDE: Quite certain.

CARSON: Did you ever meet him at the corner of Tite Street?

WILDE: Never.

CARSON: What did you want to know Wood for at all?

WILDE: I didn't want to know him at all.

CARSON: Then, why did you ask him to come round, the very first evening you met him, to dine at the Florence in Rupert Street.

WILDE: I had been asked to be kind to him and help him. I don't know whether the telegram can be procured, but Lord Alfred Douglas sent a telegram from Salisbury. He told me he knew this young man. He showed me a letter.

CARSON: You tell us that?

WILDE: Yes. It wasn't my desire to know him. He was rather a nuisance.

CARSON: Did you ever ask him to go to Tite Street?

WILDE: Never.

CARSON: Was he ever there?

WILDE: Never.

CARSON: Do you swear that?[148]

WILDE: Yes.

CARSON: Was your wife away at that time at Torquay?

WILDE: My wife was – yes, my wife was away and my children were away and the governess, and there was nobody at all at Tite Street except the caretaker.

CARSON: Your wife was away?

WILDE: Yes.

CARSON: Had you an assistant there – a butler whom you called Ginger?

WILDE: No, I had no manservant at all at the time.

CARSON: Do you say that?

WILDE: Yes.

CARSON: Was there a boy there?

WILDE: No.

CARSON: What servant had you there?

WILDE: There was merely a caretaker, a female caretaker.

CARSON: Had you ever a servant called Ginger?

WILDE: No, never.

CARSON: Never called any boy that?

WILDE: No.

CARSON: Are you quite sure of that?

WILDE: Yes, quite sure.

CARSON: Had you any boy in your employment at all?

WILDE: Not at that time, no.

CARSON: At that time there was nobody in Tite Street but the caretaker?

WILDE: Nobody there but the caretaker.

CARSON: Now, I must ask you this: did you arrange several evenings to meet Wood at the corner of Tite Street when the house was empty in this way?

WILDE: No, certainly not.

CARSON: Did he go in with you to Tite Street?

WILDE: No.

CARSON: Did you ever have any immoral practices with Wood?

WILDE: Never in my life.

CARSON: Did you ever open his trousers?

WILDE: Oh, no!

CARSON: Put your hand upon his person?

WILDE: Never.

CARSON: Did you ever put your own person between his legs?

WILDE: Never.

CARSON: You say that?

WILDE: Yes.

CARSON: I say to you that several nights in Tite Street you did that.

WILDE: I say it is entirely – absolutely untrue.

CARSON: When you went to dine at the Florence, or to supper at the Florence, did you have a private room there?

WILDE: Yes.

CARSON: Did you have any impropriety between you upon that occasion?

WILDE: No, none whatever.

CARSON: Why did you go from the Café Royal round to the Florence in Rupert Street?

WILDE: Why did I go round there?

CARSON: Yes.

WILDE: I went round there because I have been for a long time in the habit of supping at the Café Florence – I considered it a pleasant place to sup at – and also that I had been in the habit of having cheques cashed by the proprietor of the Café Florence, which I had never done at the Café Royal, so that I went round and got a cheque cashed on that occasion, and gave Mr Wood some money on behalf of Lord Alfred Douglas.

CARSON: How much did you give him on that occasion?

WILDE: About two pounds.

CARSON: Why did you do it?

WILDE: Because I had been asked by Lord Alfred Douglas to be kind to the young man whom he knew. He was in want of a situation and he wanted helping. I gave it to him for that reason.

CARSON: I suggest that you first had immoral relations with him and then gave the money.

WILDE: It is perfectly untrue. In fact, the money that I gave him, I gave him in the Café Royal and I merely got a cheque cashed for my own convenience – the next day being Sunday.

CARSON: Does it occur to you as being a strange thing to take a man of his position and give him supper and then give him money?

CLARKE: He says he gave him the money first.

CARSON: You are quite wrong. It is the other way. He said he went round to the Café Florence to change the cheque.

CLARKE: As a matter of accuracy, I was correct. He gave him the money at the Café Royal and then went round to the Florence for his convenience and changed the cheque.

CARSON: Why didn't you give him money and say, 'You can go and have supper yourself'?

WILDE: Why should I? He said he had had no supper. Why shouldn't I be kind to him?

CARSON: Do you think he wanted your presence to be kind to him?

WILDE: I don't know. He had written to Lord Alfred Douglas saying he wanted money.

CARSON: A man in a different social position?

WILDE: I don't care about different social position.

CARSON: You don't care?

WILDE: Not about different social position. If anybody interests me or is in trouble and I have been asked to help him in any way, what is the use of putting on airs about one's own social position? It is childish.

CARSON: Was he an artist?

WILDE: No, certainly not.

CARSON: A literary man?

WILDE: No. Oh, no.

CARSON: Do you recollect Wood going to live at 36 Langham Street – I think that is near Portland Place somewhere?

WILDE: I remember that he changed the place where he was

living, because he wrote to me when I was in Paris to tell me
so.

CARSON: Where did he change from?

WILDE: From where he was living at his first place to some other
place.

CARSON: You don't know where it was from?

WILDE: I don't know. I couldn't say what was the first place where
he was living. I have never been to any place that he was living
at, but I remember getting a letter from him in Paris saying
that he had changed his address.

CARSON: Have you got that letter?

WILDE: I don't think I have got that letter, no. No, I have not
got that letter. Why should I keep it?

CARSON: You haven't got it?

WILDE: No.

CARSON: When he went to 36 Langham Street used you to go to
see him there?

WILDE: No.

CARSON: Are you quite sure of that?

WILDE: Quite certain.

CARSON: Were you ever in 36 Langham Street?

WILDE: Never in my life. I was in Paris and in Torquay.

CARSON: Do you remember his moving then to Russell Street?

WILDE: No, I have no recollection of any of his movements.

CARSON: When he came to you about these letters, did you consider that he was wanting to levy blackmail from you?

WILDE: I have been told that this was his intention.

CARSON: Did you? Answer my question.

WILDE: He disarmed me by handing me the letters.

CARSON: Did you consider—

WILDE: I considered there was something wrong about it.

CARSON: Did you consider that he was trying to levy blackmail
from you?

WILDE: Yes, and I was determined to face him on the subject.

CARSON: You thought he was going to levy blackmail and you
determined to face it?

WILDE: Yes.

CARSON: And the way you faced it was by giving him sixteen pounds to go to America?

WILDE: No, that is an inaccurate description of what occurred.

CARSON: You did.

WILDE: I saw the letters. I thought he was going to produce letters of mine to Lord Alfred Douglas which might contain private things and so on – he wished to extort money. Such a trade is common in London – rampant, I should think. When I wrote those letters they were of no importance – they were of no interest to me – I didn't want them. He then told me a long story of people who wanted to get these letters out of him. I did it foolishly, but out of pure pity and kindness.

CARSON: Just let me ask you a few questions which I think you can answer very shortly. You thought these letters of no importance?

WILDE: Yes.

CARSON: You were not afraid of anything that was contained in them?

WILDE: Oh! there were things in them – family matters – that I certainly would not have liked to have had published. No one likes their private correspondence to be published – allusions to other people – slighting allusions.

CARSON: And you thought it worthwhile to give him sixteen pounds?

WILDE: I did not give him sixteen pounds for that.

CARSON: I suggest to you that you gave him thirty pounds.

WILDE: No.

CARSON: What?

WILDE: No.

CARSON: Did you give him five pounds the very next day?

WILDE: Yes.

CARSON: In addition to the sixteen pounds?

WILDE: Yes.

CARSON: What did you give him that for?

WILDE: He wrote to me or asked me to see him before he went

to America. I said, 'I have no objection at all.' He told me that his passage out cost him more than he expected and I gave him five pounds additional. I did it out of kindness.

CARSON: Do you really suggest to the jury that you gave him this twenty-one pounds out of charity?

WILDE: It is not for me to make suggestions to the jury, Mr Carson.

CARSON: Is that what you say?

WILDE: What I say is that I undoubtedly felt that his having possession of these letters – the story he told me about their being robbed from him by Allen, and all that – I really, I may candidly confess, considered that he had been behaved to rather badly from the account he gave me.

CARSON: And in consequence you gave him another five pounds.

WILDE: Yes.

CARSON: Did you have a champagne lunch with him before he went off to America?

WILDE: No, I don't think there was any champagne. I don't drink in the middle of the day.

CARSON: Lunch at the Florence?

WILDE: Yes, at the Florence.

CARSON: A farewell lunch with a man who you thought wanted to blackmail you?

WILDE: Yes, he convinced me that he had never had any intention – the letters had been stolen from him by other people.

CARSON: When had you the farewell lunch?

WILDE: That was the next day.

CARSON: Who was there?

WILDE: No one was there.

CARSON: No one there but yourself?

WILDE: No.

CARSON: Did you take a private room?

WILDE: That I forget – I think, yes. I always have a private room at the Florence.

CARSON: Any familiarities on that day?

WILDE: Oh, no! None, none at all.

CARSON: Was it there and then, when you were at the champagne lunch, that you gave him five pounds?

WILDE: Yes.

CARSON: What did you give him that five pounds for?

WILDE: Because he told me that the fifteen pounds I had given him would land him almost penniless in New York, and asked me would I give him another five pounds, which I did. I gave it to him.

CARSON: Wood went away to America?

WILDE: I believe so, yes.

CARSON: You didn't throw any obstacle in the way of his going, I suppose?

WILDE: I told him I thought it would be extremely improbable – if he could not get work in London – that he would get it in New York.

CARSON: But you gave him the money to enable him to go?

WILDE: If he wished to go. I didn't care twopence whether he stayed in London or not.

CARSON: When he was in America did he write to you for money?

WILDE: No.

CARSON: Did Taylor tell you that he wrote to him to ask you for money?

WILDE: No.

CARSON: Are you quite sure of that?

WILDE: Yes, quite certain.

CARSON: Did you know that Taylor was in communication with him when he was in America?

WILDE: No.

CARSON: Just identify it. Will you tell me whether that is Wood's handwriting? (*Handing paper to* WILDE.)

WILDE: Yes, I should think so, but I have never seen any letter of his.

CARSON: Did Wood call Taylor 'Alfred'?

WILDE: Yes.

CARSON: He was on intimate terms with him apparently?

WILDE: Oh, yes, they were great friends.

CARSON: Did he call you 'Oscar'?

WILDE: Yes.

CARSON: And what did you call Wood?

WILDE: His name is Alfred.

CARSON: Didn't you call him Alf?

WILDE: No, I never use abbreviations – I don't think so.

CARSON: You called him Alfred, then?

WILDE: Yes, Alfred.

CARSON: What did you call Taylor?

WILDE: Mr Taylor's Christian name is Alfred also.

CARSON: Did you call him by his Christian name?

WILDE: Yes, always.

CARSON: Then, I may take it that you and Wood and Taylor each called the other by your Christian names?[149]

WILDE: Yes.

CARSON: You were pretty intimate, then?

WILDE: I am afraid everybody calls me, with a few exceptions, by my Christian name.

CARSON: And do you call everybody so?

WILDE: Anybody I like, yes.

CARSON: You like it?

WILDE: Yes, I like calling people by their Christian names – yes, I do.

CARSON: Was it not a curious thing that you should think a man, with whom you were on such intimate terms as to call him by his Christian name, should come and blackmail you?

WILDE: Oh, you see, you put it from your point of view – not from mine. I had been told he was going to extort money for the price of the letters and I candidly confess that I think any gentleman, rather than have his private letters hawked about – that any gentleman would buy. That was what I was told. Then when I met him and he handed me back the letters he said, no, he had never had any intention of the kind.

CARSON: What I want to ask you is this, and what I have asked you is: did you think it a curious thing that a man with whom you were on such intimate terms as to call him 'Alfred' should try to levy blackmail?

WILDE: I don't consider that he did so.

CARSON: You told me a moment ago.

WILDE: No, I don't really think so.

CARSON: Did you not tell me a moment ago, when you first made the appointment, you thought that he was going to levy blackmail?

WILDE: Quite so.

CARSON: When you went to Sir George Lewis?

WILDE: Yes.

CARSON: When you went to Sir George Lewis about the man that you called Alfred?

WILDE: Oh, yes, certainly.

CARSON: Didn't you think that was a curious thing from your friend?

WILDE: I thought it perfectly monstrous. I didn't know whether to believe it or not. In fact, I didn't believe it. The reason I made the appointment with him was I said I didn't believe he could do anything of the kind.

CARSON: You had given him money the first time you saw him.

WILDE: Yes, by desire of a friend of mine.

CARSON: You had taken him to supper?

WILDE: Yes.

CARSON: To a private room?

WILDE: Yes, I always had a private room at the Florence.

CARSON: This man you had been so kind to – didn't you think it was a very outrageous thing for that man to come to blackmail you?

WILDE: I thought it perfectly infamous.

CARSON: You thought it was perfectly infamous?

WILDE: Yes, certainly, when I was told it.

CARSON: It was perfectly infamous and you afterwards gave him twenty pounds?

WILDE: Twenty pounds.

CARSON: Gave a farewell supper or lunch to him the day before he went to America and off he went?

WILDE: Yes, because he had told me that he hadn't any intention of blackmailing me; the whole thing was done by other people. In fact Allen, he said, had got these letters and he had got them back.

CARSON: Was Wood over to see you at the Savoy?

WILDE: I don't think so – no.

CARSON: Shortly after Wood had come to you about the letters, Allen came.

WILDE: Where?

CARSON: Didn't Allen come to see you?

WILDE: Oh, yes, but quite long afterwards.

CARSON: Some time after?

WILDE: Certainly – six weeks – I suppose six weeks or two months – I really don't know.

CARSON: Six weeks or two months?

WILDE: Six weeks I should think.

CARSON: Had you known Allen before?

WILDE: Only by sight. I had known him by reputation.

CARSON: Was he a friend of Taylor's?

WILDE: Certainly not, as far as I knew – certainly not.

CARSON: Did he bring one of the letters?

WILDE: Yes – the letter that had been sent to Mr Tree.

CARSON: You knew he had stolen that letter?

WILDE: That who had stolen the letter?

CARSON: Allen. You knew he had stolen it from Wood. Wood had told you.

WILDE: No: Wood had told me that all the letters had been recovered – there were four letters. That is what Wood had told me – he assured me of it most positively.

CARSON: Didn't he tell you that the letters had been stolen from him?

WILDE: Yes.

CARSON: Though he thought he had recovered them all?

WILDE: No, he told me he had.

CARSON: Then, when Allen came you found he had not?

WILDE: Oh! immediately – not when he came, I mean first – a copy sent to Mr Beerbohm Tree. Then anonymous letters – people calling to see me et cetera.

CARSON: You knew that he had improperly come into possession of that letter?

WILDE: Oh, yes.

CARSON: When he came in what did you say to him?

WILDE: When he came to the hall of my house—

CARSON: What did you say to him, sir, when you saw him?

WILDE: I said, 'I suppose you have come on account of my beautiful letter to Lord Alfred Douglas?'

CARSON: What position in life was Allen?

WILDE: Allen? – a blackmailer.

CARSON: A blackmailer?

WILDE: A blackmailer.

CARSON: Was he a sodomite?

WILDE: I have not the smallest acquaintance with him beyond the time—

CARSON: By reputation?

WILDE: I never heard of him except as a blackmailer.

CARSON: You knew him by reputation before?

WILDE: Yes.

CARSON: But only as a blackmailer?

WILDE: Yes, as a blackmailer.

CARSON: Then you began to explain to the blackmailer what the loss of your beautiful manuscript was?

WILDE: No, that it was not a loss any more as he had sent a copy to Mr Beerbohm Tree.

CARSON: Did you describe it as a beautiful manuscript or a beautiful letter?

WILDE: A beautiful work of art, I said.

CARSON: Now, Mr Wilde, may I ask you this question. Did you give this man that you knew as a blackmailer – whose reputation you only knew as a blackmailer – did you give him ten shillings?

WILDE: Yes.

CARSON: What did he give you?

WILDE: Nothing; he gave me nothing personally – he sent it round.

CARSON: He gave you nothing?

WILDE: No.

CARSON: But at the time you gave him ten shillings what did he give you?

WILDE: Thanks.

CARSON: He had given you nothing?

WILDE: Nothing at all.

CARSON: Why did you give this notorious blackmailer ten shillings when he gave you nothing?

WILDE: I gave it to him out of contempt. (*Laughter.*)

CARSON: Out of what?

WILDE: Contempt.

CARSON: Is that the way you show contempt – by giving ten shillings?

WILDE: Very often it is one of the best ways to show one's contempt. (*Laughter.*) It was to show the man I didn't care twopence whether he had the letter or not. When he told me he was poor and said, 'Can't you pay my cab fare back?'

CARSON: Is that the only explanation you give to the jury as to the reason why you gave a notorious blackmailer ten shillings?

WILDE: Yes, to show my contempt for him. I didn't want the letter.

CARSON: I suppose he was pleased with your contempt?

WILDE: He was apparently pleased with my kindness because he sent back the letter.

CARSON: And did you accept his thanks to you for showing your contempt?

WILDE: I hardly understand what you mean.

CARSON: He thanked you for showing your contempt?

WILDE: What motives he thought I had in giving him ten shillings, I don't know. He thanked me for giving him ten shillings. I did it really to show I didn't care twopence.

CARSON: A few minutes after he went out, did Cliburn come in?

128

WILDE: Cliburn came to the door – the hall in fact – he did not come into the house.

CARSON: You have no doubt Allen told him the way you had shown your contempt – getting ten shillings?

WILDE: He mentioned, yes, that Allen said I had been kind to him.

CARSON: And then in comes Cliburn?

WILDE: Yes.

CARSON: Did you know him before?

WILDE: No – oh, I had seen him before.

CARSON: Where had you seen him?

WILDE: On the 21st of April at the stage door of the Haymarket Theatre while I was rehearsing – a dress rehearsal of my play.[150]

CARSON: What attracted your attention to him?

WILDE: The fact that he came up and spoke to me and said to me – I had gone out for a moment to write a letter; a lady had written down to ask for a box, would like to see the production of my play – I went down because the maid of this lady was waiting.

CARSON: Tell us about him.

WILDE: Suddenly, Cliburn whom I had never seen before came up to me and said, 'I want very much to speak to you with regard to a letter of yours that Mr Allen has,' and I said, 'I am in the middle of my dress rehearsal – I cannot be bothered – and I don't care twopence about it.'

CARSON: Did you think he was a blackmailer?

WILDE: Connected – yes.

CARSON: What?

WILDE: That he was undoubtedly—

CARSON: Didn't you think the whole of them were blackmailers?

WILDE: Which?

CARSON: That were coming in about the letters. Did it never occur to you that three men coming about the same letters—

WILDE: There were not three men – there were two men.

CARSON: There were three. Wasn't there Wood?

WILDE: I thought you meant with regard to this particular letter.

CARSON: Wood, Allen and Cliburn.

WILDE: But as regards this particular letter—

CARSON: Did you think Cliburn a blackmailer?

WILDE: He had never blackmailed me.

CARSON: Did you think he was a blackmailer?

WILDE: I thought he was connected with—

CARSON: Undoubtedly connected with blackmailing?

WILDE: He made no attempt to blackmail me. He said he wished to speak to me on the subject—

CARSON: And you immediately were kind to him – another blackmailer?

WILDE: Yes; he brought me back the letter. I gave him half a sovereign.

CARSON: And you began discussing that this was a beautiful manuscript – a work of art?

WILDE: I was annoyed at the soiled way in which it was returned – yes.

CARSON: Did you tell this blackmailer that this beautiful letter was about to be published as a sonnet?

WILDE: I told that to Allen.

CARSON: Didn't you tell it to Cliburn?

WILDE: No, I didn't mention that to Cliburn – no, it was to Allen.

CARSON: It was to Allen, the blackmailer?

WILDE: He was the blackmailer. He was the one who came.

CARSON: And did you tell the blackmailer that when it was published you would send him a copy?

WILDE: Yes.

CARSON: A copy published in *The Spirit Lamp*, an Oxford magazine?

WILDE: Yes, I said, 'You give me your address; I will send you a copy,' to show my indifference in the matter.

CARSON: To show your what?

WILDE: To show him how little I cared whether he had the letter or not.

CARSON: Was that the reason?

WILDE: Shortly after I saw it—

CARSON: Hadn't you got back the letter at the time you told him?

WILDE: Most certainly not.

CARSON: No?

WILDE: Most certainly not.

CARSON: But you promised him a copy when it was published?

WILDE: I told him I didn't care about having the original – that as he had sent a copy to Mr Beerbohm Tree, I had a copy of it – the thing was going to be, or had been – indeed, at that time it had been translated already: it had been translated into French and was about to appear in a magazine published at Oxford – I mean the thing had been translated three weeks before.

CARSON: Then when Cliburn had given you the letter, you had given him half a sovereign?

WILDE: Yes.

CARSON: You began telling him about the wicked life he was leading?

WILDE: I made that perhaps unnecessary observation.

CARSON: But you did make the observation?

WILDE: Yes.

CARSON: 'I am afraid you are leading a wonderfully wicked life'?

WILDE: Yes.

CARSON: What made you think that?

WILDE: Because he had come round to the Haymarket Theatre, evidently in league with this man, though he had not in any way offended me.

CARSON: But you referred to the blackmailing, didn't you, as 'a wonderfully wicked life'?

WILDE: I didn't use the word – no.

CARSON: What?

WILDE: I did not use the word.

CARSON: Wasn't that what you meant?

WILDE: I meant generally that I thought he was being mixed up with this undoubted blackmailing. I said to him, 'What a wonderfully wicked life' – or something of that sort – 'you seem to be leading.'

CARSON: You referred to the blackmailing, that is all I wanted to know. He said, 'There is good and bad in every one of us'?

WILDE: Yes.

CARSON: And you said he was a born philosopher?

WILDE: Yes, I said that.

CARSON: And that was the termination of your conversation with the wicked blackmailer?

WILDE: He did not try to blackmail; remember that was all. He was a man who came to give me back a letter. He handed it back to me. The other man was a different affair – a perfectly different affair. But this man came to give me back this thing. I thought it very kind of him to do so – very kind.

CARSON: You have told me that you wrote a great many beautiful letters; did you ever have any one of them, excepting the one that happened to be found out, turned into a sonnet?

WILDE: I would require to read a great deal of modern poetry before I could answer that. (*Laughter.*)

CARSON: Did you ever have any letter, except the one that was found out, turned into a sonnet?

WILDE: I don't know what you mean by 'the one that was found out'.

CARSON: The one, sir, for which you gave the money you have just been telling us of.

WILDE: I gave no money for that letter.

CARSON: What?

WILDE: I gave no money for that letter.

CARSON: In reference to which you gave the money?

WILDE: I did not give money in reference to it.

CARSON: The one which you got back?

WILDE: The one which was handed back to me.

CARSON: I ask you, sir, excepting that, have you ever had a letter turned into a sonnet?

WILDE: I say I should have to look through the whole of modern poetry to answer that question.

CARSON: Can you tell me any one?

WILDE: At the present moment I cannot; I should have to go through the whole of modern poetry: I could not.

CARSON: Can you tell me any one of your letters, except this discovered letter, which was ever turned into a sonnet?

WILDE: At the present moment, no – I cannot recollect any.

CARSON: Had you ever written to Lord Alfred Douglas to preserve that letter?

WILDE: No, never.

CARSON: Therefore, sir, until it was discovered, you never thought of turning it into a sonnet?

WILDE: I never turned it into a sonnet at all.

CARSON: I did not say you did.

WILDE: When the copy was sent to Beerbohm Tree, and I saw what the letter was, then I felt at once it should be translated into a poetic form.

CARSON: You thought at once it should be translated and turned into a sonnet?

WILDE: Yes.

CARSON: Were you staying at the Albemarle Hotel in 1892 about the 25th of February?[151]

WILDE: Yes.

CARSON: At that time, am I right in saying that Messrs Elkin Mathews and Co. were your publishers?[152]

WILDE: Yes, Messrs Elkin Mathews and John Lane were my publishers.

CARSON: They carried on their business at Vigo Street?

WILDE: Yes.

CARSON: Did you in February 1892 become fond of their office boy?

WILDE: I really don't think that that is the proper form in which a question should be addressed to me, it is a begging question entirely.

CARSON: I am only asking you the question.

JUDGE: I did not catch the question.

CARSON: It was whether he became fond of the office boy, my lord.

WILDE: I say I object to your description of Mr Edward Shelley.[153]

CARSON: Then, you can say 'no'.

WILDE: Very well, then – no – no, certainly not.

CARSON: Did you become intimate with their office boy?

WILDE: I deny that that was the position held by Mr Edward Shelley to whom you refer. He was not an office boy. That is the point I object to.

CARSON: You knew to whom I was referring?

WILDE: Yes.

CARSON: What age was Shelley?

WILDE: I should think about twenty.

CARSON: I suggest to you he was eighteen.

WILDE: It is quite possible.

CARSON: A good-looking boy?

WILDE: No, I wouldn't call him so – an intellectual face – but I wouldn't call him good-looking – an intellectual face.

CARSON: Did you meet him by simply going in and out of Messrs Mathews and Lane's?

WILDE: Do you mean when I first met him?

CARSON: Yes.

WILDE: I first met him in the month of October and I was arranging for the publication of my poems with Messrs Mathews and Lane.[154] I was introduced by Mr John Lane to Mr Edward Shelley, who was then an assistant, and I consider an assistant in a bookshop occupies the position of a gentleman.

CARSON: He was selling books in a shop?

WILDE: As Mr Quaritch sells books in his shop. He ranks as a gentleman.[155]

CLARKE: Was that in 1891?

WILDE: 1892, that was – September.

CARSON: You compare Shelley with Mr Quaritch?

WILDE: When you suggest that to sell books is a sort of ignominious position, I think of a man in Mr Quaritch's position—

CARSON: You know he had from fifteen to twenty shillings a week?

WILDE: I don't know what his wages were at all. I regarded him as a gentleman. I had always seen him treated as a gentleman.

CARSON: Did you ask this lad to dine with you at the Albemarle Hotel when you were staying there?

WILDE: Oh, yes, he often dined with me.

CARSON: Wait a moment; was that for the purpose of having an intellectual treat?

WILDE: Well, for him, yes. (*Laughter.*)

CARSON: You brought him there to give him an intellectual treat?

WILDE: He had expressed a great admiration of my work. I had seen him constantly. He had written me many letters about my work. I thought it would be an act of kindness. He had gone the first night to my play. I should think as a matter of conversation between us the intellectual pleasure would be more on his side than it would be on mine.

CARSON: This boy selling the books came for intellectual pleasures?

WILDE: This young man who was connected with the publishing often dined with me there and at my own house and with my wife and elsewhere. You put the questions in the wrong way.

CARSON: Did you dine with this boy in a public room there?

WILDE: Oh, no, in my own sitting room.

CARSON: Just try and recollect. Am I right in saying you dined downstairs the first time you dined there?

WILDE: I don't think I ever dined downstairs at the Albemarle – that is my recollection – but I had a private sitting room. I don't think I ever did in my life.

CARSON: I suggest February 1892. Did you dine downstairs with Shelley?

WILDE: I hardly fancy in February. I should think it would be more probably the beginning of March.

CARSON: But at all events you were in a private sitting room afterwards with him?

WILDE: Oh, yes, he was in my private sitting room – yes. We dined there or supped there or something, I don't know.

CARSON: Alone?

WILDE: No, there was a gentleman present.

CARSON: Who were they?

WILDE: A gentleman.

CARSON: Who was he? If you do not wish to mention his name I will be satisfied if you give it to me on a piece of paper.

WILDE: His name is mentioned in one of Mr Edward Shelley's letters that will be handed to you. His name is mentioned, but I would be extremely sorry, of course, that any name should be unnecessarily mentioned.

CARSON: If you will write the name on paper and put it before me I will be quite satisfied.

WILDE: I will write it down. (*He does so.*) He is mentioned by Edward Shelley in a letter dated the 23rd of February.[156]

CARSON: Is he mentioned with reference to this dinner?

WILDE: No.

CARSON: This is the first time Shelley dined with you that I am talking of – the very first dinner?

WILDE: I don't think he ever dined with me at all. I think he supped with me. I don't think he dined with me.

CARSON: I suggest to you that he dined with you in a public room. Now, I want you to be very careful.

WILDE: I haven't the smallest recollection of that occurring.

CARSON: If he says it was so, will you be prepared to contradict it – that he dined in a public room where everybody else was dining?[157]

WILDE: I should think I am not in the habit of dining in a public room. I have all my meals in my own room. I cannot remember a single case of my ever dining in the public room.

CARSON: It would probably be much more likely to make an impression on a youth of this class to dine with a distinguished gentleman like yourself than upon you: and if he says that he dined in a public room with you, would you be prepared to contradict it – with you and he alone at one table – of course, other people there?

WILDE: I say I have no recollection of that occurring, but I should consider it extremely improbable. I cannot be asked to recollect a thing of no importance.

CARSON: Do you suggest that this gentleman, whose name you have given me, dined in company with you and Shelley on the first occasion that Shelley dined? Will you pledge yourself to that?

WILDE: My own impression was it was a supper party.

CARSON: I am not talking of a supper party.

WILDE: Yes, I have no recollection.

CARSON: It was a supper party that this gentleman was at?

WILDE: He certainly supped one night.

CARSON: I suggest to you that the supper was the next night and we are some way off that yet. Now, after dinner – whether you dined there or not – were you and Shelley alone upon this first occasion in your sitting room?

WILDE: I have no recollection of this dinner at all.

CARSON: Were you alone with Shelley the first time he came there in the sitting room?

WILDE: Oh, when he came to see me, yes, he came to see me – whether he dined with me in the public room or not, I don't know; but he took a meal, certainly, with me in my own private room.

CARSON: Now, upon that occasion had you a bedroom opening off the sitting room?

WILDE: Yes.

CARSON: Did you give him whiskies and sodas in the sitting room?

WILDE: I suppose he had what he wanted – I suppose he had whatever he wanted – I don't remember.

CARSON: Do you mean to say now, you cannot tell us about this first dining with this office boy?

CLARKE: No, I beg your pardon.

WILDE: Really, I object strongly.

CARSON: This gentleman who assisted.

CLARKE: He was an assistant of the publisher.

WILDE: Yes, and I consider to be connected in any capacity with a bookseller's shop is a high privilege.

CARSON: Can you call to mind now, this dinner that you gave?

WILDE: I cannot call to mind because I do not recollect Edward

Shelley really doing anything but sup accompanied by another gentleman, though he may have come in, he may have come in.

CARSON: Did he smoke cigarettes with you?

WILDE: Oh, I should think so, certainly, if he was in my room – I always smoke them, all day long.

CARSON: Now, I ask you, on that occasion did you keep him to sleep with you that night?

WILDE: Certainly not.

CARSON: Did he stay all night and leave the next morning at eight o'clock?

WILDE: No.

CARSON: What?

WILDE: Certainly not with me; I say no.

CARSON: Did you commence, when he was in the sitting room, embracing him?

WILDE: Certainly not.

CARSON: Did you ever embrace him?

WILDE: Never.

CARSON: Did you kiss him?

WILDE: Never.

CARSON: Did you put your hand on his person?

WILDE: Never.

CARSON: And then bring him into your bedroom?

WILDE: Never.

CARSON: Sleep in the same bed with him all night?

WILDE: Never.

CARSON: Each of you having taken off all your clothes, did you take his person in your hand in bed?

WILDE: My lord, is it not sufficient for me to give an entire denial without being exposed to the ignominy of detail after detail of an imaginary thing going on? Let it be sufficient for me to give my entire denial to that having occurred. It never did occur. Why should I be exposed before the whole court by entering into this kind of thing which cannot possibly be borne.

CARSON: Unfortunately we have—

WILDE: I appeal to his lordship.

JUDGE: Do you require further details on this point?

CARSON: No, my lord.

CLARKE: When the denial is once made—

CARSON: Did he stay there till eight o'clock in the morning?

WILDE: No.

CARSON: Did you take him the next night to the Independent Theatre at Dean Street?

WILDE: He came with me, yes, to a box occupied by myself and some other friend to the Independent Theatre. Whether it was the next night, I forget.

CARSON: Did you ask him to Tite Street?

WILDE: Yes.

CARSON: Did you take him to Earl's Court?

WILDE: I hardly know what you mean.

CARSON: To the exhibition at Earl's Court?

WILDE: I rather fancy, yes, in the month of May, I think so – yes, I think in the month of May – at least we met there.

CARSON: Did you bring him to the Prince of Wales Club?

WILDE: You mean the Lyric Club?[158]

CARSON: Yes, as it was then called.

WILDE: Yes.

CARSON: Did you take him to the Café Royal?

WILDE: Yes, dined with him, oh, yes.

CARSON: Of course, you paid for him on each occasion?

WILDE: Oh, yes.

CARSON: Did you take him to Kettner's Restaurant?[159]

WILDE: Yes.

CARSON: Had you a private room?

WILDE: On one occasion, yes, by his desire.

CARSON: What?

WILDE: On one occasion to supper by Edward Shelley's desire. He was in great trouble.

CARSON: You had a private room.

WILDE: Yes, at his wish. Yes.

CARSON: Did you take him to the Hogarth Club?[160]

WILDE: No, I am not a member.

CARSON: I do not suggest you are a member. Were you there with him? Did you bring him there and get introduced?

WILDE: I hardly understand your questions. I am not a member of the club.

CARSON: Did you take Edward Shelley with you to the club to lunch with another gentleman?

WILDE: Oh, no, I could not have done that – certainly. How could I bring a person to another man's club? I could not do it.

CARSON: I am only asking you.

WILDE: Certainly not.

CARSON: Do you undertake to say he was never with you at the Hogarth Club?

WILDE: No. He knew members of the Hogarth Club.

CARSON: Was he ever there with you at the Hogarth Club? I am not going to quarrel over who introduced him.

WILDE: Whether he ever lunched in my company at the Hogarth Club, I really cannot remember, but he might have done so because he had friends there.

CARSON: Did you ever give him money?

WILDE: Yes, on two occasions.

CARSON: What?

WILDE: On two occasions – on three occasions.

CARSON: What did you give him – how much?

WILDE: The first time – am I to state—?

CARSON: I want the amounts.

WILDE: The first time it was I think four pounds. The second time it was his railway fare to Cromer where my wife and I had asked him to stay with us. I sent his railway fare knowing he was a young man with no money. The third time I gave him five pounds. That was last year – I think last year.

CARSON: You sent him three pounds to go to Cromer but he didn't go?

WILDE: No – two pounds – I forget. Whatever the railway fare is.[161]

CARSON: He kept the two pounds?

WILDE: Yes. I wrote to him when he said he couldn't come. I wrote to him knowing how poor he was – his continual references to the struggle to support his mother or something of that kind – other claims on him that were heavy on so young a man – I said, 'Don't mind a bit to send me back this money. I am sure you will want it.'

CARSON: Now, I must ask you, did you think this young man eighteen years of age was a proper or natural companion for you to have at all these places?

WILDE: Certainly – I asked him down to my wife's house – certainly.

CARSON: Did you give him a present of your various works?

WILDE: Yes, I think I gave him four or five of them.

CARSON: You gave him one of the first copies of *Dorian Gray*?

WILDE: Yes.

CARSON: A signed copy?

WILDE: Yes.

CARSON: Signed by you?

WILDE: Yes.

CARSON: Did you put inscriptions in any of them?

WILDE: I should think in all of them.

CARSON: What did you put?

WILDE: Oh, that I don't know. I could not remember at the present moment what I wrote in the book.

CARSON: 'To dear Edward Shelley'?

WILDE: Yes, I should think so.

CARSON: What?

WILDE: I don't know; are you reading it?

CARSON: I want to know did you put that?

WILDE: I should fancy – it seems to me not in the slightest degree improbable, but I ask you to let me see the book.

CARSON: Was he 'Dear Edward Shelley'?

WILDE: Yes, certainly, because if I wrote a letter to him I called him 'Dear Edward'.

CARSON: This employee was 'Dear Edward Shelley'?

WILDE: You may take a view about him that I do not.

CARSON: Is that your handwriting?

WILDE: Yes, let me look at the book. (*A copy of the book*, The Sinner's Comedy, *is handed to him.*)[162]

CARSON: Yes, certainly.

JUDGE: Yes, he says it is his handwriting.

WILDE: I have not the smallest recollection of ever giving this book. It is not a book of mine.

CARSON: You have no doubt that it is your handwriting?

WILDE: It certainly seems to be my handwriting. I have no recollection of giving any book except my own.

CARSON: I see it states: 'From the author, August 1892, to dear Edward Shelley'.

WILDE: Yes, I remember now.

CARSON: It is not one of your books at all?

WILDE: No, not at all. That is what made me hesitate.

CARSON: I suppose it was a similar inscription to that which you had put in these other books?

WILDE: That was a joke.

CARSON: What was?

WILDE: My writing.

CARSON: What part of it was a joke?

WILDE: I will explain to you. Now I understand. I only remembered at first having given Edward Shelley my own works, as I never wrote this book at all. It was a book that belonged to me and for fun I wrote in 'From the author, August 1892, to dear Edward Shelley'. That was, such as it was, a bit of nonsense. I was not the author of the book – nothing to do with it. That is why I could not understand my having given it at first.

CARSON: Was the 'Dear Edward Shelley' nonsense?

WILDE: I don't know what you mean by 'nonsense'.

CARSON: It was your own word not mine.

WILDE: Yes. 'From the author to dear Edward Shelley'.

CARSON: I suggest, Mr Wilde, that 'Dear Edward Shelley' as a reference to a boy of that class was very familiar.

WILDE: I think that any reference to a young man passionately devoted to literature as he then was – it was a very charming thing of me to have said in that case – where I did not write the book – I mean to say it was obviously a joke. How else am I to write to people?

CARSON: Now, may I ask you why it was that you were on such intimate terms with this young Shelley?

WILDE: Because when I met him he seemed most interested in literature of my kind; because he had at that time, at any rate, high literary ambition. He desired to be a writer and also, I may say candidly, because he admired my works immensely.

CARSON: That was in consequence of his literary tastes?

WILDE: Yes.

CARSON: Did you become intimate with a young lad named Conway?[163]

WILDE: I beg your pardon.

CARSON: Did you become intimate with a young man named Conway?

WILDE: Oh, yes, at Worthing.

CARSON: What was his Christian name?

WILDE: Alfonso.

CARSON: He sold newspapers on the pier at Worthing?

WILDE: No, never to my knowledge.[164]

CARSON: What?

WILDE: Never.

CARSON: Or at the kiosk?

WILDE: No, never.

CARSON: What was he doing?

WILDE: Oh, enjoying himself in being idle.

CARSON: He was a loafer at Worthing?

WILDE: I call him a very happy, idle nature. You can call him what you like.

CARSON: He had no money?

WILDE: Oh, none. When I say none, his mother had a house at Worthing.

CARSON: No occupation?

WILDE: No, he had no occupation.

CARSON: Did you know or have you ever heard that his previous occupation had been selling newspapers?

WILDE: Never in my life.

CARSON: Would it astonish you to hear that he had so much industry?

WILDE: I think it would.

CARSON: Was he a literary character?

WILDE: Oh, not at all. (*Laughter.*)

CARSON: Was he an artist?

WILDE: No.

CARSON: What age was he?

WILDE: I suppose about eighteen – about eighteen, I should think.

CARSON: About the same age as Shelley?

WILDE: Yes, if Edward Shelley was that age. I don't know Edward Shelley's age.

CARSON: How did you come to know him?

WILDE: To know Alfonso Conway? When I was at Worthing last August, Lord Alfred Douglas and I were in the habit of going out in a sailing boat and one afternoon while this boat, which was high-beached, was being dragged down by the boatmen, Conway, and a younger boy who was in flannels, were helping to draw down the boat. I said to Lord Alfred Douglas when we reached the sea, 'Shall we bring them out for a sail?' or, 'Shall we ask them whether they would like a sail?' and he said, 'Yes.'

CARSON: Then, he was assisting you in putting out the boat?

WILDE: No, I wasn't taking that trouble. He and the boy – younger who was in flannels – amused themselves by helping the two boatmen to drag down our boat which was high-beached. I amused myself with contemplation and as they had been taking the trouble to do this and so on, I said to Lord Alfred Douglas, 'Shall we ask them whether they would like to have a sail?' and they seemed very delighted and they came out for a sail. They came out every day.

CARSON: They came out every day?

WILDE: Yes, every day.

CARSON: Did you become intimate with Alfonso?

WILDE: Oh, yes. We were great friends.

CARSON: Great friends?

WILDE: Great friends.

CARSON: Did you ask this boy that you met upon the beach to lunch with you?

WILDE: To lunch with me?

CARSON: Yes.

WILDE: He has dined with me.

CARSON: Where?

WILDE: At my house in Worthing.

CARSON: At The Haven?

WILDE: At The Haven.

CARSON: Did he also have a meal with you at an hotel there?

WILDE: Oh, yes – I remember – yes, the second day.

CARSON: At the Marine Hotel?

WILDE: Yes, he lunched with me and Lord Alfred and the other friend.

CARSON: Was his conversation literary?

WILDE: No, it was, on the contrary, quite simple and easy to be understood. (*Laughter.*)

CARSON: He was an uneducated lad, wasn't he?

WILDE: Oh, he was a pleasant, nice creature. He was not cultivated. (*Laughter.*) Don't sneer at that. He was a pleasant, nice creature. His ambition was to be a sailor.

CARSON: What was his class in life?

WILDE: If you ask me what his class in life was, his father had been an electrical engineer who had died young. His mother had very little money and kept a lodging house – at any rate she had one lodger. That he himself was the only child, that he had been sent to school where naturally he had not learned much. His desire was to go to sea as an apprentice in a merchant ship. One thing he cared about was the sea. His mother was to a certain extent reluctant for him to leave her. That was the story he told me.

CARSON: And you conceived a great fondness for Alfonso?

WILDE: A most pleasant creature.

CARSON: Now, did you ask him to meet you by appointment on the parade in the evening at about nine o'clock?

WILDE: On the parade? I didn't know there was such a place at Worthing.

CARSON: Isn't The Haven near the end of the parade?

WILDE: I have never – I don't think I have ever seen Alfonso with the exception of twice when I gave him tickets for the theatre – no, I have never seen him in the evening.

CARSON: Did you take him one evening after nine o'clock to walk towards Lancing?

WILDE: No.

CARSON: Are you quite sure of that?

WILDE: Yes, quite certain. Yes.

CARSON: Is Lancing near there?

WILDE: It is about two miles off.

CARSON: Is it a lonely road?

WILDE: I have never been there in the daytime. It is a road by the sea.

CARSON: Did you kiss him on the road?

WILDE: Certainly not.

CARSON: Did you put your hands inside his trousers?

WILDE: No, certainly not.

CARSON: And had you any familiarities with him of any kind?

WILDE: None of any kind.

CARSON: Did you give him anything?

WILDE: Oh, yes.

CARSON: Money?

WILDE: I don't think I ever gave Alfonso any money – no, I don't think so.

CARSON: No money?

WILDE: No money.

CARSON: Did you give him sums from time to time amounting to fifteen pounds?

WILDE: Good heavens! No, certainly not.

CARSON: Why should that be astonishing?

WILDE: Because it didn't happen.

CARSON: He was a poor boy?

WILDE: I don't know about that. I say his mother had a house of her own.

CARSON: Did you know his mother?

WILDE: No, I did not.

CARSON: Did you ever go into his house?

WILDE: Never.

CARSON: Did you give him a cigarette case?

WILDE: I think I might have – yes, that I might have done. I forgot about that. I remember certain things I gave him.

CARSON: What did you call him?

WILDE: Alfonso.

CARSON: Did he call you Oscar?

WILDE: No.

CARSON: Are you quite sure of that?

WILDE: Yes.

CARSON: This is the cigarette case you gave him?

WILDE: I dare say, yes.

CARSON: Did you put this inscription in it 'Alfonso from his friend Oscar Wilde'?

WILDE: Whether I wrote it or he, I don't know until I see it.

CARSON: Will you look at it?

WILDE: It is more than probable I wrote it. Yes, that is my writing.

CARSON: You gave him your photograph?

WILDE: Yes.

CARSON: Just take that please and tell me if that is your writing?

WILDE: It is sure to be on my photograph; yes, that is my writing, certainly.

CARSON: 'Oscar Wilde to Alfonso'?

WILDE: Yes.

CARSON: And you gave him a book?

WILDE: Yes.

CARSON: *The Wreck of the Grosvenor.* 'Alfonso Conway from his friend Oscar Wilde. Worthing, September 21st 1894'.[165]

WILDE: Yes.

CARSON: You gave him that?

WILDE: I gave him – well, I don't know.

CARSON: You were fond of this boy?

WILDE: I liked him. He had been my companion for six weeks.

CARSON: He had been your companion for six weeks?

WILDE: A month, I suppose.

CARSON: Would you be surprised to hear that the only occupation that he ever had was this selling of newspapers?

WILDE: I never thought Alfonso had any past. I don't know why I should be asked if I would be surprised – yes, I would be rather – from what he said to me, that would surprise me – he told me that he had no profession of any kind. Certainly that would surprise me.

CARSON: Did you give him a walking stick?

WILDE: Yes, I gave him a walking stick.

CARSON: For a newspaper boy. Just look at that! He was a newspaper boy out of employment.[166]

CLARKE: I beg your pardon.

WILDE: It is like the way you talked of Edward Shelley.

CARSON: You bought that for Conway?

WILDE: Yes.

CARSON: What did that cost?

WILDE: Five or six shillings.

CARSON: This is silver.

WILDE: Ten shillings or something.

CARSON: Fifteen shillings?

WILDE: It is not beautiful.

CARSON: It was a handsome stick for a boy of that class.

WILDE: I don't think it a beautiful stick myself. I don't think it a beautiful stick, but the choice was his. (*Laughter.*)

CARSON: It is not real art, I suppose?

WILDE: I don't think so.

CARSON: Did you bring this boy away with you to Brighton?

WILDE: Yes.

CARSON: How was he dressed?

WILDE: A suit of clothes I had given him – a suit of blue serge clothes that I had given him.

CARSON: That you had given him?

WILDE: Yes.

CARSON: What kind of a hat had he?

WILDE: That I forget; I fancy, a straw hat.

CARSON: A straw hat with a red and blue ribbon?

WILDE: Yes, with a red and blue ribbon.

CARSON: Did you select the red and blue ribbon?

WILDE: No, that belongs to the Corps – it was an unfortunate selection of his own – I mean, because I believe the colour pleased him.[167] (*Laughter.*)

CARSON: You paid for the hat?

WILDE: Yes, I did, certainly. I gave him a suit of clothes, straw hat, flannels, a book to read – I gave him a lot of things.

CARSON: You dressed him up to bring him to Brighton?

WILDE: Not to bring him to Brighton.

CARSON: You dressed him up for Worthing?

WILDE: Yes, oh, certainly. Yes, for a regatta to which he was very anxious to go.

CARSON: In order that he might look more like an equal?

WILDE: Oh, no, he never would have looked that. (*Laughter.*) No, in order that he shouldn't be ashamed, as he told me he was, of his shabby and ordinary clothes – because he desired to have flannels and blue serge and a straw hat.

CARSON: He was ashamed of his shabby clothes?

WILDE: Yes, he was, in a certain degree.

CARSON: Did he look better when he was dressed up?

WILDE: Yes, he looked much nicer, much nicer.

CARSON: You took him to Brighton?

WILDE: Yes.

CARSON: Did you take a bedroom for him?

WILDE: We stayed at the hotel.

CARSON: Did you take a bedroom for him?

WILDE: Yes.

CARSON: He had no money?

WILDE: Yes, of course. I took him as a trip to Brighton.

CARSON: Was the bedroom communicating with your own?

WILDE: That I forget; it might have been so.

CARSON: Green baize folding doors?

WILDE: Green baize folding doors?

CARSON: On the first floor?

WILDE: It was on the first floor, yes – it was on the first floor – sitting room and two bedrooms, yes.

CARSON: The Albion?

WILDE: At the Albion Hotel.[168]

CARSON: Did he come into your bed that night?

WILDE: No.

CARSON: Are you certain of that?

WILDE: Quite certain of that.

CARSON: What did you take him to Brighton for?

WILDE: I took him to Brighton because I had promised that before I left Worthing I would take him some trip, to any place where he wished to go, because he had been a very pleasant, happy, good-humoured companion to myself and my children. He wished to be at Portsmouth, because he wanted to be a sailor. I, having been abroad – to France – I came back then to Worthing. I said I couldn't take him to Portsmouth – it was too far for me to go – I was just finishing a play.[169] I said I couldn't afford the time. He then asked me whether I would take him to Brighton, as he wished to go to a theatre and that he would regard it as a trip. I expressed my surprise, he living so close to Brighton, that he should consider it as a trip. It was his own choice. If I had had time I should have brought him to Portsmouth.

CARSON: Did you go to the theatre?

WILDE: I didn't, no – I sent him.

CARSON: Did you take him to dine there at a restaurant?

WILDE: Yes.

CARSON: How was it that he was such a pleasant companion for you?

WILDE: Because he was a pleasant, bright, simple, nice nature. That is what I call him.

CARSON: A nice personality?

WILDE: I would not say for him personality, no.

CARSON: When did he go back to Worthing?

WILDE: We went back the next day.

CARSON: Did you go back with him?

WILDE: Yes.

CARSON: Did you ever take another boy to the Albion?

WILDE: I have stayed at the Albion. I don't know what you mean. Just kindly tell me exactly what you mean. I have stayed with my friends at the Albion often.

CARSON: I am not talking of friends. Did you on any other occasion bring a youth about the same age – eighteen or twenty – to the Albion?

WILDE: Lord Alfred Douglas – I stayed with him at the Albion.

CARSON: Not Lord Alfred Douglas.

WILDE: No.

CARSON: Are you sure?

WILDE: Quite sure, yes.

CARSON: No one else?

WILDE: No one else.

At 4.45 p.m. the court is adjourned until 10.30 a.m. the following day.

SECOND DAY MORNING

CARSON: You told me yesterday, I think, that you were intimate with Taylor?

WILDE: Yes.

CARSON: And you have continued intimate with him down to the present time?

WILDE: Yes.

CARSON: It was he who arranged the meeting between you and Wood with reference to the letters?

WILDE: Yes.

CARSON: At his own house?

WILDE: Yes.

CARSON: At 13 Little College Street?

WILDE: Yes.

CARSON: How long had you known Taylor then?

WILDE: Since the early part of October of the previous year.

CARSON: Used he to come to your house?

WILDE: Yes. Oh, yes, he has been there.

CARSON: And to your chambers?

WILDE: Yes.

CARSON: And to the Savoy?

WILDE: Yes.

CARSON: And you told me already that you used frequently to go to his house?

WILDE: Yes, I had been certainly seven or eight times. He gave up his house, I think, in April 1893.

CARSON: August 1893?

WILDE: August, was it?

CARSON: Yes.

WILDE: Yes.

CARSON: You used to go to tea-parties there?

WILDE: Yes.

CARSON: In the afternoon?

WILDE: Yes.

CARSON: Had he a house or was it the upper part of a house?

WILDE: It was the upper part of a house.

CARSON: Do you know what rent he paid?

WILDE: I have not the smallest idea. I shouldn't think very high.

CARSON: Do you know what accommodation he had?

WILDE: There were two storeys that he owned. It was a two-storeyed house. He owned the upper — first and second storey of the house.

CARSON: He had, I believe, a bedroom, a sitting room and bathroom and a kitchen?

WILDE: Yes, I think so, yes.

CARSON: He had no servant?

WILDE: That I don't know at all.

CARSON: Do you mean to say that you don't know?

WILDE: No, I know he had no servant. He used to open the door himself; but I understand he had someone to come in and do his work, but of that I have no knowledge.

CARSON: He used to do his own cooking?

WILDE: That I don't know. I have never dined with him there.

CARSON: Do you mean to say that you don't know that Taylor used to do his own cooking?

WILDE: No; nor if he did, should I think it anything wrong. I think it rather clever. You have asked me as a fact. I say I do not know, but I have never seen him, sir.

CARSON: I have not suggested that it is anything wrong.

WILDE: No, cooking is an art. (*Laughter.*)

CARSON: Another art?

WILDE: Another art.

CARSON: Did he always open the door for you?

WILDE: Oh, no — some of his friends were there — anybody ran down when there was a ring to open the door.

CARSON: It was either he or one of the friends who were there who opened the door?

WILDE: Yes.

CARSON: Did his rooms strike you as being peculiar at all?

WILDE: Except that they displayed more taste than is usual, I saw nothing about them.

CARSON: It was rather elaborate furniture for that class of upper part?

WILDE: I didn't say the furniture was elaborate. I said the room was in good taste.

CARSON: Was it elaborate – luxurious?

WILDE: No, I said in good taste.

CARSON: What?

WILDE: No, I didn't think there was anything in the shape of luxury.

CARSON: It didn't occur to you as being luxurious in the upper part of College Street?

WILDE: Yes, there was a piano, some photographs and some lamps. I thought them most pretty rooms.

CARSON: He never admitted any daylight into them at all?

WILDE: I really don't know what you mean.

CARSON: Were there always candles or gas light in there?

WILDE: No.

CARSON: What?

WILDE: No.

CARSON: Did you ever see the rooms lighted otherwise than by gas or candles, whether at day or at night?

WILDE: Certainly.

CARSON: You did?

WILDE: (*Gives no answer.*)

CARSON: Did you ever see the curtains drawn back from these rooms in the sitting room?

WILDE: When I went to see Mr Taylor it was in winter, usually about five o'clock at tea-time, so that there was naturally always gas; but I was always under the impression – it never occurred to me – but I am under the impression, certainly, that I have been to see him earlier in the day and certainly I think daylight was admitted.

CARSON: Are you prepared to say now that you ever saw the curtains otherwise than drawn across?

WILDE: Yes.

CARSON: You did?

WILDE: Yes.

CARSON: You are clear about that?

WILDE: Yes.

CARSON: It would not be true, then, to say that he always kept a double set of curtains drawn across the windows and day and night lighted the room with candles or gas?

WILDE: Oh, I should think quite untrue.

CARSON: What?

WILDE: I should think quite untrue. I cannot at the present moment recall.

CARSON: Can you recall any time specifically at which you ever saw daylight enter that room?

WILDE: You mean at a time when there was daylight, of course?

CARSON: Yes.

WILDE: Yes.

CARSON: You can?

WILDE: Yes.

CARSON: Who was there?

WILDE: Mr Taylor.

CARSON: Anybody else?

WILDE: I don't think anybody else.

CARSON: What?

WILDE: I don't know – no, I don't think anybody else.

CARSON: What occasion was that?

WILDE: It was, I think, in the month of March that I went to see him about twelve o'clock in the day.

CARSON: Was he up?

WILDE: Yes, he was up.

CARSON: There was no one else there?

WILDE: No one else there.

CARSON: Is that the only occasion you call to mind?

WILDE: I really cannot tell you. Such a question as this never occurred to me at all. I had been to tea with him constantly in the winter when the curtains were drawn of course.

CARSON: What?

WILDE: In the winter when at five o'clock the curtains would naturally be drawn, but I am under the impression that I went to see him in the month of March at twelve o'clock, and the curtains were open.

CARSON: Were the rooms strongly perfumed?

WILDE: I don't know how you mean – how perfumed? He used to burn perfume in his rooms – charming perfume.[170]

CARSON: Were they always highly perfumed, these rooms in College Street?

WILDE: No, I wouldn't say always.

CARSON: Can you call to mind any occasion now?

WILDE: I don't know. He was in the habit of burning perfume, as I am in my rooms.

CARSON: As you are in your rooms?

WILDE: As I am in mine – a very charming habit it is.

CARSON: Will you just tell me: did you see Wood there at tea?

WILDE: No, never.

CARSON: What?

WILDE: Except on the one occasion where I met him there, but on no other occasion.

CARSON: On no other occasion?

WILDE: No.

CARSON: Did you see Mavor there?[171]

WILDE: Yes.

CARSON: Sydney Mavor?

WILDE: Yes.

CARSON: He was a friend of yours?

WILDE: Yes.

CARSON: How old was he?

WILDE: I believe about twenty-five or twenty-six.

CARSON: Was he so old as that?

WILDE: I believe so.

CARSON: Is he a friend of yours still?

WILDE: I have not seen him for – well, for a year now, when he dined with me a year ago.

CARSON: Where is he now?

WILDE: I have not the remotest idea.

CARSON: When did you last hear from him?

WILDE: About a year ago.

CARSON: You have had no communication with him since?

WILDE: I don't think I have seen him since.

CARSON: Directly or indirectly?

WILDE: From him?

CARSON: To him or from him?

WILDE: To him? Oh, yes. I have had no communication from him at all. I asked Mr Taylor to go down there on Sunday.

CARSON: Last Sunday?

WILDE: On last Sunday, yes – to go down to the house of Mr Mavor's mother to see Mr Mavor and tell him that I wished to see him.

CARSON: Where was that? Where was he, then?

WILDE: Mr Mavor?

CARSON: Yes.

WILDE: He was away; that is what I was told. You are asking me what other people told me.

CARSON: You sent last Sunday to see him?

WILDE: Yes.

CARSON: Down to his house?

WILDE: Yes.

CARSON: Do you know where he has gone to?

WILDE: I have no idea at all.

CARSON: You were not told.

WILDE: No, I was not told – no.

CARSON: Were you told that he has disappeared within the last week?

WILDE: No, I was told that his mother said he was away and would be back on Monday.

CARSON: Did you try to see him on Monday?

WILDE: Yes – Mr Taylor went again, I think, on Monday or wrote him a letter to ask him to call at his rooms and then to come and see me.

CARSON: Well, you have found him since?

WILDE: What do you mean by finding him? I am not looking for him.

CARSON: You don't understand what I mean by asking you whether you found him?

WILDE: I object to the phrase. I have never seen Mr Mavor since. He has not called on me at Tite Street, as I wished him to do.

CARSON: Do I take it that at Mr Taylor's no one waited upon you when you were at tea except Taylor.

WILDE: Everybody waited, I should think, on everybody else. There was no servant in the room, certainly.

CARSON: Did you know whether Mr Taylor had a lady's costume there?

WILDE: I don't know at all.

CARSON: What?

WILDE: I don't know at all.

CARSON: Did you ever see him with a costume on – a lady's fancy dress?

WILDE: No, I never have – no.

CARSON: Quite sure?

WILDE: Quite sure.

CARSON: Has he told you that he had a lady's costume there?

WILDE: No, he has never told me so.

CARSON: What?

WILDE: No, he has never told me so.

CARSON: And you have never heard of it?

WILDE: No, never.

CARSON: You were constantly communicating with him by telegram?

WILDE: At what period?

CARSON: At that period – 1892 and 1893.

WILDE: No, certainly not.

CARSON: What?

WILDE: Certainly not.

CLARKE: Certainly not?

WILDE: Certainly not.

CARSON: You sent him some telegrams?

WILDE: Oh, yes.

CARSON: What was the particular business you had with Taylor?

WILDE: How do you mean?

CARSON: Had you any particular business with Taylor?

WILDE: Business? No.

CARSON: What?

WILDE: No.

CARSON: None at all?

WILDE: No business at all. He was a friend of mine.

CARSON: Was he a literary man?

WILDE: He is a young man of great taste and intelligence, and brought up at a very good English public school.

CARSON: Was he a literary man?

WILDE: I have never seen creative work from his hand.

CARSON: I am not talking of that.

WILDE: Then, what do you mean by a literary man?

CARSON: Well, used you to discuss literature with him?

WILDE: He used to listen on the subject. (*Laughter.*)

CARSON: I suppose he used to get an 'intellectual treat' also?

WILDE: Certainly.

CARSON: Was he an artist?

WILDE: Not an artist in the sense of creating anything. He was very artistic, extremely intellectual, and clever, and pleasant. I liked him very much.

CARSON: Used you to get him from time to time to arrange dinners for you?

WILDE: No.

CARSON: To meet young men?

WILDE: No.

CARSON: Are you sure of that?

WILDE: Yes.

CARSON: You have dined with him with young men?

WILDE: Oh, yes, often.

CARSON: Very often?

WILDE: What do you call 'very often'? I suppose perhaps ten or twelve times.

CARSON: At these restaurants in Rupert Street?

WILDE: Yes, and elsewhere.

CARSON: The Solferino?[172]

WILDE: The Solferino.

CARSON: The Florence?

WILDE: Yes – those are in Rupert Street.

CARSON: Always in private rooms?

WILDE: Oh, no, I have dined in public rooms too.

CARSON: Generally in private rooms?

WILDE: Yes, I prefer dining in private rooms.

CARSON: Kettner's?

WILDE: Yes.

CARSON: Would you tell me, did you send him this telegram? (*It is handed to* WILDE.)

WILDE: Oh, certainly, yes.

CARSON: Just give it back to me, please. 'Alfred Taylor, 13 Little College Street.' It is dated the 7th of March [1893] my lord. 'Could you call at six o'clock. Oscar. Savoy.'

WILDE: Yes.

CARSON: You were staying at the Savoy then?

WILDE: I was staying at the Savoy then, yes.

CARSON: 'Taylor, 13 Little College Street, Westminster.' What did you want him for at the Savoy that time?

WILDE: I wanted him because I had had an anonymous letter saying that Alfred Wood was going to blackmail me for certain letters that he had stolen from Lord Alfred Douglas.

CARSON: What you told us before?

WILDE: Yes.

CARSON: And then it was there that you arranged that he would get Wood to meet you?

WILDE: The matter was discussed there.

CARSON: When you were at Goring you also telegraphed to him?

WILDE: That I forget.

CARSON: Here it is: 'Goring. Taylor, 13 Little College Street, Westminster. August 21st 1893. Cannot manage the dinner tomorrow. Am so sorry. Oscar.'

WILDE: Yes.

CARSON: Who was Fred?

WILDE: Fred?

CARSON: Yes.

WILDE: Fred was a young man to whom I was introduced by a gentleman whose name you handed up to me on a piece of paper yesterday.

CARSON: What was his other name?

WILDE: Atkins.[173]

CARSON: You were very familiar with him, were you not?

WILDE: What do you mean by the word 'familiar'? I liked him, yes, I saw him.

CARSON: You told me yesterday you did not generally call people by their short Christian name?

WILDE: Oh, no, I always do if I like them.

CARSON: It is a special mark of liking?

WILDE: No, if I dislike a person I call him something else.

CARSON: Had you any trouble about Fred?

WILDE: Never in my life, except I have seen his name down—

CARSON: Was he a friend of Taylor's?

WILDE: Yes.

CARSON: And used you to meet there at these tea-parties?

WILDE: No, I have never seen him at Taylor's.

CARSON: Never seen him at all at Taylor's?

WILDE: No.

JUDGE: Did I understand you to say that he was a friend of Taylor?

WILDE: Yes, I know they know each other, but I don't remember having met him at a tea-party there.

CARSON: Didn't they call each other by their Christian name?

WILDE: Yes.

CARSON: And did Fred call you by your Christian name?

WILDE: Oh, yes.

CARSON: The date is the 10th March 1893. 'Alfred Taylor, 13 Little College Street, Westminster. Obliged to see Tree at 5 o'clock so don't come to Savoy. Let me know at once about Fred. Oscar.'

WILDE: Yes, may I look at that?

CARSON: Yes, certainly.

JUDGE: That is to Taylor?

CARSON: Taylor, my lord.

CLARKE: You have got back to March now?

CARSON: Yes. (*The telegram is handed to* WILDE.)

WILDE: Yes, I don't remember what I wanted to know about Fred Atkins. I don't remember what I wanted to know about him; this is in 1893, I think.

CARSON: Did you know that Taylor was being watched by the police?

WILDE: Did I know?

CARSON: Yes.

WILDE: No.

CARSON: Did you ever hear that?

WILDE: Never.

CARSON: At his rooms there?

WILDE: Never.

CARSON: Did you know that Taylor and Wood were subsequently arrested together in a raid that was made on a house in Fitzroy Square?[174]

WILDE: Do you mean this year?

CARSON: Not Taylor and Wood, Taylor and Parker.[175]

WILDE: Yes, in this year, yes.

CARSON: Last year as a matter of fact – 1894.

WILDE: Yes, last year, August 1894.

CARSON: Did you know Parker?

WILDE: Yes.

CARSON: Used you to see Parker at Taylor's rooms?

WILDE: I don't think I have ever seen him at Mr Taylor's rooms, no.

CARSON: Did you ever see Parker in Chapel Street? Taylor moved to 3 Chapel Street when he left Little College Street.

WILDE: Yes, I have seen him there, yes.

CARSON: You have seen Parker there?

WILDE: Yes.

CARSON: Was Parker living there?

WILDE: That I don't know.

CARSON: What?

WILDE: I don't know that he was – not at the time that I went to see Alfred Taylor.

JUDGE: When do you say you saw Parker in Chapel Street?

WILDE: I have seen him at Chapel Street, yes, I have gone to see Alfred Taylor there and have seen Parker there.

CARSON: Wasn't Taylor notorious for introducing young men to older men?

WILDE: No, I never heard that in my life. He has introduced young men to me.

CARSON: Wait a moment. How many young men did he introduce to you?

WILDE: You can hardly ask me to remember.

CARSON: In or about?

WILDE: Do you mean people mentioned in the indictment?

CARSON: No, young men with whom you afterwards became intimate?

WILDE: I should think six – seven – eight.

CARSON: Six, seven, or eight?

WILDE: Yes, I have constantly met young men.

CARSON: No, no, that you became intimate with?

CLARKE: Became friendly with you mean?

WILDE: Became friendly with, I think, is the better word – that I became friendly with. I think about five.

CARSON: Such men as you would call by their Christian name?

WILDE: Yes.

CARSON: That degree of intimacy?

WILDE: Yes.

CARSON: Were these young men all of about twenty years of age?

163

WILDE: I should think twenty or twenty-two, I don't really – oh, young men, yes, I like the society of young men. I delight in it.

CARSON: Had any of them any occupation?

WILDE: I don't really know. All I can say is if you would ask me with regard to the people you are mentioning, I will tell you.

CARSON: Did you give money to each or how many of those?

WILDE: Yes, to the five, yes, I have given – yes, I should think – all of the five, yes.

CARSON: All five?

WILDE: Yes, I should say money and presents.

CARSON: Did they give you anything?

WILDE: Me? – no!

CARSON: Now, amongst these five did he introduce you to Charles Parker?

WILDE: Yes.

CARSON: Then, I may take it that Charles Parker was one of the ones you became friendly with?

WILDE: Oh, yes.

CARSON: Was he a gentleman's servant out of employment?

WILDE: I have no knowledge of that at all.

CARSON: What?

WILDE: I had no knowledge of that at all.

CARSON: Did you never hear that?

WILDE: I never heard it, nor should I have minded. I don't care twopence about people's social positions.

CARSON: Even if he was a gentleman's servant out of employment you would become friendly with him?

WILDE: I would become friendly with any human being that I liked and chose to become friendly with.

CARSON: How old was Parker?

WILDE: I don't keep a census.

CARSON: I am not asking you about a census.

WILDE: I don't know what his age was.

CARSON: What about was his age?

WILDE: I should say about twenty; he was young. That was one of his attractions, the attraction of youth.

CARSON: He was seventeen.

WILDE (*somewhat petulantly*): You cannot ask me a question about which I know nothing. I don't know his age, he may be sixteen or he may be forty-five, don't ask me about it. I think he was about twenty. If you cross-examine me on the question whether he was seventeen, I have never asked him his age. It is rather vulgar to ask people their ages. (*Laughter.*)

CARSON: Was he a literary character?

WILDE: Oh, no.

CARSON: Was he an artist?

WILDE: No.

CARSON: Was he an educated man?

WILDE: Culture was not his strong point. (*Laughter.*)

CARSON: Did you ever ask this man, with whom you were so friendly, what his previous occupation was?

WILDE: I never enquire about people's pasts. (*Laughter.*)

CARSON: Nor their futures?

WILDE: Ah, that is so problematic.

CARSON: Where is he now – Parker?

WILDE: I have not the remotest idea.

CARSON: What?

WILDE: I have not the remotest idea.

CARSON: Have you lost sight of him?

WILDE: Yes.

CARSON: How much money did you give to Parker?

WILDE: Oh, I should think I have given him altogether from the time I have known him about four pounds or five pounds.

CARSON: Four pounds or five pounds?

WILDE: Yes.

CARSON: For what?

WILDE: Because he was poor, because he had no money and because I liked him. What better reason is there for giving a person money than that?

CARSON: Where did you first meet Parker?

WILDE: I first met Parker at Kettner's Restaurant.

CARSON: With whom?

WILDE: With Mr Alfred Taylor.

CARSON: Was anyone with him?

WILDE: Yes, his brother.

CARSON: What was his name?

WILDE: I forget his brother's name.

CARSON: Did you become friendly with the brother?

WILDE: Oh, they were my guests.

CARSON: What?

WILDE: They were my guests at table. I am always friendly with my guests.

CARSON: Your guests?

WILDE: My guests, yes.

CARSON: Upon the first occasion that you saw them?

WILDE: Yes.

CARSON: You had never seen Charles or William Parker before in your life and they immediately became your guests at Kettner's?

WILDE: Yes, it was Mr Alfred Taylor's birthday. I had asked him to dinner and I said, 'Bring any friends of yours that you like.' He brought these two young men.[176]

CARSON: Did you know that one of them was a gentleman's valet and the other was a gentleman's groom?

WILDE: I didn't know it, nor should I have cared.

CARSON: Nor should you have cared?

WILDE: No, I don't think twopence for social position; if I like them, I like them. It is a snobbish and vulgar thing to do.

CARSON: What enjoyment was it to you, Mr Wilde, to be dining and entertaining grooms and coachmen?

WILDE: The pleasure of being with those who are young, bright, happy, careless and amusing.[177]

CARSON: Yes, but—

WILDE (*emphatically*): I don't like the sensible and don't like the old. I don't like them.

CARSON: You had never seen these two young men before?

WILDE: Yes, I said to Mr Alfred Taylor – it was his birthday – I said, 'I will give you a dinner at Kettner's. Bring any friends you like.'

CARSON: Taylor accepted your invitation by bringing a valet and a groom?

WILDE: I don't know whether a valet and a groom. I shouldn't have cared if they were. That is your account of them not mine.

CARSON: I want to know what they were.

WILDE: Yes, I told you that I didn't know their occupations, that I saw they were two pleasant—

CARSON: Isn't that the class of person that they were?

WILDE: Was that the class?

CARSON: Yes, you could form an opinion?

WILDE: No, I thought – I am surprised to hear your description of them because they did not seem to me to have the manners connected with that class. They seemed to me both very pleasant and nice. They told me their father lived at Datchet[178] and was a man of some wealth – not wealth exactly, but a man of some fortune there, and one of them, Charles Parker, said he was anxious to go upon the stage.

CARSON: Did you call him 'Charlie'?

WILDE: Oh, yes, certainly.

CARSON: The first evening?

WILDE: Yes.

CARSON: Was it a good dinner?

WILDE: I forget the menu at the present moment.

CARSON: Yes, but I suppose it was an expensive dinner?

WILDE: Well, Kettner's is not so gorgeous in price as other restaurants. The prices are fair.

CARSON: Was it one of Kettner's best?

WILDE: Oh, yes, always. (*Laughter.*)

CARSON: Always?

WILDE: Always, certainly – Kettner at his best.

CARSON: And the best of wine?

WILDE: The best of Kettner's wine, yes.

CARSON: All for the groom and the valet?

WILDE: No, for Mr Alfred Taylor whose birthday it was, who was a friend of mine, who had brought his friends.

CARSON: Was there anyone else there?

WILDE: Oh, no! No, no.

CARSON: Of course, you did the honours in a private room to the groom and the valet?

WILDE: I beg your pardon?

CARSON: You did the honours in a private room?

WILDE: No, I say I entertained Mr Taylor and his two friends.

CARSON: In a private room?

WILDE: Certainly, in a private room.

CARSON: Could you fix the date?

WILDE: I should think March, the beginning of March 1893.

CARSON: Very well, March 1893?

WILDE: I think so.

CARSON: Did you give them an 'intellectual treat'?

WILDE: They seemed deeply impressed. (*Laughter.*)

CARSON: Now, during the dinner, did you become more intimate with Charlie than with the other one?

WILDE: I liked him the better, yes, of the two.

CARSON: And did he call you Oscar?

WILDE: Oh, yes, I told him to. I like to be called either 'Oscar' or 'Mr Wilde'.

CARSON: You put him at his ease at once?

WILDE: At once.

CARSON: Did you give them plenty of champagne?

WILDE: They had whatever they wanted.

CARSON: As much as ever they could drink?

WILDE: Oh, you can find out at Kettner's; it was no elaborate amount of drinking.

CARSON: You gave him as much as ever he could take – this valet out of employment?

WILDE: If you imply by that I forced wine on them, certainly not. They were supplied, as anybody else who dines with me, with a proper amount of wine.

CARSON: You did not stint them with the amount of wine they would drink?

WILDE (*indignantly*): What gentleman would stint his guests? (*Laughter.*)

CARSON: What gentleman would stint his valet?[179]

WILDE: His guests, sir, I strongly object to that description.

CARSON: After dinner did you say, turning to Charlie and in the presence of Taylor and in the presence of William his brother, 'This is the boy for me'?

WILDE: Most certainly not.

CARSON: 'Will you come with me?'

WILDE: No.

CARSON: Anything to that effect?

WILDE: No.

CARSON: Where did you go after the dinner?

WILDE: I went back to the Savoy Hotel.

CARSON: Did you bring him with you?

WILDE: No.

CARSON: Sure of that?

WILDE: Quite certain.

CARSON: Now, I ask you, didn't you drive him to the Savoy Hotel?

WILDE: No.

CARSON: Were you staying at the Savoy then?

WILDE: Oh, yes, I was staying at the Savoy then.

CARSON: Was your house in Tite Street shut up?

WILDE: Yes, my wife was in Italy at the time.

CARSON: Your wife was away at that time?

WILDE: Yes, she was in Italy.

CARSON: You had, I believe, at the time a sitting room and a bedroom?

WILDE: Yes.

CARSON: In the Savoy?

WILDE: Yes.

CARSON: Numbers 343 and 346?

WILDE: I have no memory for numbers whatever.

CARSON: Now, I must ask you, did you give Charlie Parker at the Savoy that evening two whiskies and sodas?

WILDE: No, he did not come back with me to the Savoy.

CARSON: Or come back after?

WILDE: No.

CARSON: Or two small bottles of iced champagne?

WILDE: I say he was not there.

CARSON: Had you whiskies and sodas that evening and iced champagne?

WILDE: That I have not really the smallest recollection of – I should not be asked the question.

CARSON: Was it a favourite drink – iced champagne?

WILDE: Is it a favourite drink of mine?

CARSON: Yes.

WILDE: Yes, strongly against my doctor's orders. (*Laughter.*)

CARSON: Never mind the doctor's orders.

WILDE: I don't. It has all the more flavour if you discard the doctor's orders. (*More laughter.*)

CARSON: I ask you, on that occasion, did Charlie Parker sleep with you for several hours?

WILDE: Certainly not.

CARSON: Or get into bed with you?

WILDE: Certainly not.

CARSON: Did you give him anything that first night?

WILDE: Nothing at all.

CARSON: Or at Kettner's?

WILDE: No, nothing.

CARSON: I mean at Kettner's?

WILDE: No, nothing.

CARSON: Gave him no money?

WILDE: No money at all.

CARSON: You didn't give him two pounds?

WILDE: No.

CARSON: Did he come to supper with you the next night at the Savoy?

WILDE: No.

CARSON: Or the next week?

WILDE: No.

CARSON: At any time?

WILDE: No.

CARSON: Do you mean to say that Parker did not come at any time to the Savoy?

WILDE: At no time did he ever come to the Savoy.

CARSON: Therefore I may take it he never had supper with you there, of course, if he never was there?[180]

WILDE: No, never.

CARSON: When did you next see him?

WILDE: I think he dined with me about a week later at Kettner's with Mr Taylor.

CARSON: Nobody else?

WILDE: I don't think anybody else was there.

CARSON: And I suppose you had the same 'Kettner's best' again?

WILDE: I forget the menu on that occasion.

CARSON: Did you give him any money on that occasion?

WILDE: No.

CARSON: When did you first give him any money?

WILDE: In the month of December 1893.

CARSON: Who arranged that second dinner?

WILDE: I did.

CARSON: You wrote and asked Parker to come?

WILDE: Yes, him and his brother to come to dinner.

CARSON: Was his brother at the second dinner?

WILDE: No, his brother – his family were out of town.

CARSON: Did you ask Taylor what these young men were?

WILDE: Do you mean to say, did I make enquiries about them? It was sufficient to me that they were friends of his.

CLARKE: As to their occupations?

CARSON: As to their occupations, yes. (*To* WILDE.) You did not ask Taylor and he did not tell you?

WILDE: He told me, or rather Parker told me himself, he was anxious to go on the stage. (*Rather loftily.*) What the other man's ambition was, I do not know.

CARSON: Did Taylor tell you where he had met them?

WILDE: No, he didn't tell me where he had met them.

CARSON: Did he tell you he had met them in St James's Restaurant?[181]

WILDE: No, he did not.

CARSON: Now, you were staying, I think, from October 1893, you told me, to April 1894 at 10 St James's Place?

WILDE: I was not staying there, no.

CARSON: But you had rooms there?

WILDE: I had rooms there, yes.

CARSON: You sometimes slept there?

WILDE: Yes. Oh, yes.

CARSON: Was your house in Tite Street shut up then?

WILDE: Oh, no, I was living in Tite Street.

CARSON: Were your rooms on the ground floor?

WILDE: Yes.

CARSON: Near the hall door?

WILDE: Yes.

CARSON: A sitting room when you went in?

WILDE: Yes.

CARSON: Immediately you went in, and a bedroom off the sitting room?

WILDE: Yes.

CARSON: Were there two hall doors to the house?

WILDE: There are two houses.

CARSON: Ten and eleven?

WILDE: Ten and eleven, yes, of course, they communicate. There are two houses.

CARSON: Did you ask Taylor to tell Charlie Parker to call there?

WILDE: Did I ask him?

CARSON: Yes.

WILDE: My impression is that Mr Taylor wrote to me and said that Charles Parker was in town and would like to see me.

CARSON: Have you got that letter?

WILDE: I have not got that letter, no. That is my impression, that

I wrote to Alfred Taylor and said to tell him that Charlie Parker could come to tea any time he liked.

CARSON: Come to tea?

WILDE: Yes.

CARSON: Afternoon tea? Was it afternoon tea?

WILDE: Yes, afternoon tea, certainly.

CARSON: Did Parker come there?

WILDE: Yes.

CARSON: To tea?

WILDE: Yes.

CARSON: How often?

WILDE: Oh, I should think five or six times.

CARSON: What was he doing there?

WILDE: Nothing. What was he doing where?

CARSON: At St James's Place?

WILDE: What was he doing?

CARSON: Yes.

WILDE: Visiting me.

CARSON: Visiting you?

WILDE: Yes.

CARSON: Was he alone?

WILDE: Sometimes he came with Mr Taylor, sometimes he was alone. I liked his society.

CARSON: Very well, we will see. Did you give him presents?

WILDE: I gave him − I forget what I gave him − I gave him a Christmas present.

CARSON: Did you give him a chain?

WILDE: A chain? No.

CARSON: A chain ring?

WILDE: No.

CARSON: A chain gold ring, you know the kind of thing I mean?

WILDE: No, I don't think that was my Christmas present. I am sure it was not.

CARSON: Did you give him a cigarette case?

WILDE: Yes, I gave him a cigarette case. That was my Christmas present.

CARSON: Did you give him money?

WILDE: Yes, I gave him three pounds – four pounds.

CARSON: Three pounds or four pounds?

WILDE: Yes.

CARSON: Was that on the occasion of various visits?

WILDE: Oh, no, no; he was hard up and asked me would I do it – I did it.

CARSON: You did it?

WILDE: Yes.

CARSON: Did you give it to him all at once?

WILDE: Yes, all at once.

CARSON: What?

WILDE: All at once.

CARSON: Was he in your bedroom at any time?

WILDE: Not that I remember.

CARSON: What?

WILDE: Not that I remember. My bedroom was off my sitting room. If you ask whether, when I was putting my coat on in my bedroom he came in, I dare say he did. I don't see why he should not, but he was never in my bedroom in the sense that you imply.

CARSON: Do you recollect as a fact his being in your bedroom?

WILDE: No, I don't recollect as a fact that he was in my bedroom. The bedroom was off my sitting room. I don't see why he should not have done it. I am not fencing with the question.

CARSON: No. Did improprieties take place between you?

WILDE: None.

CARSON: How long used he to stay on each of these occasions when he came to tea?

WILDE: An hour I think – yes.

CARSON: What was he doing all that time?

WILDE: Do you ask me what a young man does when he comes to have tea with me? He has his tea, he smokes cigarettes and I hope he enjoys it.

CARSON: Really? What I would like to ask you is this: what was there in common between you and this young man of this class?

WILDE: Well, I will tell you, Mr Carson, I delight in the society of people much younger than myself. I like those who may be called idle and careless. I recognise no social distinctions at all of any kind and to me youth – the mere fact of youth – is so wonderful that I would sooner talk to a young man half an hour than even be, well, cross-examined in court. (*Laughter.*)

CARSON: Then, do I understand that even a young boy that you would pick up in the street would be a pleasing companion to you?

WILDE: Oh, I would talk to a street Arab if he talked to me, with pleasure.[182]

CARSON: And take him into your rooms?

WILDE: If he interested me.

CARSON: Had Charles Parker, during all the time that he was there, any employment during the time that he knew you?

WILDE: None.

CARSON: Do you know how he was living?

WILDE: He told me from an allowance by his father of the smallness of which he complained. That is a habit of sons.

CARSON: Do you remember Parker taking rooms at 7 Camera Square?[183]

WILDE: I remember that he lived there. I don't remember his taking rooms. I know that was his address.

CARSON: Is it near Tite Street?

WILDE: I don't know where it is.

CARSON: What?

WILDE: I don't know where it is. It is in Chelsea. It is SW.

CARSON: Did you get him clothes?

WILDE: Parker? No.

CARSON: Did you take him to lunch at various places?

WILDE: Oh, yes, Parker has lunched with me.

CARSON: What?

WILDE: Parker has lunched with me, yes.

CARSON: At how many places?

WILDE: At the Café Royal.

CARSON: Anywhere else?

WILDE: I don't remember his lunching anywhere else.

CARSON: Did he lunch with you at St James's Place?

WILDE: Oh, yes, he has lunched with me at St James's Place. I thought you said 'take him to lunch' – he came in to lunch with me several times.

CARSON: Did he dine with you again at Kettner's?

WILDE: Yes.

CARSON: The third time?

WILDE: Yes.

CARSON: Who was there then?

WILDE: Nobody at all.

CARSON: Had you a private room?

WILDE: No, no private room.

CARSON: Are you quite certain?

WILDE: I am certain. I have a particular reason for being certain.

CARSON: Did you go then to the Pavilion?[184]

WILDE: Yes.

CARSON: And then take him back to St James's Place?

WILDE: No.

CARSON: Did you go to see him at Camera Square?

WILDE: No, I have never been to see him.

CARSON: What?

WILDE: I have never been to see him.

CARSON: Why?

WILDE: Well, it really wouldn't interest me to go and see him. It would interest him very much to come and see me. (*Laughter.*) I have never been to see Charlie Parker anywhere.

CARSON: Do you mean to say you never went to see this man with whom you were so intimate?

WILDE: Never in my life. It is a very different thing his coming to tea with me and my going to call on him. It might be a bore to go and call on him.

CARSON: Did you get up a dinner for him at the Solferino?

WILDE: I don't think he has ever dined with me at the Solferino.

CARSON: Did he ever dine with you and Atkins – that is Fred?

WILDE: Yes.

CARSON: And Taylor? Do you remember a dinner where that was the party?

WILDE: I don't remember Parker being there but he may have been.

CARSON: But you remember the occasion of a dinner?

WILDE: Certainly.

JUDGE: At the Solferino?

WILDE: Yes, the Solferino.

CARSON: That was in the spring of last year, wasn't it – 1894?

WILDE: Oh, I thought it was December 1893 but it may be January 1894.

CARSON: Do you remember Parker moving from 7 Camera Square to 50 Park Walk?

WILDE: No, I don't remember his moving.

CARSON: Do you remember his living at 50 Park Walk?

WILDE: No, I don't know where 50 Park Walk is.

CARSON: Did you not want to know where your friend was living?

WILDE: Oh, yes, 7 Camera Square; I knew because I had written to him there.

CARSON: Afterwards?

WILDE: Afterwards – he may have told me that he had changed his address, it didn't produce any particular impression on me.

CARSON: It didn't produce any impression?

WILDE: No.

CARSON: Did you write him any beautiful letters?

WILDE: I don't think I have ever written to Charlie Parker a beautiful letter – no, certainly not.

CARSON: His letters were not beautiful?

WILDE: His letters? No.

CARSON: Have you any of his letters to you?

WILDE: I have only brought one.

CARSON: Would you give it to me please?

WILDE: I think there is one.

CARSON: Give it to me.

CLARKE: I will look for it. (*The letter is produced.*)

CARSON: '7 Camera Square. Thursday. Dear Oscar, Am I to have the pleasure of dining with you this evening? If so kindly send answer per messenger or wire me to above address. I do trust it will be convenient. We can spend the evening together. With very kind regards and apologies. Yours faithfully C. Parker.'

WILDE: Yes.

CARSON: Had you no other letter of his?

WILDE: I have no other letter of his.

CLARKE: After the way in which my learned friend has spoken of this young man, I should like your lordship to look at that letter and I should like the jury to see the handwriting.

CARSON (*drily*): We will see all about that as the case goes on. Parker himself will be here and the jury will see him. That will be better.

CLARKE: They will see at all events the handwriting.

CARSON: It depends who wrote the letter. Have you any other letters of his?

WILDE: I never thought his correspondence sufficiently interesting to preserve.

CARSON: Have you any other letters?

WILDE: No, I have not. This I discovered entirely by chance.

CARSON: How was it you came to keep that one?

WILDE: It was entirely by chance. I discovered that letter entirely by chance. Naturally, I was asked by my solicitor. I cannot imagine how I came to keep it.

CARSON: I want to know in March or April of last year did you go one night to visit Parker at 50 Park Walk?

WILDE: No.

CARSON: At half past twelve at night?

WILDE: No.

CARSON: Do you know where Park Walk is?

WILDE: In Chelsea.

CARSON: Is it near Tite Street?

WILDE: Oh, no, I should think quite far away.

CARSON: Is it ten minutes' walk away?

WILDE: I never walk. (*Laughter.*)

CARSON: What drive is it?

WILDE: I have no idea.

CARSON: You never walk?

WILDE: Never.

CARSON: Then, I suppose in paying your visits you would go in a cab?

WILDE: Oh, yes, always.

CARSON: Do you generally, when you pay these visits, leave the cab outside?

WILDE: What sort of visits do you mean?

CARSON: I mean visiting, going to see some of these friends of yours?

WILDE: If I went to see any friend of mine, certainly I should keep the cab outside if it was a good cab. (*Laughter.*)

CARSON: When did you last see Parker?

WILDE: I don't think I have seen him since—

CARSON: What?

WILDE: I don't think I have seen him since February last.

CARSON: February this year?

WILDE: No, February last year.

CARSON: February 1894?

WILDE: Yes.

CARSON: Are you quite sure of that?

WILDE: That is my recollection.

CARSON: Did you ever take him to the Crystal Palace?

WILDE: Yes.

CARSON: When was that?

WILDE: That was about Christmas time 1893.

CARSON: Was that the day he lunched at St James's Place?

WILDE: Yes.

CARSON: Or one of the days?

WILDE: Yes.

CARSON: Then, you went down together?

WILDE: We went down afterwards to the Crystal Palace.[185]

CARSON: Did you ever hear what became of Parker?

WILDE: Of Parker? I heard that he had gone into the army.[186]

CARSON: Enlisted?

WILDE: Yes, enlisted.

CARSON: As a private?

WILDE: Yes, as a private.

CARSON: A private in the army?

WILDE: Yes.

CARSON: I think you told me that you didn't hear that he and Taylor were arrested together?

WILDE: I beg your pardon?

CARSON: Did you hear that he and Taylor were arrested together?

WILDE: Yes, I read that in the newspapers. Yes, I was down in Worthing at the time. I read it in the newspapers.

CARSON: When was that?

WILDE: I think in August of last year.

CARSON: That is quite right, August 1894. And did you read that at the time they were arrested they were in company with several men in women's clothes?

WILDE: My recollection of what I read in the newspapers is that two men in women's clothes drove up to the house – music hall singers it was stated – and that they were arrested outside the house, but whether there was anybody in women's clothes at the house at this concert or entertainment, whatever it was, I don't know. That you can verify by the newspaper reports. Don't ask me about that.

CARSON: You call it a concert?

WILDE: I only know what I read in the papers.

CARSON: Did you ask Taylor about it?

WILDE: Yes.

CARSON: Didn't you think it was somewhat of a serious thing that Mr Taylor, your great friend, and Charles Parker, another great friend, should be arrested in a police raid at this house?

WILDE: I, when I read it, was very much distressed, but the magistrate seems to have taken a different view because he dismissed the case.

CARSON: They were charged with felonious practices, weren't they?

WILDE: Ah, I don't know the exact charge. That you can verify for yourself.

CARSON: The magistrate fined some of those that were there?

WILDE: I don't know at all.

CLARKE: Not for felonious practices.

CARSON: No, of course not.

CLARKE: You suggest it. No magistrate could have fined anybody for that.

CARSON: Did you read the list of persons who were arrested?

WILDE: Yes.

CARSON: Walter Gilworth, waiter; Henry Roberts, servant; W. Wright, valet; Arthur Ivens, clerk; George Huckle, butler; H. Browne, tobacconist; Thomas Coombes, costumier; Sam Lee, fishmonger; J. Preston, dealer. Had you ever heard of Preston before?[187]

WILDE: No.

CARSON: Sure?

WILDE: Yes, quite certain.

CARSON: Did you never hear of Preston in connection with the Cleveland Street scandals?[188]

WILDE: No, I have never heard his name at all.

CARSON: H. J. Stephens; J. Skinner, no occupation; Charles Parker, valet; A. Taylor, no occupation; Charles Smith, butler; J. Durnback, valet; John Hands, clerk; Arthur Marling, no occupation. Isn't Marley a notorious sodomite?[189]

WILDE: I have never heard of him in my life.

CARSON: John Levers, tobacconist; Herbert Coulton, fruiterer.

CLARKE: What is the question you ask him?

CARSON: Now, I ask you: when you saw that Taylor was arrested in the company of these varied people, did it make any difference in your friendship towards Taylor?

WILDE: When I read it I was greatly disturbed and wrote to him and told him so. I didn't see him again till this year.

CARSON: Yes?

WILDE: No, it has made no difference – the fact that such a charge was brought against him and dismissed – no, it made no difference to me.

CARSON: Did he write back to you when you said that?

WILDE: Yes, he wrote back to me.

CARSON: Have you got his letter?

WILDE: No, I don't think I have got his letter.

CARSON: Are you sure?

WILDE: Yes.

CARSON: You have not got his letter?

WILDE: Yes.

CARSON: And I think you told me that this same Taylor was lunching with you on Tuesday?

WILDE: When?

CARSON: On Tuesday last.

WILDE: He was not lunching with me. He came to my house at twelve o'clock.

CLARKE: Of course, I should have interposed if I had not been under the impression that my learned friend was reading from a newspaper which Mr Oscar Wilde might have seen, but that is not so. I have asked for the paper and they hand me a police report. Of course, the important question is what was in the newspaper and what information the passage in the newspaper would convey to Mr Oscar Wilde, so that I shall ask to have the newspaper report, which it is suggested Mr Oscar Wilde could have seen, produced.

CARSON: We will produce it and put it in evidence.

JUDGE: It does not matter what the source of Mr Wilde's information was, the point is whether he knew whether these facts were brought to his knowledge in any way with a view to found the question later on.

CLARKE: Yes, my lord.

CARSON: Now, Mr Wilde, when did you first know Mr Freddie Atkins?

WILDE: In October 1892, or I think the beginning of November. It was October or November 1892.

CARSON: What was he?

WILDE: Do you mean by occupation?

CARSON: Yes.

WILDE: He told me he was connected with a firm of bookmakers, in the employment of a firm of bookmakers.

CARSON: Bookmakers?

WILDE: Yes, bookmakers.

CARSON: You did not come in contact with him through making bets or anything of that kind?

WILDE: Oh, no, certainly not.

CARSON: How old was he when you first made his acquaintance?

WILDE: I should think about nineteen or twenty, but I cannot be cross-examined about the ages of these people. He was a young man, that is quite certain.

CARSON: I do not want to know his exact age. Where were you introduced to him?

WILDE: In the rooms of the gentleman whose name you handed up to me yesterday.

CARSON: Didn't you first see him at Alfred Taylor's?

WILDE: No.

CARSON: Can you tell me the address of those rooms?

WILDE: The rooms I mentioned?

CARSON: Yes.

WILDE: They were rooms off Regent Street, I think, in Margaret Street on the ground floor. I may not be right about the address, but they were off Regent Street on the right-hand side running up from this end. My impression was it was Margaret Street.

CARSON: Did you say number 12, did you mention a number?

JUDGE: No.

WILDE: I didn't mention a number, no.

CARSON: Can you give me the number?

WILDE: No, I really can't remember the number, but I might be able to find it out.

CARSON: Was anyone present when you were introduced to him?

WILDE: Yes, I think there were several people in the room.

CARSON: Was Taylor there?

WILDE: No.

CARSON: Are you sure?

WILDE: Yes, quite certain.

CARSON: Was Taylor a friend of his?

WILDE: Of whom?

CARSON: Of Atkins?

WILDE: At that time I don't think Atkins had met Mr Taylor.

CARSON: You met him, I think, on the 18th of November 1892?

WILDE: I think at the beginning of November.

CARSON: Now, the first day you met him, did you ask him to dinner?

WILDE: No, I never asked him to dinner.

CARSON: Or to lunch?

WILDE: No, I met him at dinner, but the dinner was not mine.

CARSON: Who gave the dinner?

WILDE: It was given by the gentleman whose name you handed up.

CARSON: Where was it?

WILDE: I think at Kettner's.

CARSON: Or was it at the Florence?

WILDE: That I forget really. It might have been one or the other. It was one—

CARSON: Was Taylor there?

WILDE: Yes, I think he was there.

CARSON: How soon after you met him was that?

WILDE: How soon after I met Fred Atkins?

CARSON: Yes. Was it the very day you met him?

WILDE: No, I think it was about two days afterwards.

CARSON: Was that the whole party – Taylor, the gentleman I have mentioned—

WILDE: I think so. I really forget. I cannot remember guests. There might have been other people.

CARSON: Did you become intimate with Atkins at that dinner?

WILDE: Are you ascribing any particular meaning to the word 'intimate'?

CARSON: Did you feel friendly towards him?

WILDE: Oh, yes, certainly. I called him very good company.

CARSON: Did you call him 'Freddie'?

WILDE: 'Fred'.

CARSON: And what did he call you?

WILDE: 'Oscar'.

CARSON: He was in the employment of a bookmaker at the time?

WILDE: Yes, but he apologised and said he neglected his business.

CARSON: He said he neglected his business? That was the character he gave himself?

WILDE: Yes.

CARSON: Did he seem to you to be an idle kind of fellow?

WILDE: A what?

CARSON: An idle kind of fellow?

WILDE: An idle—

CARSON: Yes.

WILDE: Oh, yes, he seemed to me—

CARSON: An idle kind of fellow doing nothing?

WILDE: Yes, with ambitions to go on the music hall stage.

CARSON: Did you think him charming?

WILDE: I thought him very pleasant.

CARSON: Did he discuss literature with you?

WILDE: Oh, I would not allow him. (*Laughter.*)

CARSON: That was not his line?

WILDE: No, the art of the music hall was as far as he had got. (*Laughter.*)

CARSON: And did you, at that dinner, ask him to lunch the next day with you at the Café Royal?

WILDE: No.

CARSON: Did he lunch with you the next day at the Café Royal?

WILDE: No.

CARSON: What?

WILDE: No.

CARSON: How soon after?

WILDE: He never lunched with me as my guest at the Café Royal. On a certain Sunday, I think it was, I was lunching by myself; he and the gentleman whose name you handed up to me were

185

lunching in another part of the restaurant, and came over and had coffee and cigarettes with me.

CARSON: How old was this other gentleman?

WILDE: I think at that time – I should think he was twenty-four or twenty-three.

CARSON: Twenty-four or twenty-three?

WILDE: Well, yes, I should think so.

CARSON: They came over and had coffee with you?

WILDE: Yes.

CARSON: Did you upon that occasion suggest to Fred Atkins to go away with you to Paris?

WILDE: No.

CARSON: What?

WILDE: No.

CARSON: Did you subsequently suggest it to him?

WILDE: I think I should like to make a statement on that subject.

CARSON: Did you?

WILDE: I was asked by this other – yes, it is difficult for me to answer on this matter unless you allow me to explain it. The suggestion was not made by me to Fred Atkins that he should accompany me to Paris; it was made by this gentleman whose name you handed up, who was unable to go.

CARSON: That you should take him to Paris?

WILDE: No, I was going to Paris on my own account to arrange about the publication of a book of mine. The gentleman, whose name you have handed up, told me that he also was going to Paris for the purpose of trying to get some work at Dalziel's agency there – he was a very good linguist – and that he was going with Fred Atkins.[190] He suggested that we should all go together. It was arranged we should go on the Monday. On this particular Sunday this gentleman told me he was unable to go till the Tuesday or Wednesday. Fred Atkins seemed very much disappointed on account of this short stay in Paris and this gentleman said to me, 'Would you take Fred over as he seems disappointed?' and I said, 'With the greatest pleasure.'

CARSON: And you did take Fred over to Paris?

WILDE: Yes, he came with me.

CARSON: How long had you known him at that time?

WILDE: I think about a fortnight.

CARSON: You, I think, went together to Paris on the 20th of November by the Club train?

WILDE: By the Club train, certainly, yes.[191]

CARSON: Did you pay for him?

WILDE: I paid for his ticket. I was repaid afterwards. I paid for his ticket over.

CARSON: And you say it was repaid afterwards?

WILDE: Yes, by this gentleman.

CARSON: By the other gentleman?

WILDE: Yes.

CARSON: It was not repaid by Atkins?

WILDE: Oh, dear me, no, certainly not.

CARSON: Did you suggest to him that he might go in the capacity of your secretary?

WILDE: Oh, never.

CARSON: What?

WILDE: Never, never. Ridiculous. I was going over to see a French publisher on French matters. It would be childish.[192]

CARSON: I only want to know.

WILDE: No, it is childish to ask me such a question.

CARSON: Then, did you not suggest that he should go as your secretary?

WILDE: Certainly not, a most gross libel.

CARSON: It was not in that capacity that he went?

WILDE: No.

CARSON: He was going on his own business?

WILDE: Oh, no.

CARSON: Or for his own pleasure, was it?

WILDE: For his own pleasure, do you mean?

CARSON: Yes.

WILDE: Oh, no, he was coming over first with this gentleman – his friend.

CARSON: He was going merely for pleasure. So far as you know he had no business in Paris?

WILDE: Oh, none at all.

CARSON: And when you got to Paris did you take him to the same rooms you were staying at?

WILDE: Yes, certainly, he came over with me, certainly.

CARSON: Where were those rooms?

WILDE: 29 boulevard des Capucines. It is an hotel.

CARSON: You took two bedrooms on the third floor?[193]

WILDE: Three or two.

CARSON: What?

WILDE: I took three.

CARSON: You took three, do you say so?

WILDE: Yes.

CARSON: Did you take three at first?

WILDE: Yes, I ordered a third to be reserved for the gentleman who was coming over.

CARSON: Did those two bedrooms open off each other?

WILDE: All three, yes.

CARSON: Now, the day after you arrived, the 21st of November, did you ask Atkins to copy out half a page of manuscript for you?[194]

WILDE: Oh, never in my life.

CARSON: Never?

WILDE: Never.

CARSON: Did you take him to lunch at the Café Julien?[195]

WILDE: Yes, certainly. He was over there with me practically at that moment as my guest.

CARSON: Did you pay for his lunch?

WILDE: Certainly, of course, I paid. He was over there practically at the beginning as my guest; really afterwards as the guest of this gentleman. I did not want him to pay for my lunch.

CARSON: He had no means to pay for himself?

WILDE: I should certainly think not – certainly not the sort of lunch that I like.

CARSON: Now, after lunch did you suggest to him to have his hair curled?

WILDE: No, I told him I thought it would be very unbecoming to him. He suggested it himself. (*Laughter.*)

CARSON: Then, there was a conversation about having his hair curled?

WILDE: Yes.

CARSON: What did he say?

WILDE: He said he thought he would like his hair curled. I said I didn't think it would be at all becoming.

CARSON: You didn't think it would be becoming?

WILDE: Yes.

CARSON: And you were of that opinion?

WILDE: That was the conclusion I had arrived to, at that moment. I have never changed it.

CARSON: You thought he looked better without his hair being curled?

WILDE: I thought it would be silly of him to do it; it wouldn't suit him at all. I think I was quite right, too, in the opinion I expressed.

CARSON: Did he get his hair curled?

WILDE: I don't think so. I should have been very angry if he had. (*Laughter.*) I have no recollection.

CARSON: You would have been angry?

WILDE: Yes, annoyed, a silly thing for him to do.

CARSON: You would have been annoyed at your guest having his hair curled?

WILDE: I told him a silly thing to do when he went off; it wouldn't suit him. I told him it would be a silly thing to do.

CARSON: Did he get it curled?

WILDE: Certainly not in Paris when I was there.

CARSON: At Pascal's the hairdressers under the Grand Hotel?[196]

WILDE: No, I have no recollection. My impression is he didn't. It is a matter to me of no importance. I don't see why I am cross-examined on that.

CARSON: You brought him out to dinner that evening?

WILDE: Certainly.

CARSON: And I believe you gave him an excellent dinner?

WILDE: I never do anything else. I give excellent dinners.

CARSON: And plenty of wine?

WILDE (*excitedly*): That is the point exactly. You must make out whatever gentleman dines with me or guest or whatever you call him, I suppose he is not stinted with the wine. If you ask me whether I ply people with wine, I say such a suggestion is monstrous and I won't have it at all. (*Laughter.*)

CARSON: Quite so. I have not.

WILDE: Ah, but you have before.

CARSON: Have I?

WILDE: Yes.

CARSON: Did you give him as much as he cared to drink. I may take it you did, of course?

WILDE: I think I have already stated that nobody who dines at my table is stinted with wine. I never give to any excess.

CARSON: Did you then send him to the Moulin Rouge? (*Laughter.*)[197]

WILDE: Yes.

CARSON: Gave him a sovereign to go to the Moulin Rouge?

WILDE: Yes.

CARSON: Did you stay at home, Mr Wilde?

WILDE: No, I think I went to a French theatre.

CARSON: When you came back was Atkins in bed?

WILDE: I don't think he had come in.

CARSON: Did you that night, when Atkins was in bed, ask him to let you get into bed with him?

WILDE: I did not. I did nothing of the kind, nor have I ever done it.

CARSON: Did you get into bed with him?

WILDE: Never.

CARSON: Or he with you?

WILDE: Never.

CARSON: Then, I suppose if anyone said that they saw you in bed it would be a mistake?

WILDE: A mistake? It would be a most infamous lie – a mistake?

CARSON: Did the other gentleman, whose name we have had written down, come within a couple of days?

WILDE: He came, I think – yes, he came on the Wednesday.

CARSON: I should have asked you this: did you upon the next day but one after your arrival give Fred Atkins a cigarette case?

WILDE: I didn't think it was the next day. I thought it was the day we left Paris.

CARSON: But you gave him one?

WILDE: Certainly. I thought you were pinning me to a date.

CARSON: This is it? (*Producing one.*)

WILDE: I don't know at all.

CARSON: There is nothing in it – a silver cigarette case?

WILDE: A silver cigarette case.

CLARKE: There is no inscription of any kind, my lord, to differentiate it.

CARSON: How long did you stay together in Paris?

WILDE: Oh, we returned on the Saturday.

CARSON: You returned together?

WILDE: All of us, yes.

CARSON: The three of you?

WILDE: Yes.

CARSON: May I ask you, Mr Wilde, what did you bring young Atkins to Paris for?

WILDE: The invitation at first extended to him was by that gentleman who was a great friend of mine. His disappointment in not going the same day that I was going and his missing two days that he otherwise would have to spend – he said to me, 'Do you mind? – I will pay for his ticket – do you mind bringing him over?' I thought him the most pleasant, good-humoured companion on the voyage. In Paris I didn't see much of him because I had other work to do. In Paris I didn't see much of him because I had other business to do and other friends to attend to. After the gentleman whose name has been handed up arrived, I didn't dine with either of them, I think, on Wednesday, Thursday or Friday. I dined with friends of my own in Paris – we used to breakfast all three. He was not there as my guest.

CARSON: That is the only explanation you give of taking him there?

WILDE: What do you mean by 'the only explanation'?

CARSON: That is the only explanation you give to the jury?

WILDE: That is the reason why I took him.

CARSON: I only want to know: you have nothing to add to that?

WILDE: I do not require anything to be added to it, or any explanation at all.

CARSON: Tell me, shortly after coming back to London, did you write to Atkins to come to see you at Tite Street?

WILDE: Yes, I was very ill after I came back and I know I wrote to the gentleman whose name has been mentioned to ask him to come and bring Fred Atkins. Whether I wrote to Fred Atkins himself personally, I don't know. I may have. He did come. I was ill during that week.

CARSON: You were ill in bed?

WILDE: Yes.

CARSON: And did he come to see you?

WILDE: Oh, yes, they both came.

CARSON: Did he come alone up to see you?

WILDE: No, I think he came with a gentleman.

CARSON: What?

WILDE: I think that he arrived—

CARSON: Did he come on any day by himself up to see you in answer to a letter from you?

WILDE: Not by himself, I think.

CARSON: Are you quite sure about that?

WILDE: Oh, it is not a point to which I could possibly swear. My impression is that he came with a gentleman – I think both came to see me – that he came to see me when I was ill in bed.

CARSON: Would you write me the name of the other gentleman who you say was with him?

CLARKE: The gentleman referred to.

CARSON: Is it the name which you wrote down?

WILDE: Yes, he came to see me and I thought it very kind of him.

CARSON: Did you really think it was very kind of Atkins?

WILDE: Yes, I think to take the trouble to go and see anybody who is ill—

CARSON: Though you had taken him to Paris?

WILDE: Yes, it is not everybody in the world who is grateful for any kindness. It is not always found. I think it is nice. When I am ill if anybody comes to see me, I am pleased.

CARSON: Did you ask him, when he came, to give you back the letter you had written to him?

WILDE: No, certainly not.

CARSON: Nothing of that kind occurred?

WILDE: Oh, nothing at all.

CARSON: Did he give you back the letter?

WILDE: Never. I question whether I wrote to him. My impression was that I had written to the other gentleman. I thought you were questioning me about an actual letter you had in your hand.

CARSON: Did you ask him to promise that he would say nothing about going to Paris?

WILDE: Certainly not. I told him I thought it the great event of his life – that he should realise it.

CARSON: I have already asked you and I think you told me you can give me no explanation of what the meaning of it is: 'Let me know at once about Fred' – the telegram to Taylor. That was after the visit to Paris?

WILDE: Oh, that was four months after.

CARSON: Can you not call to mind what that was about?

WILDE: Oh, probably about whether he could come and dine I should think.

CARSON: What? Wouldn't you wire to him yourself? 'Let me know at once about Fred.' If you wanted him to dine you would have telegraphed to him himself?

WILDE: I don't think I knew his address then.

CARSON: What had Taylor got to do with Fred?

WILDE: Well, they were friends.

CARSON: But then, why did you wire to Taylor to know about Fred?

WILDE: Because I say I do not, at the present moment, remember what I wired to Mr Taylor about Fred Atkins for. Undoubtedly

Fred Atkins was alluded to – I don't remember what it was – whether it was I wanted to see him, or whether it was that I wanted him to dine. I don't know.

CARSON: Had you any business with him?

WILDE: No. Business? – no – of course not.

CARSON: Where was Atkins living at this time?

WILDE: I have not the smallest idea.

CARSON: You have not the smallest idea?

WILDE: No.

CARSON: Did you know where he was living when you took him to Paris?

WILDE: Yes.

CARSON: Where?

WILDE: Somewhere in Pimlico.

CARSON: What was the name of the street?

WILDE: I don't know.[198]

CARSON: Do you mean to say you did not know the name of the street?

WILDE: I don't remember his address.

CARSON: Where the lad whom you were taking to Paris lived?

WILDE: No, I do not remember his address.

CARSON: Did you ever hear of it?

WILDE: If I ever wrote to him – I have no recollection of writing to him there, but you suggested to me I had – if I ever wrote to him, no doubt I wrote to that address wherever it was – I must have.

CARSON: What was the address?

WILDE: I do not at present remember.

CARSON: You did know at the time?

WILDE: If I wrote to him certainly, yes, probably knew about where he lived.

CARSON: What did you write to him about?

WILDE: You asked me whether I had written to ask him to come and see me when I was ill. I said that I had no recollection of so doing but that it was possible that I might have done so, but my impression was that I had written to the gentleman whose name is not mentioned, but it is quite possible that I wrote to him. I don't see why I should not, but I do not remember his address.

CARSON: You don't remember his address?

WILDE: No.

CARSON: Haven't you been in correspondence with him up to the present year?

WILDE: I have written to him several times, yes.

CARSON: In the present year?

WILDE: I sent him tickets for my theatre.

CARSON: This year?

WILDE: Yes, on two occasions.

CARSON: You knew his address then?

WILDE: Oh, yes, his present address certainly.

CARSON: What is his present address?

WILDE: 25 Osnaburgh Street.[199]

CARSON: Had you ever been there?

WILDE: Yes.

CARSON: When?

WILDE: In I think it was February 1894. I know it is before a certain illness he had afterwards.[200]

CARSON: What did you go there for?

WILDE: To his house?

CARSON: Yes. Had he a house?

WILDE: No, well, to his rooms, I went there because he invited me to come and have tea with him and I went.

CARSON: To tea?

WILDE: Yes.

CARSON: Who else was there to tea?

WILDE: There was a gentleman whose name I will write on a piece of paper.

CARSON: There was a gentleman there? I probably know the name?

WILDE: Yes, a young man. You probably know the name I mean.[201]

CARSON: What age was he?

WILDE: About twenty, an actor.

CARSON: Did you go there to tea more than once?

WILDE: Yes, I think I went twice to tea.

CARSON: Did you ever give Atkins any money?

WILDE: Yes.

CARSON: How much?

WILDE: I gave him three pounds and fifteen shillings.

CARSON: What did you give him that for?

WILDE: To buy him his first song on the music hall stage.

CARSON: When was that?

WILDE: He told me that the poets who write for the music hall stage never took less and so I gave him three pounds fifteen shillings. (*Laughter.*) I remember the exact sum and I met one of the poets – I had the pleasure of meeting one of the poets.

CARSON: When was that?

WILDE: It was either – I think myself in either February or March 1893.

CLARKE: February or March what year?

WILDE: 1894; I beg your pardon.

CARSON: Used Atkins to call to see you at St James's Place?

WILDE: He came twice to see me, yes.

CARSON: By himself? Alone?

WILDE: No, I think on both occasions he would be accompanied by this young actor. He dined with me at St James's Place.

CARSON: Do you say, Mr Wilde, that never on any occasion – I will put it generally – was there any impropriety between you and Freddie Atkins?

WILDE: Never, upon any occasion.

CARSON: Did you consider him a moral, respectable young man?

WILDE: Respectability, really – I don't know what you mean.[202] I thought he was a very pleasant, good-natured fellow who was going on the music hall stage, whom I encouraged to go. I bought him a song. I used to hear him sing when I went to tea at his rooms. I went in order to hear him sing, which I did. I heard him sing at a dinner at a restaurant. I was interested in him.

CARSON: Tell me, do you know Ernest Scarfe?[203]

WILDE: Yes.

CARSON: When did you meet Scarfe?

WILDE: In December 1893.

CARSON: Who introduced you to Scarfe?

WILDE: Mr Taylor.

CARSON: How old was Scarfe?

WILDE: Well, I cannot tell you. He was a young man. I never asked him his age; that is rude.

CARSON: Was he twenty?

WILDE: I should think about twenty years of age – a young man about twenty years, I should think – not more.

CARSON: What was his occupation?

WILDE: At the time nothing.

CARSON: What had been his occupation?

WILDE: He had been in Australia in the gold diggings.

CARSON: That was a long time ago?

WILDE: Well, as far as there could be length of time in a life of that brief period.

CARSON: Did you know that he too had been a valet?

WILDE: No, I didn't know that. I thought he had been in Australia.

CARSON: Do you know he is one now – in a place now?

WILDE: Certainly not, I certainly have no knowledge of that at all.

CARSON: No knowledge of that at all?

WILDE: None.

CARSON: Did you know that his father also was a valet?

WILDE: No.

CARSON: Did he appear a well-educated young man?

WILDE: A very nice, pleasant young man. Education depends on what one's standard is. He spoke well; he wrote well.

CARSON: Did you ever meet him in society?

WILDE: Oh, never, certainly not.

CARSON: Except in the society of Taylor. You met him with Taylor frequently?

WILDE: He has been in my society. (*Laughter.*)

CARSON: But has he been in society with Taylor?

WILDE: He has dined with myself and Mr Taylor and he has been in my society, which I consider more important.

CARSON: Where did Taylor introduce Scarfe to you?

WILDE: At St James's Place.

CARSON: Had you asked him to bring him?

WILDE: No.

CARSON: What?

WILDE: No.

CARSON: How did Taylor come to bring this young man there?

WILDE: Shall I tell you?

CARSON: Yes, please.

WILDE: He told me that he knew a young man who had met on board ship going out to Australia Lord Douglas of Hawick, that he had met him – I remember Lord Alfred Douglas had mentioned to me that he had met somebody who had been in the same ship that Lord Douglas of Hawick was. He introduced him to Lord Douglas at a skating rink.[204] He brought him one day to see me. I had never heard of him. He simply came in.

CARSON: It was quite unexpected?

WILDE: It was not a shock.

CARSON: The manner of his visit was quite unexpected?

WILDE: Yes, I had not asked him to bring anybody.

CARSON: Was it in the evening?

WILDE: No, it was in the afternoon.

CARSON: Did he spend the evening with you?

WILDE: Oh, no, certainly not.

CARSON: Or with Taylor in your presence, in your company?

WILDE: Oh, no.

CARSON: Did you ask him to call again?

WILDE: I asked them both to dine with me.

CARSON: That day?

WILDE: Oh, no, I don't know when. I cannot fix a day.

CARSON: Did you ask Scarfe to call again?

WILDE: Not to call again on me. I asked them both to dinner

about four or five days afterwards. I mean, I fixed a date at the time.

CARSON: Where did you dine – Kettner's?

WILDE: I suppose Kettner's, probably – yes, Kettner's.

CARSON: Was Taylor there?

WILDE: Yes.

CARSON: Taylor and Scarfe?

WILDE: Yes.

CARSON: Nobody else?

WILDE: I don't think anybody else.

CARSON: Nobody else?

WILDE: Nobody else.

CARSON: Had you a private room?

WILDE: I forget whether it was in a public or a private room, I forget. It might have been a private room, I forget.

CARSON: Did you take him back with you that night to St James's Place?

WILDE: No.

CARSON: After dinner?

WILDE: No.

CARSON: Did you ever kiss him?

WILDE: Never in my life.

CARSON: Or caress him in any way?

WILDE: No.

CARSON: Or attempt to have indecencies with him?

WILDE: Never in my life.

CARSON: Why did you ask him to dinner?

WILDE: Because I am very good-natured, because it is one of the best ways perhaps of pleasing anybody, particularly anyone not in one's social position, to ask him to dine. (*Laughter.*)

CARSON: Did you give him any money?

WILDE: No, I did not give Scarfe any money.

CARSON: You never gave Scarfe any money or any presents?

WILDE: Oh, yes, I gave him a cigarette case. It is my custom to present cigarette cases. (*Laughter.*)

CARSON: This was it? (*He produces it.*)

WILDE: I have given so many cigarette cases I cannot verify them. It was a cigarette case. Whether it is that or no, I don't know. Yes, for a Christmas present I gave it to him.

CARSON: When did you last see Scarfe?

WILDE: In the month of January of this year – no, in the month of February of this year.

CARSON: Where did you see him?

WILDE: At the Avondale Hotel.

CARSON: Did he dine with you there?

WILDE: Yes.

CARSON: Was he in employment then?

WILDE: Yes.

CARSON: Where? Well, I will not ask for the name, of course. What employment had he?

WILDE: He told me he had a clerkship. I don't know that it is necessary to give the address – in St Paul's Churchyard.[205]

CARSON: Yes, I know. Now, tell me, when did you first get to know Sydney Mavor?

WILDE: In, I think, the beginning of, well, I think it was September 1892.

CARSON: How old was he?

WILDE: I say my impression was Sydney Mavor was twenty-five.

CARSON: Is this his photograph? (*He produces the photograph.*)

WILDE: Yes, that is his photograph, yes; but that, I think, is taken at a somewhat earlier period than I have seen him. That could be verified by the photographer. He was much older looking than that when I saw him. However, photographers flatter.

CARSON: And was it Taylor introduced Mavor to you?

WILDE: No.

CARSON: Who?

WILDE: Well, the gentleman whose name has not been mentioned.

CARSON: What?

WILDE: The gentleman whose name has been handed up.

CARSON: The gentleman who went to Paris?

WILDE: Yes.

CARSON: The same man who introduced you to Atkins you say?

WILDE: Yes.

CARSON: Do you know where that gentleman is who introduced you to him?

WILDE: At the present moment?

CARSON: Yes.

WILDE: No, I do not know.

CARSON: Do you know whether he is in this country?

WILDE: I don't. I have not heard from him for eighteen months or two years.

CARSON: Mavor, I think you told me, used to be at tea at Taylor's?

WILDE: I think I have met him there, yes. Oh, yes, yes. I have – I know – yes.

CARSON: Did you give him any money?

WILDE: Oh, no, never.

CARSON: Never?

WILDE: Never.

CARSON: Did you ever give Taylor any money to give to him?

WILDE: Oh, never, never.

CARSON: Never?

WILDE: Oh, never.

CARSON: Were you present when Taylor gave him any money?

WILDE: To Sydney Mavor?

CARSON: Yes.

WILDE: Never in my life.

CARSON: Did Taylor ever tell you he gave him money?

WILDE: Never. Oh, never. I don't know what you mean – money.

CARSON: Did you give him a cigarette case?

WILDE: No, I don't think I gave him a cigarette case, no.

CARSON: You did not give Mavor a cigarette case?

WILDE: No, I don't think so.

CARSON: You dealt at a shop in Bond Street for a good many of these cigarette cases?

WILDE: At Henry Lewis, yes.

CARSON: And another shop?

WILDE: Oh, Thornhill's, yes.

CARSON: Can you give the date when you first met Mavor?

9. Sidney Mavor, one of the more 'respectable' young men whose company Wilde enjoyed between 1892 and 1895, but who later denied that any 'indecencies' had taken place between them.

WILDE: Well, my impression is that it was September 1892.

CARSON: Didn't you tell Thornhill to send a cigarette case value four pounds eleven shillings and sixpence to Mavor on the 3rd of October?[206]

WILDE: If it is there, it was a cigarette case. I knew I had given him something.

CARSON: To S. A. Mavor?

WILDE: Yes, S. A. Mavor.

CLARKE: What date do you say?

CARSON: The 3rd of October 1892; four pounds eleven shillings and sixpence. What did you give him the cigarette case for?

WILDE: Why do I give people whom I like presents? Of course if I like them, I like giving them presents. I like doing it.

CARSON: You had only known him a month?

WILDE: I think that is quite long enough to express admiration or interest. A present that I give, might have been on a birthday or anything – it is absurd to go on like this about it – a present I usually give to anybody I like.

CARSON: Anybody you like when you have known them a month?

WILDE: Oh, a month – it doesn't require that.

CARSON: Did you invite him to dine?

WILDE: Oh, yes.

CARSON: At an hotel in Albemarle Street?

WILDE: Invite him to dine at an hotel in Albemarle Street?

CARSON: What?

WILDE: He stayed with me at an hotel in Albemarle Street.

CARSON: He stayed with you?

WILDE: Yes.

CARSON: He stayed a night there?

WILDE: He stayed a night there, yes.

CARSON: When was that?

WILDE: That was, I think, in October.

CARSON: After you had given him the cigarette case?

WILDE: After I had, yes.

CARSON: I suggest to you it was the 19th of October?

WILDE: That it was the 19th?

CARSON: Yes.

WILDE: Oh, yes, I dare say it was in October. I know I was coming back from Scotland. I was on my way through London.

CARSON: And you stayed yourself one night at this hotel?

WILDE: Yes.

CARSON: And you asked Sydney Mavor to stay there too?

WILDE: Yes, he met me at the station when I arrived and knew that I was going through London, going to stay at the Albemarle, and he came and we dined and stayed there.

CARSON: And you both only stayed there the one night?

WILDE: Oh, yes, that was all.

CARSON: Was he living in London at the time?

WILDE: Somewhere near London. Oh, yes, in London, certainly, in London.

CARSON: Notting Hill, I think?

WILDE: Yes, Notting Hill or West Kensington, certainly, yes.

CARSON: Did your bedrooms communicate?

WILDE: Of that I have not the smallest recollection.

CARSON: What?

WILDE: I have no recollection of that; they may or may not.

CARSON: What did he stay there that night for?

WILDE: He stayed there because I had asked him to meet me at the station. He came there and I asked him to stay with me – I was going to stay – for companionship.

CARSON: But he didn't stay the night for companionship, did he?

WILDE: Not the night, it was an amusement, a pleasure to him to stay with me at an hotel.

CARSON: But was it any pleasure at night?

WILDE: It was the pleasure of the evening passed with me and next morning we met at breakfast.

CARSON: Is that the reason he stayed with you?

WILDE: Yes, I like to have people staying with me, I like it.

CARSON: Did you pay for him?

WILDE: Oh, yes, certainly – I had asked him.

CARSON: Did any indecencies take place between you?

WILDE: Oh, none at all, none at all.

CARSON: Did he ever stay with you again?

WILDE: I don't think ever again, no.

CARSON: You have stayed many times in hotels in Albemarle Street since then?

WILDE: Oh, many times.

CARSON: I want to know weren't the three rooms you had there a sitting room and two bedrooms 26, 27 and 28?[207]

WILDE: Yes, I don't remember the numbers of the rooms.

CARSON: They were communicating?

WILDE: Yes, a set of rooms, two bedrooms and a sitting room.

CARSON: Did you take the room for him?

WILDE: Certainly, the bedroom for him.

CARSON: You both came to the hotel together?

WILDE: Yes.

CARSON: You did not enter his name in the hotel book?

WILDE: I have never been asked at the Albemarle Hotel to make any entry either of my own name or anybody's.

CARSON: Did you give them the name?

WILDE: I am sure I must have said it to the servants.

CARSON: It is not entered.

WILDE: Yes, that is nothing. I don't suppose my name is entered; my name is not entered in my handwriting. I have never been asked to.

CARSON: He never stayed with you another night?

WILDE: No.

CARSON: For companionship?

WILDE: I object to your using that phrase.

CARSON: You said it.

WILDE: You asked me why he stayed with me. I said because I was on my way through London. There was no one at home. It was pleasant for me to have a companion. It was pleasant for him to stay at a smart, nice hotel.

CARSON: He could have got home to Notting Hill in twenty minutes or half an hour?

WILDE: Yes, it amused him to be my guest, it is a very nice, charming hotel.

CARSON: Had he luggage with him?

WILDE: Yes.

CARSON: Did you tell him to bring his luggage?

WILDE: Yes.

CARSON: And to stay the night.

WILDE: Oh, yes, I had invited him.

CARSON: And to stay the night?

WILDE: Yes.

CARSON: Did you ever after that have him to dine with you again?

WILDE: Yes.

CARSON: Where?

WILDE: What date are you talking of?

CARSON: October 19th.

WILDE: Oh, yes, he often dined with me after that.

CARSON: Where?

WILDE: I suppose Kettner's – the Solferino – he certainly dined with me three or four times.

CARSON: Was Taylor there?

WILDE: Yes.

CARSON: Taylor was generally at the dinners he was at?

WILDE: Though – I don't remember particularly whether he was but—

CARSON: Frequently?

WILDE: Frequently? There were not frequent dinners. He dined with me also the last time I saw him at the beginning of last year – he dined with me.

CARSON: Was Mavor very intimate with Taylor?

WILDE: That I couldn't tell you. I had not met him in Taylor's rooms, but I had seen him there as I was for a very short time in London only, about two months or so.[208]

CARSON: Did you know he used sometimes to stay with Taylor?

WILDE: No, I never knew that – no.

CARSON: Did you know Walter Grainger?[209]

WILDE: Yes.

CARSON: What was he?

WILDE: A servant at Lord Alfred Douglas's rooms in Oxford.

CARSON: In Oxford?

WILDE: Yes.

CARSON: High Street, Oxford?[210]

WILDE: Yes.

CARSON: How old was he?

WILDE: I should think about sixteen.

CARSON: You used to go down to those rooms, Mr Wilde, sometimes?

WILDE: They were the rooms of Lord Alfred Douglas and Lord Encombe. I constantly stayed from Saturday to Monday, I think, certainly three times from Saturday to Monday.[211]

CARSON: In 1893?

WILDE: In 1893, yes.

CARSON: Were you on familiar terms with Grainger?

WILDE: What do you mean by 'familiar terms'?

CARSON: I mean to say did you have him to dine with you or anything of that kind?

WILDE: Never in my life.

CARSON: What?

WILDE: No! It is really trying to ask me such a question. No, of course not. He waited on me at table; he did not dine with me.

CARSON: I thought he might have sat down. You drew no distinction.

WILDE: Do you think that in the case of Lord Alfred Douglas and Lord Encombe's rooms that would have happened with the servant?

CARSON: You told me yourself—

WILDE: It is a different thing – if it is people's duty to serve, it is their duty to serve; if it is their pleasure to dine, it is their pleasure to dine and their privilege.

CARSON: You say not?

WILDE: Certainly not.

CARSON: Did you ever kiss him?

WILDE: Oh, no, never in my life; he was a peculiarly plain boy.

CARSON: He was what?

WILDE: I said I thought him unfortunately – his appearance was so very unfortunately – very ugly – I mean – I pitied him for it.

CARSON: Very ugly?

WILDE: Yes.

CARSON: Do you say that in support of your statement that you never kissed him?

WILDE: No, I don't; it is like asking me if I kissed a doorpost; it is childish.

CARSON: Didn't you give me as the reason that you never kissed him that he was too ugly?

WILDE: *(warmly)*: No.[212]

CARSON: Why did you mention his ugliness?

WILDE: No, I said the question seemed to me like – your asking me whether I ever had him to dinner, and then whether I had kissed him – seemed to me merely an intentional insult on your part, which I have been going through the whole of this morning.

CARSON: Because he was ugly?

WILDE: No.

CARSON: Why did you mention the ugliness? I have to ask these questions.

WILDE: I say it is ridiculous to imagine that any such thing could possibly have occurred under any circumstances.

CARSON: Why did you mention his ugliness?

WILDE: For that reason. If you asked me if I had ever kissed a doorpost, I should say, 'No! Ridiculous! I shouldn't like to kiss a doorpost.' Am I to be cross-examined on why I shouldn't like to kiss a doorpost? The questions are grotesque.

CARSON: Why did you mention the boy's ugliness?

WILDE: I mentioned it perhaps because you stung me by an insolent question.

CARSON: Because I stung you by an insolent question?

WILDE: Yes, you stung me by an insolent question; you make me irritable.

CARSON: Did you say the boy was ugly, because I stung you by an insolent question?

WILDE: Pardon me, you sting me, insult me and try to unnerve me in every way. At times one says things flippantly when one should speak more seriously, I admit that, I admit it – I cannot help it. That is what you are doing to me.

CARSON: You said it flippantly? You mentioned his ugliness flippantly; that is what you wish to convey now?

WILDE: Oh, don't say what I wish to convey. I have given you my answer.

CARSON: Is that it, that that was a flippant answer?

WILDE: Oh, it was a flippant answer, yes; I will say it was certainly a flippant answer.

CARSON: Did ever any indecencies take place between you and Grainger?

WILDE: No, sir, none, none at all.

CARSON: Now, I think you went down in June 1893 to stay at Goring?

WILDE: Yes, I took a house there, yes.

CARSON: A place called 'The Cottage'?

WILDE: The Cottage, Goring – yes.

CARSON: Did you bring over Grainger from Oxford to attend on you there?

WILDE: Oh, yes, he was under the butler there. I had been asked – he asked me to get him a place. He had asked me at Oxford. He told me he was leaving those lodgings and asked me whether I could get him a place. When I took this house at Goring, it was suggested to me it would be a kindness to have Walter Grainger to attend.

CARSON: When he was there, Mr Wilde, did you ask him to come into your bedroom?[213]

WILDE: Never in my life.

CARSON: Or into your bed.

WILDE: No.

CARSON: Had he the bedroom next to yours?

WILDE: He had at first, yes; it was a very tiny house. There was great difficulty in distributing the servants.

CARSON: And so he had the bedroom next to yours?

WILDE: Yes; upstairs slept the butler in one room and the maid servants. Then, there were three other bedrooms, one was occupied by Lord Alfred Douglas, one by myself and a very tiny little one was occupied by Walter Grainger. Subsequently, on the arrival of my children, Walter Grainger slept in a sort of outhouse.

CARSON: But before your family arrived, as I understand, he had a bedroom next to yours?

WILDE: Yes.

CARSON: Do you know where the butler is that you had there?

WILDE: I have no idea at all.

CARSON: Now, Mr Wilde, you were staying at the Savoy, I think, from the 2nd of March 1893 to the 29th of March?

WILDE: Yes, if those are the dates, I know I stayed there in March some days.

CARSON: I think you told me at that time your house was shut up?

WILDE: My wife was away, my house was shut up part of the time; then my children came back. My wife was away in Italy at the time.

CARSON: Did you ever bring any boys into your bedroom at the Savoy?

WILDE: No, sir.

CARSON: What?

WILDE: No.

CARSON: Did you know a man at the Savoy Hotel, a masseur named Miggie?[214]

WILDE: There was a masseur there; I forget his name.

CARSON: Midgie or Miggie – I don't know how they pronounce it – used he occasionally to go in and massage you in the mornings?

WILDE: Yes.

CARSON: Will you say, Mr Wilde, when he came in, did he find a boy in your bed?

WILDE: Never.

CARSON: He has been a long time at the Savoy, hasn't he?

WILDE: I don't know how long he has been; I don't know.

CARSON: Had he been massaging you long?

WILDE: No; about ten days. I was very ill when I was at the Savoy. If there is any date you can correct me. I was very ill and I had been recommended massage, so I was massaged every morning, or a great many mornings.

CLARKE: Will you mention the time of year?

CARSON: It was March 1893. (*To* WILDE.) You changed your rooms, I think, at the Savoy at that time?

WILDE: Oh, yes, I changed my rooms.

CARSON: When you had been there a few days?

WILDE: Yes.

CARSON: You went into other rooms?

WILDE: Yes.

CARSON: Was it from there, when you were there, that you wrote that letter which we had produced yesterday saying you had got a sitting room looking out on the Thames?

WILDE: Yes.

CARSON: And you say in neither of these rooms, neither the one you had first – the bedroom you had first – or the bedroom that you got upon the second occasion – in neither of them did you ever bring a boy?

WILDE: No, never.

CARSON: And there never was a boy in your bed there?

WILDE: Oh, never, never, certainly not.

CARSON: You have gone frequently to this place in Paris, haven't you?

WILDE: Oh, yes, yes, often.

CARSON: When were you last there – the same house, I mean, that you had Atkins at?

WILDE: I think in January; I forget really what year.

CARSON: February 1893, I suggest to you.

WILDE: Yes, I was, February 1893.[215]

CARSON: Did you go on any subsequent occasion to get in there and find it was too full and could not get in?

WILDE: No.

CARSON: What?

WILDE: No.

CARSON: Did you go on any subsequent occasions there at all?

WILDE: No, I don't think I did.

CARSON: Did you apply for rooms there and were you told it was full, whether by letter—?

WILDE: Never in my life – no.

CARSON: What?

WILDE: Never.

CARSON: Mr Wilde, upon any of these occasions – I am not talking of the time Atkins was there – did you bring boys into your bed?

WILDE: Never.

CARSON: Or a boy?

WILDE: Never.

CARSON: At this hotel?

WILDE: Never.

CARSON: Never on any occasion or into your sitting room?

WILDE: Let me ask you what you mean – what you limit the word boy to – I mean, to what age?

CARSON: Lads.

WILDE: Oh, yes – no.

CARSON: About twenty.

WILDE: About twenty.

CARSON: Eighteen to twenty?

WILDE: Oh, I have many friends in Paris from eighteen to twenty.

CARSON: And you used to bring them there?

WILDE: I don't know about bringing – they used to call on me and see me.

CARSON: Late at night?

WILDE: No, they would call at teatime or dinner time – any time.

CARSON: Used any of them to come late at night, twelve or one o'clock?

WILDE: Oh, no, I don't think anyone has ever called on me at such an hour – certainly not.

CARSON: And stayed there till four or five in the morning?

WILDE: Certainly not.

CARSON: What?

WILDE: Certainly not.

CARSON: Only one question more. It would take some time probably to get him, but you would know the waiter who waited upon you there in Paris if you saw him?[216]

WILDE: I don't know whether I should.

CARSON: You were there very frequently.

WILDE: Yes, I don't know that I should recognise him.

CARSON: He used to take you in coffee every morning?

WILDE: I stayed so many times, at least I stayed on three or four different occasions, and always had different rooms. I don't know whether I should remember him.

OSCAR WILDE *is re-examined by* SIR EDWARD CLARKE.

CLARKE: You were first asked whether you were aware that Lord Queensberry objected to your acquaintance with his son being continued. Will you kindly take those letters into your hand and tell me first: were those letters written by Lord Queensberry? (*The letters are handed to* WILDE.)

WILDE: Yes.

CLARKE: Secondly, will you answer this question 'yes' or 'no': were those letters communicated to you by the persons who received them?

WILDE: Yes.

CLARKE: Thirdly, were those letters the only—

WILDE (*interposing*): If you will allow me – in the case of one, it was not by the person to whom it was addressed.

CLARKE: Very well, but still it was communicated to you?

WILDE: Oh, yes, it was brought to me.

CLARKE: Was it from those letters that you gathered the statement, which you made to my learned friend, that Lord Queensberry objected to your continued intimacy?

WILDE: Yes.

CLARKE: I put those letters in, my lord.

CARSON: They are going to be read, I suppose?

CLARKE: I will read them. The first letter is from the Marquess of Queensberry to Lord Alfred Douglas. It is dated 'Carter's Hotel, 14 & 15 Albemarle Street, W. Sunday, 1st April'.

Alfred – It is extremely painful to me to have to write to you in the strain I must, but please understand I decline to receive any answers from you in writing in return. After your recent, hysterical, impertinent ones, I refuse to be annoyed with such, and I decline to read any more letters. If you have anything to say, do come here and say it in person. Firstly, am I to understand that, having left Oxford as you did, with discredit to yourself, the reasons of which were fully explained to me by your tutor, you now intend to loaf and loll about and do nothing? All the time you were wasting at Oxford I was put off with an assurance that you were eventually to go into the Civil Service or to the Foreign Office, and then I was put off with an assurance that you were going to the Bar. It appears to me that you intend to do nothing. I utterly decline, however, to just supply you with sufficient funds to enable you to loaf about. You are preparing a wretched future for yourself, and it would be most cruel and wrong for me to encourage you in this.

Secondly, I come to the more painful part of this letter – your intimacy with this man Wilde. It must either cease or I will disown you and stop all money supplies. I am not going to try and analyse this intimacy, and I make no charge; but to my mind to pose as a thing is as bad as to be it. With my own eyes I saw you both in the most loathsome and disgusting relationship as expressed by your manner and expression. Never, in my experience, have I seen such a sight as that in your horrible features. No wonder people are talking as they are. Also, I now hear on good authority, but this may be false, that his wife is petitioning to divorce him for sodomy and other crimes. Is this true, or do you not know of it? If I thought the actual thing was true, and it became public property, I should be quite justified in shooting him at sight. These Christian English cowards and men, as they call themselves, want waking up.

Your disgusted so-called father,

QUEENSBERRY

That is dated the 1st of April.

WILDE: Naturally.

CLARKE: How long was that after the interview at the Café Royal, the second interview with Lord Queensberry of which you spoke when you had parted on friendly terms?

WILDE: I should think about three days or four days.

CLARKE: There is a statement in that letter: 'I hear on good authority that his wife is petitioning to divorce him on the grounds of sodomy and unnatural crimes.' Is there the slightest foundation for that statement?

WILDE: Not the slightest.

CLARKE: The next is dated 'Tuesday, 3rd April, Carter's Hotel, 14 & 15 Albemarle Street, W', again addressed to Lord Alfred Douglas. 'You impertinent young jackanapes. I request you will not send me such messages through the telegraph—'

CARSON: Where is the telegram that Lord Alfred Douglas sent to his father? Put it in. It is only fair.

CLARKE: My lord, I will put in at once the telegram. 'To Queensberry, Carter's Hotel, Albemarle Street. What a funny little man you are. Alfred Douglas.' The answer is:

You impertinent young jackanapes. I request you will not send me such messages through the telegraph. If you send me any more such telegrams, or come with any impertinence, I will give you the thrashing you deserve. Your only excuse is that you must be crazy. I hear from a man at Oxford that you were thought crazy there, and that accounts for a good deal that has happened. If I catch you again with that man, I will make a public scandal in a way you little dream of; it is already a suppressed one. I prefer an open one, and at any rate I shall not be blamed for allowing such a state of things to go on. Unless this acquaintance ceases, I shall carry out my threat and stop all supplies, and if you are not going to make any attempt to do something, I shall certainly cut you down to a mere pittance, so you know what to expect,

QUEENSBERRY

The next is a letter from Lord Queensberry to Mr Alfred Montgomery, the father-in-law of Lord Queensberry, the father of

215

Lady Queensberry who divorced him. This is dated from 'Skindles, Maidenhead Bridge, Berks. Friday, 6th, Morning, 6 o'clock'. That is Friday the 6th of July, my lord:

Sir. I have changed my mind, and as I am not at all well, having been very much upset by what has happened the last ten days, I do not see why I should come dancing attendance upon you. Your daughter is the person who is supporting my son to defy me. She won't write, but she is now telegraphing on the subject to me. Last night, after hearing from you, I received a very quibbling, prevaricating message from her, saying the boy denied having been at the Savoy for the last year; but why send the telegram unless he could deny that he had been there with Oscar Wilde at all? As a matter of fact he did, and there has been a stinking scandal. I am told they were warned off, but the proprietor would not admit this. This hideous scandal has been going on for years. Your daughter must be mad by the way she is behaving. She evidently wants to make out that I want to make out a case against my son. It is nothing of the kind. I have made out a case against Oscar Wilde and I have to his face accused him of it. If I was quite certain of the thing I would shoot the fellow on sight, but I can only accuse him of posing. It now lies in the hands of the two whether they will further defy me. Your daughter appears now to be encouraging them, although she can hardly intend this. I don't believe Wilde will now dare defy me. He plainly showed the white feather the other day when I tackled him – damned cur and coward of the Rosebery type. As for this so-called son of mine, he is no son of mine, and I will have nothing to do with him. He may starve as far as I am concerned after his behaviour to me. His mother may support him, but she shan't do that here in London with this awful scandal going on. But your daughter's conduct is outrageous, and I am now fully convinced that the Rosebery–Gladstone–Royal insult that came to me through my other son, that she worked that – I thought it was you. I saw Drumlanrig here on the river, which much upset me.

That was the eldest son who died since.

It shall be known some day by all that Rosebery not only insulted me by lying to the Queen which she knows, which makes her as bad as him and Gladstone, but also has made a lifelong quarrel between my son and I.

QUEENSBERRY

The next one was written from Scotland to Lord Alfred Douglas on the 21st of August 1894:

I have received your postcard, which I presume is from you, but as the writing is utterly unreadable to me have been unable to make out hardly one sentence.[217] My object of receiving no written communication from you is therefore kept intact. All future cards will go into the fire unread. I presume these are the 'hyerogliphics' [*sic*] of the OW posing [sodomites] club, of which you have the reputation of being such a shining light. I congratulate you on your autography; it is beautiful and should help you get a living. I don't know what at but, say, crossing-sweeping. My friend I am staying with has made out some of your letter, and wished to read it to me, but I declined to hear a word. However, according to his advice I shall keep it as a specimen, and also as a protection in case I ever feel tempted to give you the thrashing you really deserve. You reptile. You are no son of mine and I never thought you were.

QUEENSBERRY

The next letter, the last, is the 28th of August 1894, 26 Portland Place W. It is to Lord Alfred Douglas:

You miserable creature. I received your telegram by post from Carter's and have requested them not to forward any more, but just to tear any up, as I did yours, without reading it, directly I was aware from whom it came. You must be flush of money to waste it on such rubbish. I have learned, thank goodness, to turn the keenest pangs to peacefulness. What could be keener pain than to have such a son as yourself fathered upon one? However, there is always a bright side to every cloud, and whatever is is light [*sic*]. If you are my son, it is only confirming proof to me, if I needed any, how right I was to face every horror and misery I have done rather than run the risk of bringing more creatures into the world like yourself, and that was the entire and only reason of my breaking with your mother as a wife, so intensely was I dissatisfied with her as the mother of you children, and particularly yourself, whom, when quite a baby, I cried over you the bitterest tears a man ever shed, that I had brought such a creature into the world, and unwittingly had committed such a crime. If you are not my son, and in this Christian country with these hypocrites, 'tis a wise father who knows his own child, and no wonder on the principles they intermarry on, but to be forewarned is to be forearmed. No wonder you have fallen a prey to this horrible brute. I am only sorry for you as a human creature. You must 'gang your ain gait'. Well, it would be rather a satisfaction to me, because the crime then is not to me. As you see, I am philosophical and take comfort from anything; but, really, I am sorry for you. You must be demented; there is madness on your mother's side, and indeed few families in this Christian country are without it, if you look into them. But please cease annoying me, for I will not correspond with you, nor receive nor answer letters, and as for money, you sent me a lawyer's letter to say you would take none from me, but anyhow, until you change your life I should refuse any; it depends on yourself whether I will ever recognise you at all again after your behaviour. I will make allowance; I think you are demented and I am very sorry for you.

QUEENSBERRY

Mr Wilde, were those the letters which conveyed the wish, that it is suggested came to your knowledge, that Lord Queensberry had, that you should cease your acquaintance with his son?

WILDE: Yes.

CLARKE: And having regard to the contents of those letters and the nature of those letters, did you or did you not think it right to take any notice of that wish?

WILDE: Would you kindly repeat your question, Sir Edward?

CLARKE: Having regard to the character of those letters, did you or did you not think it right to disregard the wish that was referred to?

WILDE: I thought it right to entirely disregard it.[218]

CLARKE: And I think I asked you before, your friendship with Lady Queensberry and the sons continues to the present time?

WILDE: Yes.

CLARKE: Now, you have been asked some questions which I must go through. I must just ask you two or three questions with regard to the literary matters. With respect to *The Chameleon*, you have told us the extent of your connection with that book.

WILDE: Yes.

CLARKE: As to *Dorian Gray*, it is suggested to you that in consequence of objections to the character of the book as it was published in America, it was altered with a view to purge or tone it down for the purpose of the English publication. Is there any ground for that?

WILDE: No, I would not use the word 'purge' or 'tone down'. I can point the passage out. Yes, it was pointed out to me that a certain passage in *Dorian Gray* – pointed out to me by Mr Walter Pater – he said, 'I think there that the veil of mystery that makes this book interesting – that there, some people reading there would definitely say, "Here is the sin."' I respected his opinion more than that of anybody I had ever met.

JUDGE: I did not quite catch it: 'People would say, "Here is—".' You said something?

WILDE: Yes, 'Here is the definite sin of Dorian Gray', my idea having been to write a book with a certain atmosphere about it.

CLARKE: I believe, Mr Wilde, that Mr Walter Pater wrote you several letters upon the subject of the book?

WILDE: Yes.

CARSON: Would that be evidence?

CLARKE: The fact that he wrote letters?

CARSON: You cannot mention the subject, but just the fact that he wrote letters.

CLARKE: I beg your pardon.

CARSON: I beg yours.

JUDGE: What is the objection?

CARSON: I submit the witness cannot give evidence of the contents of these letters, my lord.

JUDGE: No, he can refer to the subject matter of them, though.

CLARKE: I believe Mr Pater wrote you several letters with regard to this book and in deference to his opinion you modified one passage?

WILDE: Not in consequence of anything said in any letter of his – in consequence of what he said one afternoon in my house.

CLARKE: At all events in deference to that, there was one passage modified which you are prepared to show if necessary?

WILDE: Yes.

CLARKE: The book being published was, I think, very widely reviewed indeed?

WILDE: Yes, very widely.

CLARKE: And was reviewed by among others Mr Pater himself?

WILDE: Yes, by Mr Pater himself.

CLARKE: In the *Bookman* of November 1891. I believe your attention was called to a criticism upon the book which was published in the *Scots Observer*?

WILDE: Yes.

CLARKE: To which you yourself replied?

WILDE: Yes.

CLARKE: My lord, only a fragment of that letter was read and I just want to read it. Your letter was written to the editor of the *Scots Observer* dated the 9th of July 1890:

Sir, You have published a review of my story, *The Picture of Dorian Gray*. As this review is grossly unjust to me as an artist, I ask you to allow me to exercise in your columns my right of reply. Your reviewer, sir, while admitting that the story in question is 'plainly the work of a man of letters', the work of one who has 'brains, and art, and style', yet suggests, and apparently in all seriousness, that I have written it in order that it should be read by the most depraved members of the criminal and illiterate classes. Now, sir, I do not suppose that the criminal and illiterate classes ever read anything except newspapers. They are certainly not likely to be able to understand anything of mine. So let them pass, and on the broad question of why a man of letters writes at all let me say this. The pleasure that one has in creating a work of art is a purely personal pleasure, and it is for the sake of this pleasure that one creates. The artist works with his eye on the object. Nothing else interests him. What people are likely to say does not even occur to him. He is fascinated by what he has in hand. He is indifferent to others. I write because it gives me the greatest possible artistic pleasure to write. If my work pleases the few, I am gratified. If it does not, it causes me no pain. As for the mob, I have no desire to be a popular novelist. It is far too easy. Your critic then, sir, commits the absolutely unpardonable crime of trying to confuse the artist with his subject-matter. For this, sir, there is no excuse at all. Of one who is the greatest figure in the world's literature since Greek days Keats remarked that he had as much pleasure in conceiving the evil as he had in conceiving the good. Let your reviewer, sir, consider the bearings of Keats's fine criticism, for it is under these conditions that every artist works. One stands remote from one's subject-matter. One creates it, and one contemplates it. The further away the subject-matter is, the more freely can the artist work. Your reviewer suggests that I do not make it sufficiently clear whether I prefer virtue to wickedness or wickedness to virtue. An artist, sir, has no ethical sympathies at all. Virtue and wickedness are to him simply what the colours on his palette are to the painter. They are no more, and they are no less. He sees that by their means a certain artistic effect can be produced, and he produces it. Iago may be morally horrible and Imogen stainlessly pure, Shakespeare, as Keats said, had as much delight in creating the one as he had in creating the other.

It was necessary, sir, for the dramatic development of this story to surround Dorian Gray with an atmosphere of moral corruption. Otherwise the story would have had no meaning and the plot no issue. To keep this atmosphere vague and indeterminate and wonderful was the aim of the artist who wrote the story. I claim, sir, that he has succeeded. Each man sees his own sin in Dorian Gray. What Dorian Gray's sins are no one knows. He who finds them has brought them.

In conclusion, sir, let me say how really deeply I regret that you should have permitted such a notice as the one I feel constrained to write on to have appeared in your paper. That the editor of the *St James's Gazette* should have employed Caliban as his art-critic was possibly natural. The editor of the *Scots Observer* should not have allowed Thersites to make mows in his review. It is unworthy of so distinguished a man of letters.

I am, etc.

OSCAR WILDE

There was, I think, a violent attack upon the book in the *St James's Gazette?*[219]

WILDE: Yes, a most violent attack.

CLARKE: A passage was read yesterday from *The Picture of Dorian Gray* but the answer was not read.

CARSON: That is because that part is not in *Lippincott's.*

CLARKE: Whether it is in *Lippincott's* or not, my lord, I must read the passage that my learned friend read yesterday in order to read the answer.

CARSON: What page?

CLARKE: Page 224. The painter speaking to Dorian says,

'Why is it that so many gentlemen in London will neither go to your house nor invite you to theirs? You used to be a friend of Lord Staveley. I met him at dinner last week. Your name happened to come up in conversation, in connection with the miniatures you have lent to the exhibition at the Dudley. Staveley curled his lip, and said that you might have the most artistic tastes, but that you were a man whom no pure-minded girl should be allowed to know, and whom no chaste woman should sit in the same room with. I reminded him that I was a friend of yours, and asked him what he meant. He told me. He told me right out before everybody. It was horrible! Why is your friendship so fatal to young men? There was that wretched boy in the Guards who committed suicide. You were his great friend. There was Sir Henry Ashton, who had to leave England, with a tarnished name. You and he were inseparable. What about Adrian Singleton, and his dreadful end? What about Lord Kent's only son, and his career? I met his father yesterday in St James's Street. He seemed broken with shame and sorrow. What about the young Duke of Perth? What sort of life has he got now? What gentleman would associate with him?'

That was the passage read yesterday.

CARSON: It is right to say the rest of it is not in the first edition of *Lippincott's*. This is put in.

CHARLES GILL: All this is now written in? The whole of it?

WILDE: That is the alteration I made – the alteration I made is in the answer.

CLARKE: If you please, then, that is the alteration you made:

'Stop, Basil. You are talking about things of which you know nothing,' said Dorian Gray, biting his lip, and with a note of infinite contempt in his voice. 'You ask me why Berwick leaves a room when I enter it. It is because I know everything about his life, not because he knows anything about mine. With such blood as he has in his veins, how could his record be clean? You ask me about Henry Ashton and young Perth. Did I teach the one his vices, and the other his debauchery? If Kent's silly son takes his wife from the streets, what is that to me? If Adrian Singleton writes his friend's name across a bill, am I his keeper? I know how people chatter in England. The middle classes air their moral prejudices over their gross dinner-tables, and whisper about what they call the profligacies of their betters in order to try and pretend that they are in smart society, and on intimate terms with the people they slander. In this country it is enough for a man to have distinction and brains for every common tongue to wag against him. And what sort of lives do these people, who pose as being moral, lead themselves? My dear fellow, you forget that we are in the native land of the hypocrite.'

'Dorian,' cried Hallward, 'that is not the question. England is bad enough, I know, and English society is all wrong. That is the reason why I want you to be fine. You have not been fine. One had a right to judge of a man by the effect he has over his friends. Yours seem to lose all sense of honour, of goodness, of purity. You have filled them with a madness for pleasure. They have gone down into the depths. You led them there. Yes: you led them there, and yet you can smile, as you are smiling now. And there is worse behind. I know you and Harry are inseparable. Surely for that reason, if for none other, you should not have made his sister's name a by-word.'

I think substantially, my lord, that closes the passage.

CARSON: That is left out: 'Dorian, Dorian, your reputation is infamous.'

CLARKE: That is the substance of it. Now, to pass to the other matters. You have said that several of these young fellows, whose names have been mentioned here, were introduced to you by Alfred Taylor?

WILDE: Yes.

CLARKE: When did you first know Alfred Taylor?

WILDE: In October 1892, I think so, yes, October – (*a pause*) – 1893 it must be – no, I think it must be—

CLARKE: It must have been 1892, I think?

WILDE: 1893, yes.

CLARKE: I think you must have known him in October 1892?

WILDE: October 1892 yes, yes I remember.

CLARKE: Were you introduced to him by the gentleman whose name has been written down and referred to?

WILDE: Yes.

CLARKE: I quite concur in omitting names in this case which are not absolutely necessary, but is that gentleman a gentleman of position and repute?

WILDE: A gentleman of high position, good birth and good repute.

CLARKE: How long is it since you saw him?

WILDE: Oh, March or February 1894. I have not seen him, of course, he has not been in England for two years.

CLARKE: He has not been in England for two years?

WILDE: No.

CLARKE: And has not been available for the purpose of coming here in this case?

WILDE: Oh, impossible. I have not heard from him for a year and a half.

JUDGE: You last saw him, I understand, a year ago?

WILDE: Oh, more than that, my lord, two years ago.

CLARKE: At the time that you were introduced to Alfred Taylor, was Alfred Taylor living at this 13 Little College Street?

WILDE: Yes.

CLARKE: Did you know anything about his having any occupation or the extent of the means which he had at his control?

WILDE: Alfred Taylor?

CLARKE: Yes.

WILDE: No, I knew that he had lost a great deal of money that he had inherited, but that he had still a share in a very important business.

CLARKE: Did you know where Alfred Taylor had been educated?

WILDE: Yes.

CLARKE: Where?

WILDE: At Marlborough School.

CLARKE: Was he a well-educated young man?

WILDE: Yes, certainly.

CLARKE: Had he any accomplishments?

WILDE: Yes, he plays the piano very charmingly.

CLARKE: And you from time to time went to see him?

WILDE: Yes.

CLARKE: And were introduced by him to different other persons?

WILDE: Yes.

CLARKE: You have continued your acquaintance with Alfred Taylor?

WILDE: Yes.

CLARKE: Had you at the time of your introduction to him, or have you ever had since, any reason to believe that Alfred Taylor was an immoral and disreputable person?

WILDE: None whatsoever.

CLARKE: You have been asked some questions, Mr Wilde, as to whether you saw in August of last year a notice in the paper with regard to Alfred Taylor and Charles Parker having been with other persons arrested?

WILDE: Yes.

CLARKE: Do you happen to remember in what newspaper you saw it?

WILDE: I think it was in the *Daily Chronicle.*

CLARKE: Do you remember the extent of the information that you got? You have not the paper at hand at this moment. What was it that you saw in the paper?

WILDE: That a raid had been made by the police on a house, I think in Fitzroy Street, that two men had driven up to the house in female attire, that they were at once arrested. The police then entered the house where they found dancing and singing going on and arrested everybody who was there.

CLARKE: And that among the persons arrested—?

WILDE: Oh, yes, that among the persons arrested were Mr Alfred Taylor and Charles Parker.

CLARKE: Did you gather what was the charge made against them when they were before the magistrates?

WILDE: Oh, yes.

CLARKE: What was it?

WILDE: The charge was, as well as I remember – I don't remember the exact wording of these things – assembling there for an unlawful and felonious purpose.

CLARKE: Did you also ascertain what was the result of the charge so far, at all events, as Parker and Taylor were concerned?

WILDE: Yes, it was dismissed by the magistrate.

CLARKE: And I think you told us that some other people were fined. Of course, they could not be fined for that offence. I do not know whether you know for what it was that they were fined or whether you gathered that?

WILDE: I have no recollection at all.

CLARKE: My lord, we cannot ascertain immediately what the fines were inflicted for. I thought it was for having music and dancing only. (*To* WILDE.) You say that upon seeing that in the papers you were much distressed about it and I think you said you wrote to Mr Taylor?

WILDE: Yes.

CLARKE: You haven't his reply? Did he write to you in answer?

WILDE: He did. I have not got the letter.

CLARKE: But whether he wrote to you, or whether he gave you any account of it afterwards, or told you afterwards what had happened, what was the explanation which he gave you?

WILDE: He told me that it was a benefit concert that he had been given a ticket for, that when he arrived at the house there was dancing going on and he was asked to play the piano, that two music hall singers were expected to come in costume and they were not in the house, I think he said, at the time, but suddenly the police entered and arrested everybody.

CLARKE: And knowing that the charge had been dismissed and hearing Taylor's account of how it had happened, was there the slightest impression left upon your mind of imputation of blame to Taylor?

WILDE: None. I thought it a most monstrous thing – the arrest at the time. It seemed to me so. I was extremely sorry for him.

CLARKE: Now, I understand that of the persons whose names have been mentioned, several were introduced to you by Taylor?

WILDE: Yes.

CLARKE: I will take first the case which my learned friend referred to, which is not connected with Taylor, but the case of Shelley. It was put to you Shelley was an office boy, or something of that kind. Who first introduced you to Shelley?

WILDE: I was introduced to Edward Shelley by Mr John Lane, publisher.[220]

CLARKE: Was Mr John Lane publishing your book?

WILDE: Yes.

CLARKE: That is Mr John Lane of the firm of Mathews and Lane who are publishers at the Bodley Head at Vigo Street?

WILDE: Yes.

CLARKE: Were you informed upon that introduction, or did you ascertain whether this young man was a young man of literary tastes and ambitions himself?

WILDE: Mr Lane introduced me to Mr Edward Shelley and I shook hands with Mr Edward Shelley in Mr Lane's presence. He said, 'This is Mr Edward Shelley. He gives me great help, without whom I could not bring out my books' – something of that kind – something graceful. I happened, two or three days afterwards, to go into the shop again and I had a long talk about literature with Shelley.

CLARKE: With Edward Shelley?

WILDE: Yes.

CLARKE: Did you find him a person who had a certain amount of literary information and taste?

WILDE: A great deal of cultivation and a great desire for culture; a very interesting personality.

CLARKE: Did you from time to time go to this place at Vigo Street while the publication of your works was proceeding?

WILDE: Oh, often, yes, for a period extending over years.

CLARKE: Did you on many occasions find Shelley the only person in charge of the place?

WILDE: Yes.

CLARKE: And on those occasions did conversations upon literary subjects take place between you?

WILDE: Oh, yes, yes.

CLARKE: In February of 1892 I think the play of *Lady Windermere's Fan* was produced?

WILDE: Yes.

CLARKE: And did you give Mr Shelley some tickets?

WILDE: Yes, I gave him a ticket for the first night, a dress circle ticket.

CLARKE: On the evening of the first performance and after the play, which I think was a great success, Mr Wilde—

WILDE: It was a great success, yes.

CLARKE: Did you stop with some gentlemen – some friends?

WILDE: Yes.

CLARKE: And was Mr Edward Shelley at your invitation one of the party?

WILDE: I think so, but I am not quite sure. I am not quite sure of that but I think he was. I am not quite sure.

CLARKE: If you please, perhaps I ought to have asked you these questions. You have said that Mr Shelley was a person of literary information and of literary taste?

WILDE: Yes.

CLARKE: Was Mr Shelley, or did he profess to be, a great admirer of your own works?

WILDE: Yes, he was very well acquainted with all my works and very appreciative of them.

CLARKE: And you gratified that appreciation by presenting him with copies of your books?

WILDE: Oh, yes. I gave him, I think, three of my books.

CLARKE: It seems to me that in the copies of your works which are produced here as having been given by you to Mr Edward Shelley, the flyleaf upon which any inscription would have been written has been torn out. Did you ever write an inscription in any book given by you to Mr Edward Shelley which you would have the smallest objection to the whole world reading and seeing?[221]

WILDE: Never in my life, never.

CLARKE: I believe you went to Paris soon after the first performance of *Lady Windermere's Fan*?

WILDE: Yes.

CLARKE: And returned from Paris, I think, in the month of April 1892?

WILDE: Yes.

CLARKE: After your return did Mr Shelley dine with you at Tite Street?

WILDE: Yes.

CLARKE: With Mrs Wilde?

WILDE: Yes.

CLARKE: Was he in every way a gentleman whom you were content to introduce to your wife at your own table?

WILDE: In every way.

At this point the Court is adjourned for luncheon.

WILDE *does not appear until a few minutes after the Court has reassembled.*

WILDE: My lord, I hope you will allow me to offer my apologies for being late. The clock at the hotel where I was lunching was wrong and I regret it extremely.

WILDE *is further re-examined by* SIR EDWARD CLARKE.

CLARKE: Will you kindly just look at these letters and see if they are in the handwriting of Edward Shelley and if they are, will you kindly hand them back to me and then I will ask you a question.

WILDE: Yes, Sir Edward, these are in the handwriting of Edward Shelley.

CLARKE: Upon hearing the contents of the plea in this case, did you search for letters that you might have from Edward Shelley?

WILDE: Yes, I searched for the letters.

CLARKE: You found these letters and produce them?

WILDE: Those are all that I have found. There are many that I have torn up.

CLARKE: I want to read these letters. The first is 'Sunday evening, February 21st 1892, 3 Hildyard Road, Earls Court, SW':

Dear Mr Oscar Wilde, I must again thank you for the *House of Pomegranates* and the theatre ticket. It was very good of you to send them to me and I shall never forget your kindness. What a triumph was yours last night! The play was the best I have seen on the stage, such beauty of form and wit that it adds a new phase of pleasure to existence. Could Lady Blessington live now, the conversations would make her jealous.[222] George Meredith might have signed it. How miserably poor everything seems beside it, except of course your books: but then your books are a part of yourself. Mr B—— is a charming fellow. He quite agrees with these opinions.

Mr Wilde you know the name I have expressed only by an initial?[223]

WILDE: Oh, yes, very well.

CLARKE: Is that a gentleman of position and repute?

WILDE: Of position and repute.

CLARKE: Good repute?

WILDE: Very good repute.

CLARKE: Was he the gentleman who has been mentioned as having, on one occasion at all events, dined with you and Mr Shelley?

WILDE: Supped with me and Mr Shelley.

CLARKE: There is no reason except a desire to avoid pain which prevents me mentioning his name in this case.

WILDE: It was a desire to avoid pain to his family with whom I am on terms of most intimate friendship. If I might be allowed to say this, Sir Edward, I had given Mr Edward Shelley a seat in the dress circle next to this other friend of mine and had written to my friend to say: 'You will find a cultivated young man – his name is Edward Shelley – sitting beside you; pray talk to him.' I wanted to give him a companion.

CLARKE: And this gentleman and Mr Edward Shelley both supped with you afterwards?

WILDE: Not on that night, Sir Edward, subsequently.

CLARKE (*continuing*):

Mr B—— is a charming fellow. He quite agrees with these opinions. Could you favour me with his address? He gave me his card and I arranged to write or call upon him. Unfortunately the card has disappeared and I can do neither. I shall ask him to dine with me shortly and go to a theatre afterwards,

EDWARD SHELLEY

The next is 'Vigo Street, October 27th':

My dear Oscar, Will you be at home on Sunday evening next. I am most anxious to see you. I have called this morning, but I am suffering from nervousness, the results of insomnia and am obliged to remain at home. I have longed to see you all through the week. I have much to tell you. Do not think me forgetful in not coming before, for I shall never forget your kindness, and I am conscious that I can never sufficiently express my thankfulness. Please write a little note about Sunday.

Believe me, ever yours,

EDWARD SHELLEY

'3 Hildyard Road, Earls Court, SW, Sunday evening. My dear Oscar, I have decided to decline Mr Lane's offer of assistance.' That is dated 'January 8th 1893':

I cannot accept money of him. It was wrong of me even to have hesitated and now I wish to ask a favour of you. Will you, if you are not in town at the time of the performance, give me your seat at the Independent Theatre on the evening when Ibsen's *Ghosts* is performed. I'm very anxious to see this play and would esteem it a great favour if you will oblige me in this matter. People are beginning to clamour for *The Sphinx* and *Salomé* and you really must publish the latter before I leave Vigo Street. Ricketts called me and asked me for your address and I am convinced from his manner that something dreadful may happen unless he receives the manuscript of *The Sphinx* shortly.

Believe me ever yours,

EDWARD SHELLEY

Was *The Sphinx* a poem of yours?

WILDE: It is a poem of mine that was published by Messrs Mathews and Lane.

CLARKE: I believe you had read it to Mr Edward Shelley?

WILDE: I had given him the manuscript in the first instance in the month of January as he desired to see it. He had shown it to Mr Lane and Mr Mathews, and then they made me an offer to publish it with drawings and designs by Mr Ricketts – a most distinguished, if not the most distinguished of younger artists – and that is the gentleman alluded to who was anxious to see the manuscript to prepare his designs.[224]

CLARKE: As to *Salomé*, which it mentions, that was the French play which had, I hear, been written. I forget who published that play?

WILDE: It was printed in France but Messrs Mathews and Lane were anxious to have their name on the title page as well as the name of my French publishers and I had engaged that they should have so many copies – five hundred copies – with their name on them conjointly with that of the French publisher.[225]

CLARKE: That was a matter of business arrangement that was pending at that time?

WILDE: Yes, it was published, I think, about two months afterwards.

CLARKE: The next is 'March 27th 1893. 3 Hildyard Road, SW':

My dear Oscar, I have had a very horrible interview with my father and have been told to leave the house. I am on the verge of despair. I am sick and tired, body and soul, of my harsh existence. I am anxious to do work of some sort. My hopes in one direction are gone and my parents accuse me of idleness. It is monstrous. It is unjust. I am only too anxious to find employment of some nature but cannot succeed in doing so, and so I am eating the bitter food of charity and contempt. The stupid, brutal insults of Vigo Street are preferable to this.[226] I do not – cannot – think that I am entirely deficient in ordinary ability. Here am I stranded and without hope. I do not ask for more than sufficient to live upon, and by strict economy I can live upon six pounds per month, but even this I cannot obtain. Forgive my poor silly egoism – but I am in torture and do not know what to do.

Believe me ever yours,

EDWARD SHELLEY

If this note causes you any annoyance, do not, I implore you, answer it.

That is dated March 1893. At that time had he left the employ-ment of Messrs Mathews and Lane do you remember?

WILDE: Yes, I think at that time he had left that employment.

CLARKE: And was looking out for another situation?

WILDE: Was very anxious to get another situation, a situation with a publisher.

CLARKE: Now, the next is '3 Hildyard Road SW, Wednesday, April 25th 1894':

> Dear Oscar, I want you to help me if you will. I am living in absolute poverty and have lost my health and strength through trying to keep myself on four pounds three and four pence per month.

That is a salary of fifty pounds a year. Do you know where he had been getting that sum?

WILDE: In some commercial house in the city.[227]

CLARKE (*continuing*):

> Oscar, I want to go away and rest somewhere. I think in Cornwall for two weeks. I am determined to try and live a Christian life and I accept poverty as part of my religion, but I must have health. I have so much to do and for my mother and brothers and for myself – I mean my art. I am an artist: I know that I am. Will you see whether you are able to lend me ten pounds until Christmas. I can repay it by that time. I must have rest. I am weak, ill, people laugh at me. I am so thin they think me strange. Forgive me for asking this of you. I must have health and strength. I wait your reply.
>
> > Believe me always yours sincerely,
> > EDWARD SHELLEY

Did you or did you not lend him the ten pounds?

WILDE: My own impression is that after that letter I saw him. Would you tell me the date?

CLARKE: The 25th of April 1894.

WILDE: I certainly lent him five pounds, certainly, about that time, or gave it to him, I should say. I do not lend money. I give it.[228]

CLARKE: When a man asks you to lend him money, you know what it means?

WILDE: I give the money.

CLARKE: That is the 25th of April. You said at that time he had got his fifty pounds a year at some office in the city?

WILDE: Yes, a commercial office, not a publisher's office.

CLARKE: The next letter I have gives the name of that office; it is at '1 Dunster Court, Mincing Lane, London, 14th June 1894':

My dear Oscar, I shall be very thankful if you will use your influence on my behalf and try and get me some employment in a publisher's or a newspaper office. I simply cannot live much longer in my present manner. I cannot live upon the money I receive for my work and I have to borrow from my parents who cannot afford to lend me money. You have position and power in London. Will you try to get me something to do. I think I have talent for work connected with books. I would gladly work for a year for seventy-five pounds if anyone would give me the position. I will accept nothing from the viper—'

Then a name is mentioned I need not read.[229]

WILDE: He complains of the treatment of some previous employer of him.

CLARKE: He mentions the name of a previous employer:

He hurt me too much. I despise him, but I cannot forget. Use your power on my behalf. I have others depending upon me and at present I am taking the food from their mouths and it is hateful. Let God judge the fact. If you like to use your power now for me I shall thank you all my life. Do help me.

Believe me, yours sincerely,

EDWARD SHELLEY

Please write to 3 Hildyard Road and say whether you will try and help me. I must know whether you will try.

The next is 'June 15th 1894, 3 Hildyard Road. Dear Oscar, I wish to thank you for your letter.' You had replied to him?

WILDE: I had answered the letter at once.

CLARKE (*continuing*):

I shall be very grateful if you will use your influence on my behalf. I again apologise for having obtruded my private worries upon you, but I am feeling ill and weak and scarcely know what I am about. I hope to leave Mincing Lane at the end of July. I have existed for more than ten months upon four pounds three shillings and fourpence per month. I dare not do it any longer. My strength is almost gone. I must stop myself before it is too late. If my means will allow I shall take two rooms in Chelsea and read with a coach at night. I, too, will know everything. You have deadly enemies in London. Hence the *Daily News* article.

Is that same article about the play?

WILDE: It is an article not quite appreciative on the poem called *The Sphinx*.[230]

CLARKE (*continuing*):

Permit me to thank you again for your courtesy and kindness to me. I must also thank you on behalf of my mother. Believe me ever sincerely, Edward Shelley.

The other is the 28th of August 1894, '3 Hildyard Road, SW, August 28th 1894':

Dear Oscar, You must ignore my telegram, for a meeting would only cause pain. I am trying to live according to my light but the life is sometimes too hard to bear. Only those who have given up all that was pleasant in the world and who have effaced self can realise what Christianity really is. The world becomes a void, empty prison to them. You realised this when you wrote. 'The Star Child'.

Was that a poem of yours?

WILDE: It was a prose poem published in the *House of Pomegranates*.

CLARKE (*continuing*):

Poor Charley Hinxman died at Bournemouth after a fortnight's delirium, preceded by a year's illness.[231] His death has caused a gap in my life. I cannot realise that he has gone. I wrote to Lane asking him to give me work some days ago, but I feel I cannot go back to him and I am writing to him tonight to tell him so. Even were he to offer me work I feel I could not go back. The loss he has put me to is beyond his power to repair. I am frequently in the East End and have traversed the region known as Leman Street, Whitechapel. The sight of those poor hungry souls is a never-to-be-forgotten one. I am afraid sometimes that I am not very sane. I feel so nervous and ill. Goodbye.

Always yours,

EDWARD SHELLEY

Will you please send me your *Sphinx*. 'And sweet to hear the

cuckoo mock the spring while the last violet loiters by the well.'[232]
I agree with the *Athenæum* reviewer.[233]

Are those the letters you have found?

WILDE: Those are all the letters I have been able to find.

CLARKE: Was there ever any relation between you and Edward Shelley other than that which you have described as the relation between a man of letters and a person who admired his poetry and works, and had been brought into connection with him in business matters?

WILDE: Never upon any occasion, never.

CLARKE: With regard to Alfonso Conway at Worthing, when was it you went down to Worthing?

WILDE: I think the 1st of August I went there.

CLARKE: And about how long did you stay there?

WILDE: I stayed, I think, two months at Worthing.

CLARKE: Did you stay there continuously or did you leave Worthing to go to London for a time and go back there?

WILDE: No, I went once to Dieppe; that was for four days. I came up to London once for a day to see a theatrical manager.[234] But I was there continuously with the exception of four or five days.

CLARKE: What house was it that you had at Worthing or rooms? Did you have a home?

WILDE: Yes, it was a house; my wife and my children and myself lived in a furnished house that we had taken from a friend of my wife's.[235]

CLARKE: It was a furnished house that was taken for a time?

WILDE: Yes.

CLARKE: Did your wife and your boys go to Worthing at the same time you did?

WILDE: Yes.

CLARKE: And remained there during your stay?

WILDE: At the beginning. Some time in September – I can hardly say exactly when – both my boys had returned to school; my wife returned to town with them to prepare them for going back to school and I stayed on for, I fancy, a fortnight after that.

CLARKE: And did Mrs Wilde rejoin you?

WILDE: No, she went visiting in the country.

CLARKE: You have told us, with regard to this boy, the circumstances under which you met him. He was not at that time in any employment so far as you know?

WILDE: None at all.

CLARKE: Did you ever hear of his having been employed as a newspaper boy?

WILDE: No, I had no idea; no, certainly not. I never heard of it, nor had any idea that he had any connection with literature in any form. (*Laughter.*)

CLARKE: So far as your information went as to his desires or wishes as to employment, what was that desire and wish?

WILDE: Oh, an intense desire to go to sea in the Merchant Service as an apprentice.

CLARKE: And did he go out from time to time sailing with you?

WILDE: He used to go out every day after I met him with myself, with my son, with my son's friend and with other friends who were there. We went out every morning and bathed from this boat and fished in the afternoon.

CLARKE: Was Mrs Wilde acquainted with Conway?

WILDE: Oh, yes.

CLARKE: Did she see Conway?

WILDE: Oh, yes, constantly.

CLARKE: Where?

WILDE: After bathing we would return to the beach. My wife would meet us, that is my son and myself and my son's friends, and, of course, I introduced Conway to her – she knew him quite well. He had also been to a children's tea at our house while my wife was there. He was a great friend of my son's as well as myself.

CLARKE: When did you leave Worthing?

WILDE: I fancy about the 2nd or 3rd of October I went round to Brighton.

CLARKE: Have you ever seen Conway since then?

WILDE: No, I have never seen him since then – no. I have written to him one letter.

CLARKE: Do you remember when that was?

WILDE: Writing the letter?

CLARKE: Yes.

WILDE: I think it was in the month of November last. It was with reference to his becoming an apprentice in the Merchant Service. I had consulted a gentleman, who was a great friend of mine who has many ships and so on, and asked him the circumstances under which it could be done, and I wrote to Conway and told him the circumstances of the case.

CLARKE: Now, I want to ask you a question or two with regard to Wood. When was it you first saw Wood?

WILDE: That was in the month of January, at the end of the month of January 1893.

CLARKE: Was it at Taylor's rooms?

WILDE: No, at the Café Royal.

CLARKE: You have seen him, I think, at Taylor's rooms?

WILDE: Only on one occasion.

CLARKE: On one occasion?

WILDE: On the occasion of the letters.

CLARKE: Only on the occasion of the letters?

WILDE: That was the only time.

CLARKE: Then, who introduced Wood to you?

WILDE: If I may make my answer a little long, there was no actual introduction took place. I was staying with Lady Queensberry at Salisbury. While I was there Lord Alfred Douglas showed me a letter from Wood asking him whether he could help him in any way to obtain employment and stating that he was out of employment and asking him could he assist him in any way.

CARSON: He has told us all this already. I think that has all been said.

CLARKE: I will take it shortly because you have been good enough to tell us all that before, but that was the way you were introduced to him?

WILDE: Lord Alfred asked me if I would see him, and sent a telegram to Wood and said I would be at the Café Royal between nine and ten, and would give him something from Lord Alfred.

CLARKE: At that time you had no knowledge at all about Wood except that?

WILDE: Except that – that is all.

CLARKE: What his occupation was or what he had been or anything of that kind?

WILDE: I understood him to have been a clerk – yes, a clerk. He was out of employment. It was a clerkship he wanted.

CLARKE: I think I have very little more to ask you. With respect to these young men whose names have been mentioned, who were introduced to you by Alfred Taylor or through Alfred Taylor, they from time to time joined at teas or dinners or lunches at which you were present?

WILDE: Oh, they have always been my guests with, I think, one or two exceptions.

CLARKE: Have you any idea of what the occupation had been of Charles Parker or his brother?

WILDE: No, none whatsoever. They told me they were up in London looking for employment. Charles Parker was anxious to go upon the stage.

CLARKE: I think you mentioned that so far as their position was concerned you understood that the father was at Datchet some time and that he was a man of means and making an allowance to his sons?

WILDE: Yes, he was represented as being a man of means.

CLARKE: There was one person whose name has been mentioned – Atkins—

WILDE: Yes.

CLARKE: He, I understand, was introduced to you by a gentleman whose name has been passed along on paper but has not been mentioned?

WILDE: Yes.

CLARKE: Was that the first time you knew of Atkins at all?

WILDE: The first time, yes.

CLARKE: Now, with regard to these persons, when they were introduced to you, had you any reason whatever for suspecting them of being immoral or disreputable persons?

WILDE: None whatsoever.

CLARKE: With regard to either of them, has there ever come to your knowledge anything to show you that they were disreputable persons and have you, in spite of that, continued the intimacy or the friendship?

WILDE: Nothing has ever come to my knowledge with regard to either of them that led me to believe anything at all against their character, unless you count it against the character of Charles Parker that he was arrested on a charge which the magistrate dismissed and I saw his name in the paper; but having read the case I didn't think there was anything against him. I do not happen to have seen him since.

CLARKE: And apart from that matter of those two persons having been arrested—

WILDE: Not those two – but Charles Parker.

CLARKE: I will leave out Alfred Taylor – you are quite right because I have already dealt with that – but apart from the fact that Charles Parker had been arrested and the charge against him had been dismissed, has there been anything at all to bring to your mind the idea that these persons were persons of disreputable lives?

WILDE: Nothing whatsoever.

CLARKE: As to Charles Parker I will just ask you this: having special reference to something. Have you ever seen Charles Parker in your life at the Savoy Hotel?

WILDE: Never in my life.

CLARKE: Have you ever in your life been at number 7 Camera Square?

WILDE: Never in my life

CLARKE: Have you ever in your life been to 50 Park Walk?

WILDE: Never in my life.

CLARKE: With regard to Walter Grainger whose name has been mentioned as having been at Goring, how long was he with you?

WILDE: I should think two months; during part of the time when my own servant, I think, went home to his parents under certain circumstances. I think two months he was in my service – I had been away some of that time, for three weeks I should say, I had been away about three weeks or a month.

CLARKE: He went away for some time, did he?

WILDE: Yes.

CLARKE: Will you answer this 'yes' or 'no'; was he to your knowledge in ill health during part of that time?

WILDE: Yes.

CLARKE: I think there is only one question I have to ask you on another matter. How was it that after the interview with Lord Queensberry on the 30th of June and these further letters coming to your knowledge, that you did not then take steps against Lord Queensberry?

WILDE: On account of the very strong pressure put upon me by the Queensberry family – very strong pressure that I did not feel able to resist.

CLARKE: Did you early in July have an interview with a Member of Parliament who represented the Queensberry family?[236]

WILDE: On the Wednesday following the Saturday on which Lord Queensberry's visit to my house occurred I had an interview with a member of Lady Queensberry's family who is a Member of Parliament.

CLARKE: On that occasion did you express any intention of your own?

CARSON: I do not think, my lord, that could be in any sense evidence.

JUDGE: No.

CLARKE: I will not carry it further. At all events, you have told us it was the strong pressure of the Queensberry family.

WILDE: Great pressure from Lady Queensberry that I felt I could not resist at the moment.

CARSON: There was one letter read by my learned friend which refers to a postcard sent by Lord Alfred Douglas. It is a letter in answer to a postcard and I desire to have that postcard in.

CLARKE: I object for reasons which will become obvious to your lordship in a moment. My lord, the letter which I put in from Lord Queensberry is this:

> I have received your postcard – which I presume is from you – but the writing is quite unreadable to me and I have been unable to make out hardly one sentence. My object of receiving no written communication from you is therefore kept intact. All future cards will go into the fire unread. My friend, who is staying with me, has made out some of your letter and wished to read it to me, but I declined to hear one word.

My lord, if this were in answer to that card, I should at once myself put it in as evidence, thinking it proper to go in: but inasmuch as it is not an answer to that card – I will hand up to your lordship the letter – I submit this postcard cannot be put in evidence.

CARSON: I submit, with great respect, to explain the conduct of Lord Queensberry in reference to the letter – if it was nothing else but to bear out what he states about the legibility – I have a right, my lord, to put in this card. It is not to be left as if this letter were written without anything causing it to be written.

JUDGE: The point is whether that card was brought to the notice of Lord Queensberry.

CARSON: He said he received the card.

CLARKE: But that it was illegible.

JUDGE: I will just read the letter.

CARSON: I think he says part of it was read.

CLARKE: He says, 'I declined to hear it.'

JUDGE: I think there is evidence that he saw sufficient of the contents of the postcard to justify the card being read.

CARSON: This is it: 'As you return my letters unopened—'

CLARKE: But he says it is illegible.

CARSON: The point has been ruled upon.

JUDGE: I think he saw enough of it.

CARSON (*continuing*):

> As you return my letters unopened I am obliged to write on a postcard. I write to inform you that I treat your absurd threats

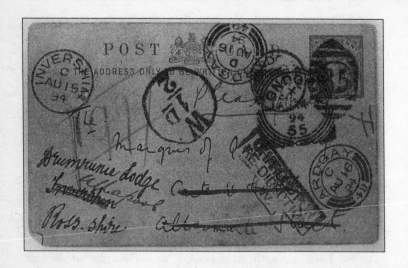

10. Lord Alfred Douglas's 'unreadable' postcard threatening to shoot his father if assaulted by him. It is written first horizontally and then continued across the card from bottom to top.

with absolute indifference. Ever since your exhibition at OW's house, I have made a point of appearing with him at many public restaurants such as the Berkeley, Willis's Rooms, the Café Royal etc. and shall continue to go to any of these places whenever I choose and with whom I choose. I am of age and my own master. You have disowned me at least a dozen times and have very meanly deprived me of money. You have therefore no right over me, either legal or moral. If OW has to prosecute you for libel in the criminal courts you would get several years' penal servitude for your outrageous libels. Much as I detest you, I am anxious to avoid this for the sake of the family, but if you try to assault me I shall defend myself with a loaded revolver which I always carry, and if I shoot you or if he shoots you, we should be completely justified as we should be acting in self-defence against a violent and dangerous rough, and I think if you were dead not many people would miss you. A.D.[237]

My lord, there are two letters in the course of the correspondence which I would ask to read. There is one from Mr Humphreys, solicitor to Mr Wilde, and the answer of Lord Queensberry to him.

CLARKE: I will make no difficulty about it. If my learned friend's time has not come for putting in evidence, I will put in evidence myself anything which my learned friend thinks fit.

CARSON: Very well.

CLARKE: And if I had known that that card was so legible and had known its contents, there would have been no discussion as to whether it was to have been put in. If you will let me have these letters I will put them in. The 11th of July 1894 is a letter from 'Messrs Humphreys, Son and Kershaw, Giltspur Chambers, Holborn Viaduct, EC to the Marquess of Queensberry':

My Lord Marquess, We have been consulted by Mr Oscar Wilde with respect to certain letters written by your lordship, in which letters you have most foully and infamously libelled him, and also your own son, Lord Alfred Douglas. In those letters your lordship has mentioned exalted personages and Mr Oscar Wilde, not being desirous of wounding their feelings by a publication of your letters, has instructed us to give you the opportunity of retracting your assertions and insinuations in writing, with an apology for having made them. If this be done at once, it may prevent litigation, but unless done forthwith no other course will be left open to us but to advise our client the proper course to adopt to vindicate his character.

Awaiting your reply by return of post, we have the honour to be yours obediently,

C.O. HUMPHREYS, SON AND KERSHAW

Then 'Skindles, Maidenhead, July the 13th. Sir, I have received your letter here –' I will hand that in and read the copy:

– with considerable astonishment. I certainly shall not tender Mr Wilde any apology for letters I have written to my son. In those letters I made no direct accusations but implied, as I did to Mr Oscar Wilde's face the other day, that to pose as a certain thing and to give occasion for a most odious scandal which is the talk of the town, was as bad as the actual thing, and that I was determined to put a stop to it as far as my son was concerned. As to your allusion that in my private letters to my son I had mentioned exalted personages, I am at a loss to understand what you mean, as I have no recollection of doing so.

Lord Queensberry was perfectly right in that, that there is not in any of the letters connected with this case, or so far as I know in existence, any reference to any exalted personages having anything to do with the matters which are being investigated here.[238]

JUDGE: There are names mentioned in the letters.

CLARKE: Names are mentioned but absolutely without any reference to the matter with which we are dealing. (CLARKE *continues to read the letter*):

However with Mr Wilde's horrible reputation, I can afford to defy him to publish any private letters I have written to my son. You are quite at liberty to take any steps you please.

That obliges me to put in another letter. (*To* WILDE.) You were aware, were you not, that Lord Queensberry had an interview after that with Mr Humphreys?

WILDE: Yes.

CLARKE: Here is a letter the 18th of July from Lord Queensberry to Messrs Humphreys dated 'Skindles, Maidenhead Bridge, Berks':

> Sir, Since seeing you this morning I have heard that the revolver has been given up. I shall therefore not insist in taking the step I threatened to do tomorrow morning, of giving information to the police authorities.

It is possible that that is explained, my lord, by the postcard that has been read.

JUDGE: Yes.

CLARKE (*continuing*):

> However, if this is to go on, and I am openly to be defied by Mr Wilde and my son by further scandal in public places, I shall have no other resort than to do as I threatened and give information at Scotland Yard as to what has happened.
>
> Yours faithfully,
>
> QUEENSBERRY

CLARKE: I presume the contents of that letter were repeated to you about the giving information to Scotland Yard and so on?

WILDE: Yes.

CLARKE: And you took no notice of it whatever?

WILDE: None whatsoever, none.

JUROR: May we ask a few questions, my lord?

JUDGE: You had better tell me what the questions are. (JUROR *writes on a piece of paper, which is handed to his lordship.*)

JUDGE: Yes, you can ask that, certainly.

JUROR: Can you tell us whether the editor of *The Chameleon* was a personal friend of yours?

WILDE: I had never seen him at the time when he wrote to me from Oxford to ask me to contribute to this magazine. I had never seen him till that time. I subsequently saw him, I think, in the month of November in London, in rooms of a friend at the Albany.[239] I had written to him that I really had nothing to give him. I was engaged in work of a more serious character. Being invited to meet him at lunch, I came in afterwards. He then begged me to give him anything at all and I said that I could give him, if he liked, some aphorisms out of my plays and others unpublished. I may say that some of the aphorisms quoted yesterday by Mr Carson were out of the play at present performing at the Haymarket Theatre – the one about pleasure for pleasure and there was no complaint in the box office about immorality in the play which was performed before the public.[240] (*Laughter.*)

CLARKE: Are we to understand that this *Chameleon* was for private circulation?

WILDE: No, not for private circulation. I do not think so, at least.

CLARKE: We will hand up a copy. They will see that only one hundred copies were to be printed, but so far as these one hundred copies were to go, they would be for public circulation.

JUROR: Were you aware of the nature of this article 'The Priest and the Acolyte' before its publication? Had you ever seen it or heard anything about it?

WILDE: Nothing whatsoever. It came upon me as a most horrible shock. I had heard nothing whatever about it.

CLARKE: At this stage of the case that is the evidence for the prosecution.

CARSON: Having regard to what Sir Edward Clarke has said as to that being all the evidence 'at this stage', I understand his case is closed and that he must make his whole case now?

JUDGE: Yes.

CLARKE: Subject, of course, to this: that evidence may be given with regard to which I should ask, perhaps, to call evidence in rebuttal.

JUDGE: It may possibly be that some evidence is sprung upon you.

CLARKE: I do not think there will be any difficulty about it because I am quite certain that, although strictly I might not be entitled to claim it, I would not desire to call it, unless the circumstances were such as would certainly induce your lordship to allow it.

JUDGE: Broadly, I think you are bound to close your case now, but I will reserve, if the emergency arises, the discretion of allowing you to call further evidence.[241]

EDWARD CARSON *opens the case for the defence.*

CARSON: May it please your lordship, gentlemen of the jury, appearing in this case for Lord Queensberry, I cannot but feel that a very grave responsibility rests upon me in putting this case before you as best I can. So far as Lord Queensberry is concerned, as to any act he has done, as to any letter he has written, or as to the card which has put him in his present position, he withdraws nothing. He has done what he did premeditatedly and he was determined, at all risks and at all hazards, to try and save his son. Gentlemen of the jury, whether he was right or whether he was wrong, you have probably now, to some extent, information upon which you can found a judgement. But I must claim for Lord Queensberry that, not withstanding the many elements of prejudice which my learned friend Sir Edward Clarke thought fit in his opening speech to introduce into the case, Lord Queensberry's conduct in this respect has been absolutely consistent all through, and if the facts which he stated in his letters as to Mr Wilde's reputation and as to Mr Wilde's acts were correct, then I say not only was he justified in doing all he could to put a stop to what must, or at least most probably might, prove a disastrous acquaintance, but he was bound to take every step which could suggest itself to him to bring about at once such an enquiry as would lead at all events to the acts and doings of Mr Wilde being made public. Gentlemen of the jury, it was said that the names of eminent persons and distinguished persons were introduced in Lord Queensberry's letters. For my own part I say with absolute sincerity that I am very glad those letters have been read here, and, if I may say so, I think Sir Edward Clarke took a very proper course in having those letters read, because the impression suggested apparently had been at some time that the names of those distinguished persons were in some way or other in Lord Queensberry's letters mixed up with his charges against Mr Oscar Wilde. But now that the letters are before the court and the jury, if there ever was any impression of that kind drawn, or if any such suggestion had been made upon previous occasions to that effect, it is quite clear from the letters themselves that the matters connected with these distinguished individuals were quite distinct from the allegations as regards Mr Oscar Wilde. They were brought in, in no connection whatsoever with reference to those allegations. They were purely political matters rising out of the fact, as is apparent from the letters themselves, that one of Lord Queensberry's sons, the late Lord Drumlanrig, had been made a member of the House of Lords of which Lord Queensberry is not a member, and that Lord Queensberry, whether rightly or wrongly, felt aggrieved that that should be an honour conferred upon his eldest son while it was not given to him; and therefore it was that the names of eminent politicians and statesmen happened to be introduced at all. But, gentlemen of the jury, as I said before, from the beginning to the end, Lord Queensberry has been influenced as regards Mr Oscar Wilde by one hope and one hope alone – namely that he might save his own son.

Now, what is Mr Oscar Wilde's own case? His case is that up to a certain date, at all events, whenever he met Lord Queensberry, Lord Queensberry was upon terms of friendship with him. As he told you, the last time he had seen him prior to the interview at Tite Street and prior to those letters, which have been given in evidence here, when he met him at the Café Royal, friendly relations seemed to have existed between the parties and nothing appears to have happened in the nature of a personal quarrel or personal dispute of any kind between Lord Queensberry and Mr Wilde, which would render Lord Queensberry to be liable to the accusation that in what he was doing in this case, in protesting against this intimacy between his son and Mr Wilde, he was actuated by anything like malice or spite by reason of any disagreement which had happened between Mr Oscar Wilde and himself.

Gentlemen of the jury, Mr Wilde's character became known to Lord Queensberry – the character which he had gained from his writings, to which I will call attention in a moment; scandals in connection with the Savoy Hotel, which you will have proved before you before the case is over; the general character, which a man in Mr Wilde's position must necessarily have won for himself when he was leading the kind of life which even he has confessed to, and it is only a small portion of it in evidence. He had been going about with men – young men who were not his co-equals in station, who were not his coevals in age. He had been associating with men, who, I think it will be proved before this case is over beyond all doubt, were well-known as some of the most immoral characters in London. I refer above all to Taylor – a notorious character as the police will tell you; and I must remind you of the fact that at an early hour today I put the question direct to Mr Wilde as to whether Taylor's house was anything more than a mere den for introducing men to these lads, and as to whether Taylor was anything more than a procurer of these lads for sodomitic purposes. And Taylor upon Tuesday last is found in company with Wilde in his house in Tite Street, and my learned friend Sir Edward Clarke does not venture to put him in the box there to explain how it was he came to introduce these various boys and to give him an opportunity of asking him the course of life he led. Taylor is found afterwards at Fitzroy Square in company with Parker, arrested with a number of notorious characters on suspicion by the police. My learned friend says there was an acquittal upon that occasion. Yes, but the police do not act in this way without very grave reason and without very grave suspicion. It may be that the police might be unable to obtain such evidence as would lead to a conviction upon the more serious charge which was made against these men. But I certainly should have thought that when Taylor was found in the company of these people, and when the police thought fit to interfere in that way, after the evidence that has been given that he was practically the right-hand man of Wilde in all these orgies with artists and valets, that at least we might have had an opportunity of cross-examining Mr Taylor and hearing some explanation from him of what was really going on in Fitzroy Square at the time that he was arrested. Gentlemen of the jury, Taylor is the pivot of this case. I say that for the simple reason that when you hear these various witnesses examined and when, one after the other, they are unfortunately compelled to tell you here about the filthy and immoral practices of Mr Oscar Wilde, surely the man who introduced these men to Oscar Wilde is, above all others, the man who could have thrown some light upon their antecedents and some light upon his object in introducing these men to Mr Oscar Wilde. Mr Oscar Wilde undertakes to prove sufficient here to send the Marquess of Queensberry to gaol and to have him branded as a criminal; and I say above all things it was for Mr Oscar Wilde, when so much was proved by his own admissions as regards this man Taylor – and we certainly did not at all mince matters in dealing with his connection with Taylor – it certainly lay upon him, if he had any witness in the case, who could bear out his innocence of the charges that are made in this plea of justification, to call him and that one man was Taylor and that man is not and will not be produced by my learned friend.

But we heard a great deal of a gentleman whose name was written down upon each occasion. When it was convenient to introduce somebody, this was the name that Mr Oscar Wilde gave because he was out of the country; but Taylor is in the country – Taylor is still a friend of Wilde. Nothing has happened, as he says, to interrupt his friendship. Where is Taylor? He is not produced and indeed, gentlemen of the jury, I am not surprised. You will hear from these witnesses – and let me say that nothing can be more painful than to have to ask witnesses, who are some of them procured by Taylor and some of them procured by Wilde for evil purposes, nothing can be more painful than to ask them to go through the various descriptions of the manner in which Wilde acted towards them – but you will hear a good deal more about Taylor from these witnesses as the case proceeds. You will hear the kind of life that this man Taylor lived, the extraordinary den that he kept in Little College Street with its curtains always drawn, the luxurious hangings of his windows, his rooms gorgeously and luxuriously furnished with the perpetual change of varied perfumes and the altogether extraordinary life that he was leading there; the daylight never admitted; always the shaded light of candles or of lamps or of gas. And when you hear the extraordinary way in which he kept these rooms and, put together with that, the extraordinary company that was there at these 'innocent afternoon tea-parties', I think you will come to the conclusion I am right when I say that Taylor is the pivot of this case in which the true relation of Mr Wilde to these various practices must turn.

But before I come to an examination of the evidence in the case, I mean the evidence as regards these various young men, let me say a word as regards the position which Mr Wilde takes up in reference to the publications upon which he has been examined and cross-examined, and let me contrast that with the position he takes up in reference to these men who were from time to time introduced to him or picked up by him. As regards literature his standard was a very high one. His works were not written for the Philistines nor for the illiterate. His works could really only be understood by the artist and he was indifferent as to what the ordinary individual thought of them or how the ordinary individual might be influenced by them. He took such a high standard of art as an artist in that box yesterday, that whenever anything corrupt was pointed out to him in these various books he said, 'Oh, you may put that meaning upon it, but then an artist would understand it in a different sense.' In relation to his books he was a complete artist. In relation to his books he wrote only in the language of an artist for artists. Gentlemen of the jury, contrast that with the position he takes up as regards these lads. He picks up with Charlie Parker, who was a gentleman's servant and whose brother was a gentleman's servant. He picks up with young Conway, who sold papers on the pier in Worthing and he picks up with Scarfe, who I think also was a gentleman's servant; and when you come to confront him with these curious associates of a man of high art, his case is no longer that he is dealing in regions of art, which no one can understand but himself and the artistic, but his case is that he has such a magnanimous, such a noble, such a democratic soul (*laughter*) that he draws no social distinctions, and it is exactly the same pleasure to him to have a sweeping-boy from the street – if he is only interesting – to lunch with him or to dine with him, as the best educated artist or the greatest *littérateur* in the whole kingdom.

Gentlemen, I say his position in this respect is absolutely irreconcilable. Observe the reason which influenced him in trying to get out of these passages in his own works – which go to the full extent of justifying every word that Lord Queensberry wrote about him – when he tries to get out of those, it is necessary to say, 'That is not language which amongst us artists would be understood in the sense you mean,' but when you ask him about his associates, he would say, 'Well, I have a right to have such associates as these and I do have them for an innocent purpose, because I dream, no longer in their cases in the language peculiar to artists, but I accommodate myself to the ideas, the tastes and the wishes of even the valets and the newspaper boy that I pick up at Worthing.' Gentlemen of the jury, I think if we had rested this case alone on Mr Wilde's literature we would have been absolutely justified in the course we have taken. When I say 'we', I mean Lord Queensberry. What was this literature?

First let me ask you to consider what Lord Queensberry undertakes to prove. He undertakes to prove that Mr Wilde was posing as a sodomite. I do not think I have any fault to find with the definition that my learned friend Sir Edward Clarke gave to that term. Lord Queensberry took care in all his letters to use exactly the same phrase and to persistently state that he did not accuse Mr Wilde of committing the actual felony

– that would be a matter which would subject Mr Wilde to very serious consequences if it were true – but of 'posing as a sodomite' and I think you will say that that really meant that Mr Wilde, by his acts and by his writings, was putting himself in that position that people might naturally and reasonably infer from the writings and the course of life he was adopting, that he, Mr Wilde, was either in sympathy with, or addicted to, immoral and sodomitic habits.

Now, gentlemen of the jury, let me very briefly refer to this literature. I take up first *The Chameleon*. I am not going to say for a moment that Mr Wilde is accountable for everything that appears in *The Chameleon*; that would be an absurd and extraordinary proposition. But I do most emphatically say this, and I submit it to your judgement, that if a gentleman is willing to contribute to a publication which is, in its essence – not merely in that one article, as I will show you, but in others – which is, in its essence, a teaching of sodomitic practices and gives as his contribution aphorisms or 'Phrases and Philosophies for the Use of the Young', such as I have directed attention to in my cross-examination – and you find those matters published without any public demur on the part of a man like Mr Oscar Wilde, I do say that he does, to that extent at all events, acquiesce in his name going along with and his own contribution going with the contributions that are in this paper. It is all very well to tell me that he went to the editor and that he complained of this article to the editor. Why didn't he publish his condemnation of him? Why didn't he say to the public, 'I, Oscar Wilde, disapprove of the other articles in this paper and I knew nothing about them at the time I gave my contribution of "Phrases and Philosophies for the Use of the Young"'? I will tell you why he didn't do it. He only complained of 'The Priest and the Acolyte' as being inartistic. He never complained of the immorality of 'The Priest and the Acolyte'. He knows of no distinction – he said so over and over again and he has published it under his own hand – he knows of no distinction between a moral and an immoral book and he cares for none. Nor does he care whether an article in its very terms and in its very essence is blasphemous. All he says is that he doesn't approve of it from an artistic and literary point of view. Therefore it is that the disapproval, that he expressed to the editor of this extraordinary magazine, was not a disapproval of anything which was contained in the article itself; it was a disapproval of it from a literary point of view and a complaint that it was not up to the standard of art which he attempts to attain to. Now, gentlemen of the jury, what is that article? What is this article 'The Priest and the Acolyte'? It is the story, as you were told yesterday, of the priest who falls in love, and I use the term advisedly, with the acolyte – the boy who was attending him at the Mass. I am not going to read you any portion of this story, but all I can say is that the description in it of the admiration that the priest had for this boy and the description of his beauty, of his intense feeling towards him, if it would call to mind anything, would call to mind especially those two letters which unfortunately Mr Oscar Wilde has written among others to Lord Alfred Douglas. It is exactly the same idea, exactly the same notion, that runs through that story of 'The Priest and the Acolyte', of a man using towards a man the language which men sometimes use, and perhaps legitimately use, towards women. That is the idea, the essential idea, in the descriptions all through. And, gentlemen of the jury, when the priest describes the beauty of this boy, when he tells him of his love and shows him his passion, the unfortunate boy, dominated by the priest – and I will show you afterwards that this is exactly the same idea that runs through *Dorian Gray* – the unfortunate boy being dominated by the priest is found by the rector afterwards in his bedroom and the priest makes the kind of defence that Mr Wilde made in the box yesterday. He says, 'Oh, the world does not understand the beauty of this love.' But not being able to persuade the rector and the public of the beauty of this love, they resolve to die together upon the altar. The priest administers poison to the acolyte and takes it himself, using upon the occasion the sacred words of the sacrament that belong to the

Church of England, and there, as it says, 'in one long passionate embrace' the priest and the acolyte die together. Gentlemen of the jury, I asked Mr Wilde did he think that was blasphemous and Mr Wilde said he did not think so. Well, I refer to that for this reason: that if you find running through Mr Wilde's own works afterwards the same idea, if you find Mr Wilde himself in his conduct with Lord Alfred Douglas, in the communications which we have proved here in evidence, adopting the same language and the same idea – and I shall have a word to say presently about what Mr Wilde calls these two beautiful letters and which I call disgusting letters – I say when you find the same idea running all through, have you the slightest doubt that same kind of mind that wrote this *Chameleon*, wrote these letters to Lord Alfred Douglas? But, gentlemen of the jury, unfortunately this point as to *The Chameleon* does not rest upon this story of 'The Priest and the Acolyte' and these 'Phrases for the Young' that Mr Wilde has referred to. There is unfortunately in it – and I fear it shows some justification for the frightful anticipation that Lord Queensberry had as regards his own son – a poem called 'Two Loves' produced in this same volume with Oscar Wilde's own 'Phrases for the Young' – a poem by Lord Alfred Douglas which Mr Oscar Wilde admits he showed him at some time or another, prior to its being published in this magazine, and which poem, my learned friend reminds me, Mr Wilde describes as beautiful. I have read it. Any person can read it and there is no difficulty in seeing in it that the whole object and the whole idea of it is to draw the distinction between what the world calls 'love' and what the world calls 'shame', one being the love that a man bears towards a woman, and the other being the unholy shame that a man ought to have if he ventures to transfer that kind of love and that kind of passion to a man. That is the idea all through Lord Alfred Douglas's poem, and is it not a terrible thing to think that that young man, upon the threshold of his life, having been these several years in the company, aye, under the domination of and adored and loved by Oscar Wilde as would appear from these letters that have been given here – is it not a horrible thing to think that there to the public he makes known the results of his education and the tendencies of his own mind upon this subject, this frightful subject of the passion of man for man? Gentlemen of the jury, you cannot, by saying that Mr Wilde disapproved of 'The Priest and the Acolyte', get rid, so far as this case is concerned – and I say nothing more – of the effect on the case of this periodical *The Chameleon*, when Mr Wilde, without demur so far as the public was concerned, allowed these immoral phrases of his – for they were nothing else – to be published to the public in conjunction with the poem by Lord Alfred Douglas and in conjunction with 'The Priest and the Acolyte'. I ask you, gentlemen of the jury, if the case stood alone upon that, was Mr Oscar Wilde posing as a sodomite in the sense I have mentioned to you? I put it to you to make it your own personal question: if any one of you had a young son and you knew that he, under the domination and out of his acquaintanceship with Mr Wilde, had written a contribution in this *Chameleon* with Mr Wilde, what under those circumstances would be your own feeling? What would be your own suggestion? What would be the horror you would feel as regards what might be the result of your own son of being associated in that way with persons who are making such contributions to public literature?[242]

Gentlemen of the jury, I pass away from *The Chameleon* and I come to the book called *Dorian Gray*. I have no doubt that everyone in court who listened yesterday to the description given by Sir Edward Clarke of *The Picture of Dorian Gray* must have been enchanted by the eloquent picture which he, in so brief a time, drew of this novel. But his picture was an outline and had omitted all the horrid details. But, gentlemen of the jury, *Dorian Gray* – and I am not now going to refer to these passages to which I called Mr Wilde's attention yesterday – *Dorian Gray* is important in this case in two ways. *Dorian Gray* is the tale of a young man – a beautiful young man, for his description is given here – beautiful in person who by conversation with one who had great literary power and who had great power of speaking in epigram, just as Mr Wilde has, by exactly the same kind of teachings as are to be found in the 'Phrases and Philosophies for the Use of the Young', had opened the eyes of Dorian Gray to what they were pleased to call 'the delights of the world' and there is only one passage that I would call your attention to, to show you the way in which the eyes of this innocent young man were supposed to be opened by his conversation with Lord Henry Wotton, who was the individual to whom I have referred. It is at page twenty-six.[243]

'And yet,' continued Lord Henry, in his low, musical voice, and with that graceful wave of the hand that was always so character-istic of him, and that he had even in his Eton days, 'I believe that if one man were to live out his life fully and completely, were to give form to every feeling, expression to every thought, reality to every dream — I believe that the world would gain such a fresh impulse of joy that we would forget all the maladies of mediævalism, and return to the Hellenic ideal — to something finer, richer, than the Hellenic ideal, it may be. But the bravest man amongst us is afraid of himself. The mutilation of the savage has its tragic survival in the self-denial that mars our lives. We are punished for our refusals. Every impulse that we strive to strangle broods in the mind, and poisons us. The body sins once, and has done with its sin, for action is a mode of purification. Nothing remains then but the recollection of a pleasure, or the luxury of a regret. The only way to get rid of a temptation is to yield to it. Resist it, and your soul grows sick with longing for the things it has forbidden to itself, with desire for what its monstrous laws have made monstrous and unlawful. It has been said that the great events of the world take place in the brain. It is in the brain, and the brain only, that the great sins of the world take place also. You, Mr Gray, you yourself, with your rose-red youth and your rose-white boyhood, you have had passions that have made you afraid, thoughts that have filled you with terror, day-dreams and sleeping dreams whose mere memory might stain your cheek with shame—'

'Stop!' faltered Dorian Gray, 'stop! you bewilder me. I don't know what to say. There is some answer to you, but I cannot find it. Don't speak. Let me think. Or, rather, let me try not to think.'

For nearly ten minutes he stood there, motionless, with parted lips, and eyes strangely bright. He was dimly conscious that entirely fresh influences were at work within him. Yet they seemed to him to have come really from himself. The few words that Basil's friend had said to him – words spoken by chance, no doubt, and with wilful paradox in them – had touched some secret chord that had never been touched before, but that he felt was now vibrating and throbbing to curious pulses.

Music had stirred him like that. Music had troubled him many times. But music was not articulate. It was not a new world, but rather another chaos, that it created in us. Words! Mere words! How terrible they were! How clear, and vivid, and cruel! One could not escape from them. And yet what a subtle magic there was in them! They seemed to be able to give a plastic form to formless things, and to have a music of their own as sweet as that of viol or of lute. Mere words! Was there anything so real as words?

Yes; there had been things in his boyhood that he had not understood. He understood them now. Life suddenly became fiery-coloured to him. It seemed to him that he had been walking in fire. Why had he not known it?

With his subtle smile, Lord Henry watched him. He knew the precise psychological moment when to say nothing. He felt intensely interested. He was amazed at the sudden impression that his words had produced, and, remembering a book that he had read when he was sixteen, a book which had revealed to him much that he had not known before, he wondered whether Dorian Gray was passing through a similar experience. He had merely shot an arrow into the air. Had it hit the mark? How fascinating the lad was!

Gentlemen, in the story from that day onwards down to the last scene which Sir Edward Clarke spoke of, that boy's life, commencing there and then with the corruption implanted in his mind from his conversation with Lord Henry Wotton, on and on became more and more corrupt until all the vices that can be imagined were the vices in which he indulged. Gentlemen, Mr Oscar Wilde yesterday told me that there were passages in that book which might refer to the vice of sodomy, at least might be taken to refer to it by those who do not understand the artistic bearing of the language. I could have understood that as a defence or as a justification for Mr Wilde's publishing his book, if he had taken care that the book never came into the hands of those who would only put the ordinary meaning on the language – if it only came into the hands of those who would only put the artistic meaning which he says has to be put upon the language. But Mr Wilde admitted to me as regards the publication of that book, and indeed it was the case of Sir Edward Clarke, that it has been published at every bookstall – published no doubt in this purged form – but also published and sold originally for one shilling in the original edition out of which I took the various passages yesterday – published in *Lippincott's Magazine* in America, my friend says, but I think that the magazine is also sold very largely in this country.[244] Therefore, gentlemen of the jury, I am not going to dwell further upon this book of *Dorian Gray*, but I am going to say this, and I believe that anybody who reads it will say that I am justified in what I am saying, it is the story of a man corrupted by another man and who by such corruption is brought to commit, or the book suggests he has committed, this sodomitic vice of which we will hear a good deal more, probably, before this case closes, and if you come to the conclusion that *Dorian Gray* is a book of the kind that I have already told you – and you will remember the passages that I read out yesterday – if you come to the conclusion that it was a book of that character, then I ask you, what is the answer to our plea of justification here? What is the answer to our plea that Mr Wilde was even, by the publication of that book – and *a fortiori* by the publication of that book – taken in connection with the fact that he had a contribution in *The Chameleon*, under the circumstances I have already described, what answer, I ask, is there to our plea of justification that he was actually posing as a sodomite, in the sense which I have already told you? And when I am told here that Lord Queensberry, who was trying to free his son from the influence of this man, is to be sent to gaol because he wrote this card, I say that Lord Queensberry was not only justified but he was bound, if he had known of nothing else as to what is contained in these two documents which I hold here, justified in taking any step that he thought was necessary for putting an end to the acquaintance between his son and Mr Wilde and was more especially justified when – having given Mr Wilde full notice for the reasons that he stated at the time, being the same reasons that he states now, that he no longer wished that intimacy to continue – his son, unfortunately under Mr Wilde's influence, set his parent's authority at naught and determined to carry on, in spite of his remonstrances, the same intimacy as existed before, an intimacy which can only be described as the domination of Mr Wilde over this unfortunate Lord Alfred Douglas.[245]

Gentlemen, I pass from the literature and come upon another branch of the case about which, in many respects, there is no dispute. I must say yesterday, when my learned friend was opening the portion of the case which referred to the letter which has been called a sonnet, it did occur to me that a more thinly veiled attempt to cover the real nature of this letter and its history has never been attempted in a court of justice. I really have some difficulty in understanding why Sir Edward Clarke referred to the matter at all. I rather think he thought that we knew more about this letter and that he had better give an explanation of it. I certainly knew nothing about this letter, but if that was my friend's idea, his explanation was futile, because the letter which we did possess he had no explanation for. But what is this ridiculous explanation as regards this letter written to Lord Alfred Douglas? A man of the name of Wood, said my learned friend, intimated in some way or another to Oscar Wilde that he had taken out of a coat that was given him by young Douglas, certain correspondence that passed between Oscar Wilde and Lord Alfred Douglas. 'A man of the name of

Wood'? Why, he was 'Alfred'. He was one of the bosom companions of Wilde; he was one of the friends of Taylor; he was one of the lot – he was one of the Little College Street lot – 'a man of the name of Wood,' said my learned friend Sir Edward Clarke. Well, that would be a very convenient way, no doubt, to introduce the case if there was nothing more about Wood. But who was Wood? Wood was the man 'Alfred' whom Mr Wilde, the first day he met him, knowing nothing whatever about him and finding him merely a man who was in poor and impoverished circumstances, immediately asks to one of Kettner's best dinners that same evening and after a while, having entertained him over and over again, becomes so intimate with him – indeed, I am not sure that the intimacy did not spring up on the very first occasion – that they called each other by their Christian names. It is 'Alfred'; it is 'Oscar'. And this is the man who gives an intimation in some way or another to Mr Wilde that he has got Douglas's letters. Well, the first thing one would rather expect would be this: if this was a really respectable gentleman, such as Mr Wilde tells us now he was, an absolutely respectable gentleman, there would have been no difficulty whatsoever in his coming up and handing these letters over to Wilde or to Douglas. The letters were not the property of Wilde at that time; they were the property of Douglas. But when Wilde's friend 'Alfred' gets possession of the letters, the first thing we hear of is not: 'Look here, Oscar, here are some letters which came into my possession,' or 'Look here, Alfred, did you get any letters? If so please give them back to me.' The first intimation we get is that Wilde goes down to Sir George Lewis, a very eminent solicitor in London, and he asks Sir George Lewis to send a friendly note to his friend Alfred. This friend Alfred got the friendly note and reciprocating the friendly feeling which Mr Oscar Wilde had shown in going to Lewis, he refuses to answer the note and he refuses to see Sir George Lewis. What was the cause of the strained relations between Wilde and this man Wood? How came it about that the mere fact of one of Wilde's bosom friends having a letter or two of his should lead to all this roundabout method of trying to get back these letters? What is the reason of it? It could not be that there was any previous relationship between Wood and Wilde which put Wilde into a little difficulty. That might be suggested, but Mr Wilde says nothing of the kind had ever occurred. But I only mention it in this context because, when I tell you that previous to the possession of these letters, Wilde had been carrying on his filthy and abominable practices with this man Wood, you then get the key to the whole situation. He was not the innocent friend assisted by Wilde out of the largeness of that great heart which he has told us in the box that he has. (*Laughter*). He was one of the men introduced by Taylor with whom Wilde had carried on immoral practices. When Wilde heard that the man with whom he had been carrying on immoral practices had got the letters – you see, if Wood wished to turn against Wilde, the letter would be a strange corroboration of the fact that Wilde was given to these immoral practices. That was the reason of Wilde's anxiety to get the letters at any cost. That was the reason why Wilde goes to Sir George Lewis. What other reason can be suggested? Wood would not see Sir George Lewis. He thought perhaps Sir George Lewis would be too clever for him, and so Wilde then telegraphs or gets Taylor to come and see him at College Street. Taylor could have thrown some useful light upon this matter. Taylor could have given us some little information about it. Taylor could have given us some idea as to what took place between him and Wood. Indeed, I rather think that Taylor could have told us the whole matter. But, at all events, at Little College Street, Wood met Wilde, and I believe Taylor was present. Now, here again, there may be little discrepancies between Mr Wood and Mr Wilde in their evidence. Taylor would have been very useful to show which of them was telling the truth. He has been on Tuesday last in close conversation with Wilde in Tite Street. He is his bosom friend up to the present moment. But he will not examine him. Well, they go to Little College Street and certainly an extraordinary interview takes place. Mr Wilde told us yesterday he thought his friend Alfred had come to blackmail him. I must say he treated him very considerately being under that impression. He comes in and he tells him the story about these letters. They had been stolen from him and it turns out that Wood had really no letters, at least we are told letters of no importance at all, but such as he had he handed them back to Wilde. He tells Wilde that a notorious blackmailer of the name of Allen had unfortunately got one of the letters.

CLARKE: That is not so.

CARSON: Mr Wilde thought at that time they were all the letters. But what is Wilde's case? Wilde's case is that these letters were not of the slightest value – they were not of the slightest incriminating character – the ones that he got back from this man, and being under the impression that the man had come in to blackmail him, and because he gave him letters which were not of the slightest value, he at once gives him sixteen pounds. Now, what did he give him that sixteen pounds for? What does any gentleman in the box there think that Wilde gave to Wood sixteen pounds for upon that occasion? I will tell you. The one thing that Wilde was anxious for was that Wood should leave the country and go to America and he gives him sixteen pounds. The next day he meets him, I think, at a lunch at the Florence – he invites him to lunch at the Florence. They have a farewell lunch in a private room and he gives him another five pounds out of his deep gratitude for the companionship that Wood had given him at some previous period, and there and then, having had the farewell lunch at the Florence, Wood is shipped away to America and I suppose Wilde hoped he never would see him again. But he is here and he will be examined before you.

Gentlemen of the jury, you know this kind of explanation is trifling with common sense, trifling with reason, but that is not the whole story of this 'beautiful letter' and having got this letter from Wood, some time afterwards comes in Allen. 'Allen,' says Wilde, 'I had never seen before, but of one thing I was certain—'

JUDGE: Meantime he had received a copy from Mr Beerbohm Tree.

CARSON: I thank your lordship for reminding me. Meantime somebody had sent a copy, or what purported to be a copy, to Mr Beerbohm Tree, who had in hand one of Mr Wilde's plays, and Mr Beerbohm Tree at once sent for Mr Wilde and gave him the copy. Now, gentlemen of the jury, I am sure you will allow me to say as regards Mr Beerbohm Tree, as his name has been introduced into this matter, that so far as I can see Mr Beerbohm Tree acted in every way that was perfectly right having received that communication.

CLARKE: There is no question about that.

CARSON: I take leave to make that statement because I have had a communication this morning by cable from Mr Beerbohm Tree saying that, even there in America, he has seen his name introduced into the matter, and substantially stating that his whole connection with Mr Wilde is what I stated yesterday.[246]

JUDGE: There is not the slightest ground for making any suggestion whatever adverse to Mr Beerbohm Tree.

CARSON: It is only fair in this case there should be no misapprehension on that point. I spoke to my friend Sir Edward Clarke about it and he at once agreed with me and his lordship entirely agrees with me that Mr Beerbohm Tree's action was exactly what it ought to have been.

JUDGE: He acted with the most perfect propriety.

CARSON: Mr Beerbohm Tree sent for Mr Wilde. He gave him a copy of the letter and Mr Wilde, being in possession of the copy of the letter, began to think, 'Now the letter is discovered, how will I get out of it?' A short time afterwards Allen, the blackmailer, calls and he has the most extraordinary conversation with Allen, the blackmailer. He spoke to him about the letter. He told him that it was no matter now that he had a copy, that it was really a beautiful sonnet, and that he intended to have it published in some magazine which was shortly coming out at Oxford.

JUDGE: *The Spirit Lamp.*

CARSON: Gentlemen of the jury, I should like to know when did Oscar Wilde make up his mind to publish this letter to Lord Alfred Douglas as a sonnet, because I asked him specially, when he was sending it to Lord Alfred Douglas, did he even ask Lord Alfred Douglas to preserve it, and he said he did not, and so far as he would know, it would be put into the waste-paper basket or would be torn up. But, you see, the moment it was discovered, it was necessary that he should make a case in connection with it as the blackmailer had it, and he at once makes up his mind that it would be a splendid way for him to get out of the matter by saying, 'Oh, this is not a real letter at all, it is a poem; it is a sonnet, a prose poem.' It was 'a valuable manuscript', which he had never asked Lord Alfred Douglas to keep at all, and which he never, so far as he was concerned, could have published unless he got it back in some way or other from Lord Alfred Douglas. But he makes up his mind when it is discovered: 'Well, I will say, "This is not an ordinary letter," and what I will do will be this,' – and no doubt he did make up his mind to this course – 'I will make a clean breast of the whole thing, and I will publish it as a poem in this magazine *The Spirit Lamp*,' which is published at Oxford by, I believe, Lord Alfred Douglas. He tells all this to Allen, the blackmailer. Now, gentlemen of the jury, let us just for one moment see what this 'valuable sonnet' this 'manuscript' is. It is dated 16 Tite Street, Chelsea SW. 'My own boy, Your sonnet is quite lovely. It is a marvel that those red, rose-leaf lips' – that 'red rose' is a term that Lord Henry Wotton uses to young Dorian Gray upon the occasion which I have told you of already – 'that those red, rose-leaf lips of yours should be made no less for music of song than for madness of kissing.' Now, I take leave to say, so far as I can see, there is nothing beautiful in the idea at all. To my mind it is absolutely disgusting. Assuming that it is a poem, that it is a sonnet addressed by a man of forty years of age – or I should say at that time he was not quite forty – to a boy of about twenty, I say that to address even a sonnet to him and to talk of him as having 'red, rose-leaf lips made no less for music of song than madness of kissing', is disgusting. But even if you come to the conclusion that it is beautiful, as Mr Wilde says, and that it is poetic, I do not think the resources of Mr Wilde's intellect would fail him if he attempted to recall or repeat something equally beautiful. 'Your slim gilt soul walks between passion and poetry. I know Hyacinthus, whom Apollo loved so madly, was you in Greek days' – that is an allusion to a classical relation between Hyacinthus and Apollo, which it is not necessary to repeat – 'Why are you alone in town and when do you go to Salisbury?' – this occurs to me as being a very ordinary kind of language – I have not seen the French into which this was translated.[247] I do not know how they rendered it. 'Why are you alone in town and when do you go to Salisbury? Do go there and cool your hands in the grey twilight of Gothic things, and come here whenever you like. It is a lovely place.' I do not know whether that means Tite Street.

CLARKE: No, that is a mistake in the copy.

CARSON: I am told it was from Torquay, but the copy they gave me was from Tite Street. 'Come here whenever you like. It is a lovely place – it only lacks you. But go to Salisbury first. Always with undying love, yours Oscar.' Gentlemen of the jury, I ask you, now, to put yourselves in the position of a parent, who hears of a man so dominating his son twenty years younger than him, that he ventures to address to him this abominable piece of disgusting immorality. You may believe, if you like, that this was written as a sonnet to be published; I am sure I shall envy your credulity if you do. But it is the case made, and no doubt the eloquence of my friend may induce you to believe a great many things and he may lead you to believe that that is a sonnet. If so, he and I, each no doubt as advocates take an entirely different view of the document. But the beautiful sonnet, unfortunately for his case, happens to be the one letter that was disclosed to the public. The other three, Mr Wilde told you, he destroyed. That had been known to the public by being sent to Mr Beerbohm Tree, but it is an extraordinary thing that the only letter that Mr Wilde is able to refer us to, that was ever published as a sonnet, is the one letter which became known to the public. Now, gentlemen of the jury, I do not see it is for you, however, any great difference between that 'beautiful letter' and the other letter that Mr Wilde wrote from the Savoy Hotel when he was carrying on further immoralities, which will be proved to you up to the hilt in the course of this case – when his wife was away in Italy – when he had shut up his house in Tite Street and he had gone down to stay at the Savoy Hotel and had taken a suite of rooms; although, I must say, from one fact that is stated on the face of it and from his letter itself I should have thought it would have been better for Mr Wilde to stay at Tite Street and that is the fact that he says his bill there is forty-nine pounds for a week and that he fears he must leave and he has no money and no credit. Well, I should have thought that a gentleman having a house in Tite Street and having no money and no credit might have very well managed to do there in a very quiet way without having a suite of rooms at the Savoy Hotel. But here is the letter: 'Savoy Hotel, Victoria Embankment, London, WC. Dearest of all Boys, Your letter was delightful, red and yellow wine to me' – there was a letter written by Douglas to him which was red and yellow wine that was never published as a sonnet – 'but I am sad and out of sorts, Bosie, you must not make scenes with me. They kill me. They wreck the loveliness of life. I cannot see you, so Greek and gracious, distorted by passion' – the 'Greek' is the same idea he had brought into the other – 'I cannot listen to your curved lips saying hideous things to me. Don't do it. You break my heart. I'd sooner . . .' – then there is something I cannot decipher[248] – '. . . than have you bitter, unjust and horrid. I must see you soon. You are the divine thing I want, the thing of grace and genius, but I don't know how to do it. Shall I come to Salisbury? There are many difficulties. My bill here is forty-nine pounds for a week! I have also got a new sitting room over the Thames. But you, why are you not here, my dear, my wonderful boy? I fear I must leave; no money, no credit, and a heart of lead. Ever your own Oscar.' What does a man mean in writing that letter to a boy twenty years younger than himself? It can mean only one thing, unfortunately. I am not here to say that anything has ever happened between Mr Oscar Wilde and this young man. God forbid. But I say it permits to the conclusion that Wilde has conceived this vile, abominable passion towards this young man, which is just in keeping with the tone and character of the persons of whom he wrote in his book *Dorian Gray*. I say in addition it shows this: that this young man was in the unfortunately dangerous position that he acquiesced in the domination of Wilde – a man of great ability and of great attainments – a dangerous position for a young man who eventually wrote 'Two Loves', the poem to which I have called your attention, in *The Chameleon*. I want to know, when that letter has been written by Wilde to Lord Queensberry's son and Lord Queensberry protests, are you going to send Lord Queensberry to gaol? You may say, if you like, that his letters were impassioned; you may say, if you like, that his letters were written in a tone which a calm man would not use, and you may say, if you like, that his publishing this matter in the way in which he did, by leaving a card at the Albemarle Club, was a way of which you did not approve. Before you condemn him, read that letter and tell me that the gorge of any father ought not to rise if he believes, as is proved now, that his son was so dominated by Mr Oscar Wilde that he allowed him to make love to him – a filthy, abominable love – the love contained in that correspondence. We are always told when we come into courts of justice that the man who is charged – charged often under difficult circumstances – ought to have done this and ought to have done that and ought to have done the other. What would you have done? What was he to have done? He says he wrote to his son and he wrote to Wilde, and he told them that if he met them he would create a scandal; and his own son under the influence of Wilde, writes back to him and tells him, 'Recollect. I your son – because you ask me to give up Wilde in the case – I your son, if you come near us, so dominated am I by Wilde, I will shoot you.' Well, Lord Queensberry was determined to bring the matter to an issue. What other way had Lord Queensberry of bringing the matter to an issue than the one which he has adopted? He might have written a letter, as I think Sir Edward Clarke suggested, to the committee of the club; he might have done it in many other ways. But he chose the one way which you have before you and he did that most deliberately, and he is not afraid to abide by the issue which is raised in this court.

Gentlemen, Allen did not give the letter on that occasion. Allen was a notorious blackmailer and Allen was given ten shillings. Said Mr Wilde, 'I gave him that to show him my contempt for him.' Well, it is on a par with all the rest of Mr Wilde's paradoxical conduct, as I suppose he would call it, that he gives the man whom he knew as a notorious blackmailer and who had brought him nothing, a half-sovereign. Do you believe that he gave it to show his contempt? Gentlemen, you know very well that he gave it to keep Allen friendly. Allen goes out and Allen apparently meets Cliburn who has the letter, and Cliburn goes in almost immediately afterwards with the letter and he gives up the letter to Mr Wilde and he gets, I think, half a sovereign for the letter. There is the history of that letter.[249] Sixteen pounds paid to Wood – five pounds the day after. Wood shipped to America. Allen and Cliburn coming in each paid a sum of ten shillings. No doubt they were easily dealt with because they really were, to use a common phrase, 'bluffed' by Mr Wilde about the copy that was to be published; and, of course, as everybody, as Mr Tree and others would have seen this letter, there was no real value to be attached – no premium value to be attached – to the possession of it. Well, as I have said before, gentlemen of the jury, the whole story as regards that letter can only be explained when you hear Wood's evidence. Wood will describe to you – I am not going to anticipate it now – how time after time Mr Oscar Wilde, almost from the commencement of their acquaintance, adopted filthy and immoral practices with him. When you hear that, I think you will say that you have the key to the whole mystery as regards this letter, and you will see that the suggestion with which my learned friend Sir Edward Clarke thought it necessary to open up the facts, that this was a mere matter of Mr Wilde wanting to publish a valuable manuscript upon which he set considerable store, is only a desperate suggestion that is made because, of course, the letter would have to be brought before you in any event as it had been made public.

At 4.20 p.m. the court is adjourned until 10.30 a.m. on the following day.

EDWARD CARSON *resumes his opening speech for the defence.*

CARSON: If your lordship pleases, gentlemen of the jury: yesterday
when it came to the usual time for adjourning the court, I had
dealt as fully as I intend to deal with the question of Mr Wilde's
connection with the literature that has been produced in this
case and also with the fact of those letters, one of which was
produced by him and one of which was produced by us, and I
almost hoped that I had sufficiently demonstrated upon those
to you – which are not questions really in dispute in this matter –
that so far as Lord Queensberry is concerned, he was absolutely
justified in bringing to a climax in the way he did, this question
of the connection between Mr Oscar Wilde and his son.

I have unfortunately a more painful part of the case now to
approach. I have to comment upon the other evidence which is
supplemental to what I may call the clear and admitted facts.
It will be my painful duty to bring before you these young men
one after the other to tell their tale. It is, of course, even for
an advocate, a distasteful task, but gentlemen of the jury, let
those who are inclined to condemn these men for allowing
themselves to be dominated, misled, corrupted by Mr Oscar
Wilde, remember the relative positions of the two parties, and
remember that they are men who have been more sinned against
than sinning. Gentlemen, I am not going in any great detail
now to criticise the evidence of Mr Oscar Wilde in relation to
the several transactions as to which I have cross-examined him.
There are general observations applicable to all the cases. There
is, in point of fact, a startling similarity between each of them
upon his own admissions, which must lead you to draw a most
painful conclusion. There is the fact that in not one of these
cases were the parties upon an equality in any way with Mr
Wilde; they were none of them really educated parties with

whom he would naturally associate; they were none of them his equal in years; and there was, you must have observed, a curious similarity in the ages of each and every one of them. Gentlemen of the jury, Mr Wilde said there was something beautiful about youth and something charming which led him to adopt the course of life he did in relation to these young men. Has Mr Wilde been unable to find more suitable companions, who would be at the same time young and who would at the same time have all the charm that he wishes so much to associate with, in youths of his own class? The thing is absurd. His excuse in the box, there, was only a travesty of what is the reality of the facts. Now, who were all these young men? Of Wood I have already spoken. Wood – of whose past history Wilde pretends that he knew nothing – Wood, so far as he knew, a clerk out of employment. Who was Parker? He professes the same ignorance as regards Parker, that he knew nothing about his antecedents. Who was Scarfe? Exactly in the same way he knows nothing about him, except that he was out of employment; and as regards Conway, that he met him by chance upon the beach at Worthing. Gentlemen of the jury, there is an extraordinary similarity in the history of all these cases. All these young men of some eighteen to twenty years of age, perhaps one or two of them a year or two more, the manner of the introduction to Wilde, the way in which Wilde treated them subsequently, the giving to them of money, and the giving to them of presents one and all, are in the same category, all leading up to the same conclusion: that there was something unnatural, something unexpected – what you would not expect in the relations between Wilde and these gentlemen.

Take first the case of Parker. How did Wilde get to know Parker? Parker was a gentleman's servant. We do not wish to introduce names into this case which we can avoid, but Parker was a gentleman's servant – the name can be either handed up or told, and there need be no mystery about it – who was out of employment. He and his brother, one evening in a restaurant in Piccadilly, met Taylor, and Taylor came and addressed them and within a day or two Wilde gives his dinner to Taylor upon his birthday, and he says to Taylor who is one of his bosom friends, 'Bring anyone you like.' What an idea Taylor must have had of Wilde's tastes; when invited to a birthday dinner and told to bring any guests he likes, he brings a groom and a valet. Why, gentlemen, what if that one fact is true – and it is true beyond all doubt, because the main features of it have been admitted by Mr Wilde himself – why did Mr Taylor first speak to these young men in the restaurant in Piccadilly at all, if Taylor was the class of man that Wilde has pretended he was in the box here? And what was the meaning of Taylor if he knew that Wilde was moral and upright and the artistic and literary man that he undoubtedly was – what was his meaning in bringing these two men to dine with him at this birthday dinner? Gentlemen of the jury, there can be no explanation to these matters, there can be no explanation but the one that Taylor was the procurer for Wilde, as he undoubtedly was, and you will hear from this young man Parker, who will have to tell his unfortunate story to you. He will tell you he was poor, he was out of place, he had no money and, of course, unfortunately he fell a victim to Wilde, and he will tell you that upon the very first evening that they met – and indeed Mr Wilde himself has led up to what was the result – because he, just fancy, upon the very first evening they met, Wilde addressing the valet as Charlie, and Parker addressing Wilde, the distinguished dramatist – whose name was being mentioned, I suppose, in every circle in London for the distinction he had gained by his plays and by his literature – and, just fancy, the valet at the dinner addressing him as 'Oscar'. I do not at all wish to say anything about Mr Wilde's theories of putting an end to social distinctions. It may be a very noble and a very generous instinct in some people to wish to break down all social barriers. I know nothing about that, but I do know one thing, one thing that is plain in this case: that Mr Wilde's conduct was not regulated by any very generous instincts towards these young men. If Mr Wilde wanted to assist Parker, if Mr Wilde was interested in him, if Taylor was interested in him, and if Taylor wanted to do him a good turn, do you think it is any benefit for a man in Mr Wilde's position in society and his position in literature, even with a view to assisting a young man of Parker's class in life, do you think it is any benefit to take him to a restaurant and to prime him with the best of champagne and to give him the most luxurious dinners, is that the way a generous charity or a generous sympathy would be extended by one man towards another in the position in which Parker was, gentlemen of the jury? Of course, all that ridiculous excuse of Mr Wilde will not bear one moment's examination. He knew, of course, that up to the hilt he would be traced to have been over and over and over again with Parker, that Parker would have been traced to be dining and lunching in his company, to be going to his rooms, to be going to the Savoy. He knew that all that would be demonstrated by witness after witness if he ventured to deny it, and so he makes a clean breast of the whole thing and he asks the jury to say, 'Yes, but that was all perfectly innocent – aye, more – a generous action for my part.' Gentlemen of the jury, upon that evening, the first evening that they met, Wilde, having given them plenty of champagne and having otherwise treated them, as he says a gentleman always does those whom he asks to dinner, he suggests to this young man to drive home with him to the Savoy Hotel and, I must say, I think we have had no explanation up to this from Mr Wilde himself as to what he was doing with this suite of rooms in the Savoy Hotel at all. It is a very large hotel and it is probably a very easy kind of place to move about in, and Wilde, of course, had no difficulty, even without the people in the hotel suspecting anything at that time, in bringing Parker into his rooms and Parker will tell you how, when he got into his rooms, he was primed with whiskies and sodas and with iced champagne, which Mr Wilde indulges in, contrary to the directions of his doctor; and being primed with that, he will tell you how he was brought to bed by Mr Wilde and he will tell you of the shocking immoralities which he was led to perpetrate on that occasion. Was there the slightest truth, said my learned friend to Mr Wilde, in the statement in Lord Queensberry's letter that there had been a scene in the Savoy Hotel or a scandal in connection with the Savoy Hotel? 'None whatsoever,' says Mr Wilde. Yes, but, gentlemen of the jury, isn't it an extraordinary thing that, writing as far back as the month of June or July 1894, Lord Queensberry refers to this scandal in the Savoy Hotel? There may have been no open scene in Wilde being turned out, but men cannot live this kind of life without gossip going abroad and without reports being circulated in the circles in which they mix. When you hear the evidence that comes now from the Savoy Hotel, which no doubt gave rise to the gossip which Lord Queensberry had heard, you will wonder not that the gossip reached Lord Queensberry's ears, but you will wonder that this man Wilde has been tolerated in society in London for the length of time that he has, bringing boys into the Savoy Hotel. And a respectable man who has been there for years will be produced before you, the masseur Migge, whom I asked Mr Wilde about, who will tell you that he was astonished upon going unexpectedly one morning into Mr Wilde's room to find a boy lying in his bed. And the servants, some of them in the same hotel, will be brought and they will tell you the disgusting filth in which they found the bedclothes on more than one occasion. Was it any wonder that scandal reached Lord Queensberry, whose son was living for a portion of the time at the Savoy Hotel? Well, there is Parker.

I am not going through the various details of Parker's connection with Wilde. What did Wilde want with Parker? He wanted him only for his immoral purposes and then he dropped him, and Parker has since enlisted in the army and I am sure, I hope and trust, that now that he has entered into the service of his country where he will be kept under discipline, his experiences of the past – and his last experience was being arrested with Taylor in the raid in Fitzroy Square – the experience of the past may be, as I believe it has been, a lesson to him in the future, because I am told that, at all events since he has entered the army, he has not had a single black mark against his name, and he now bears there an excellent character. But it is not for me to set up Parker, it is not for me to say that Parker is a respectable, credible witness. Wilde tells you that Parker was a highly respectable man and it does not lie in Wilde's mouth to say one word against Parker as a witness in this case. He comes here and he will come here with great reluctance. Tracked out and asked the truth which was brought home to him by the knowledge that we had, he has to tell the truth, and I regret that he has to come here, and I regret that I shall have to examine him in connection with my learned friends to prove all this before a prurient public, who will be in no wise benefited by hearing the details of his evidence. Gentlemen, that is Parker.

I take now in contrast to the case of Parker, the case of Conway – Alfonso Conway. Why I am now taking Conway in contrast to the other case is for this reason: Conway was not procured by Taylor, but was procured by Wilde himself. Wilde at the time was living in Worthing and he had not Taylor at hand when these horrible lusts came upon him to procure a boy and so let us see how he gets at poor Conway. Now, was there ever a more audacious story confessed in a court of justice than that confessed by Wilde in relation to Conway? What is it? He sees a boy upon the beach at Worthing; he knows nothing whatsoever about him except that he is a boy there assisting about the different boats. His real history, as Wilde proved to you, is this: he had previously sold newspapers at Worthing at the pier at one of these kiosks, and I must say that I do not think a more flippant answer ever was given by a witness than what Mr Wilde said yesterday. When he was asked if he knew anything about Conway being previously connected with selling newspapers, he told us he did not know that he had had any previous connection with literature. No doubt he thought in many of his answers he was making very smart repartee and probably that he was scoring off counsel who was cross-examining, or something of that kind, but Conway is upon the beach and he helps Mr Wilde to take out his boat and through that an intimacy springs up. Now, if you had not heard it proved by Mr Wilde himself, could you have believed that within a day or two that boy was lunching with Wilde, was brought to his house and if Wilde's evidence is true, which I hope sincerely it is not, was introduced to his children and to his family. At the time when he first met Conway, it appears his wife was not at Worthing, but I rather gathered from him that his children were. At all events, he said that at some time or other Conway had been in association with his children, an extraordinary fact – this young man Conway of twenty being told to you to be in association with two little boys of eight and nine – well, you find Conway lunching! Now, what happens? Of course, Wilde could not bring about this boy, there or anywhere else, looking in his extraordinary condition, and what does he do? And – now, it is really here that the disgraceful audacity of the man comes in – he procures him a suit of clothes and he dresses him up like a gentleman and he puts some of these public school colours, something of that kind, upon his hat and he makes him look as if he were a proper person to be associating with him. Really, really, gentlemen of the jury, the thing is past belief. It is almost past belief if we had proved that as against Mr Wilde you would have almost not believed it. But Mr Wilde knew that we had the witnesses to prove it all, we had all the things here to produce as you saw and Wilde dare not deny it. What did he dress Conway up for? I venture to say that if he was really anxious to assist Conway, the very worst thing he could have done was to take Conway out of his proper sphere and to begin, as he did with Parker, giving him champagne lunches, taking him to his hotel, treating him in a manner which, of course, Conway in the future could never expect to live up to. I could understand the generous instincts of a man who would say, 'Here is a smart boy at Worthing whom I have met at the pier. I will try and get him employment; I will educate him; I will give him some money; I will try and assist him in any way I can,' but is it any assistance to a boy like Conway to do as

Wilde did, to take him up and dress him and take him about giving him champagne lunches and all the rest of it?[250] (*Here* CARSON *pauses.*) Would your lordship excuse me for a moment?

CLARKE *and* CARSON *confer together inaudibly.*

CLARKE: Would your lordship allow me to interpose at this moment and make a statement which, of course, is made under a feeling of very great responsibility? My learned friend, Mr Carson, yesterday addressed the jury upon the question of the literature involved in this case and upon inferences to be drawn from admissions made with regard to letters by Mr Oscar Wilde yesterday, and my learned friend began his address this morning by saying that he hoped yesterday that he had said enough dealing with those topics to induce the jury to relieve him from the necessity of dealing in detail with the other issues in this case. My lord, I think it must have been present to your lordship's mind that those who were representing Mr Oscar Wilde in this case had before them a very terrible anxiety. They could not conceal from themselves that the judgement that might be formed of that literature and of conduct which has been admitted, might not improbably induce the jury to say that when Lord Queensberry used the words 'posing as sodomite', he was using words for which there was sufficient justification to entitle a father, who used those words under these circumstances, to the utmost consideration and to be relieved from a criminal charge in respect of that statement. And, my lord, with it, in our view, and in our clear view, that that might probably be the result – not improbably be the result upon that part of the case – I and my learned friends who desire to be associated with me in this matter, had to look forward to this, that a verdict given in favour of the defendant upon that part of the case might be interpreted outside as a conclusive finding with regard to all parts of the case, and the position in which we stood was this: that without expecting to obtain a verdict in this case, we should be going through day after day, it might be, with long evidence, an investigation of matters of the most appalling character. In those circumstances, I hope your lordship will think that I am taking a right course, which I take after communicating with Mr Oscar Wilde, and that is to say that having regard to what has already been referred to by my learned friend in respect of the matters connected with the literature and the letters, I feel that he could not resist a verdict of 'not guilty' in this case – 'not guilty' having reference to the words 'posing as'. In those circumstances I hope your lordship will think that I am not going beyond the bounds of duty, and that I am doing something to save, to prevent, what would be a most terrible task, however it might close, if I now interpose and say that on behalf of Mr Oscar Wilde I would ask to withdraw from the prosecution, and if your lordship does not think at this time of the case and after what has taken place that I ought to be allowed to do that on his behalf, my lord, I am prepared to submit to a verdict of 'not guilty' having reference, if to any part of the particulars at all, to that part of the particulars which is connected with the publication of *Dorian Gray* and the publication of *The Chameleon.* I trust, my lord, that that may make an end of the case.

CARSON: My lord, I do not know that I have any right whatsoever to interfere in any way in the application that my learned friend has made to your lordship. I can only say as far as Lord Queensberry is concerned that if there is a verdict of 'not guilty', a verdict which involves that he has succeeded in his plea of justification, I am quite satisfied. Of course, my lord, my learned friend would admit that we must succeed upon that plea in the manner in which he has stated, and that being so, it will rest entirely with your lordship as to whether the course suggested by my learned friend is to be taken.

JUDGE: Inasmuch as the prosecutor in this case is prepared to acquiesce in a verdict of 'not guilty' against the accused, I do not think it is any part of the function of the judge or the jury to insist on going through prurient details which can have no bearing upon the matter which is already concluded by the assent of the prosecutor to an adverse verdict. But as to the jury putting any limitation upon the verdict, the justification is a justification of a charge which is 'posing as sodomite'. If that is justified, it is justified; if it is not, it is not; and the verdict of the jury upon it must be 'guilty' or 'not guilty' and I understand the prosecutor assents to a verdict of 'not guilty'. There can be no terms; there can be no limitation; the verdict must be 'guilty' or 'not guilty'. I understand him to assent to a verdict of 'not guilty' and, of course, the jury will return that verdict.

CARSON: Of course, my lord, the verdict will be that the plea of justification is proved and is for the public benefit.

JUDGE: Of course, that involves it.

CLARKE: The verdict is 'not guilty'.

JUDGE: The verdict, I take it, is 'not guilty', but it is arrived at by that process. Of course, I should have had to tell the jury the two things to be established there – had to be established – that the justification set up was true, that is: that it was true in substance and in fact, that the prosecutor had posed as a sodomite; and I should also have had to tell them that they would have to find that that statement was published in such a manner as to be for the public benefit. If they found those two issues in favour of the defendant, then he would not be guilty. The verdict will be 'not guilty' and that is, I understand it, the verdict with the assent of the prosecutor, that the jury are invited to return.

The jury confers briefly.

JUDGE: Gentlemen of the jury, your ultimate verdict will be 'not guilty', but there are other matters which have to be determined by reference to the specific findings on the plea of justification, and, as I have told you, that plea involves two things: that the statement is true in fact and that the publication was for the public benefit. Those two facts you will have to find, and then having found those in favour of the defendant, your verdict will be 'not guilty'; but you will have to say whether you find the plea of justification proved or not.

The jury confers for a few minutes without leaving the box.

CLERK OF THE COURT: Gentlemen, do you find the plea of justification in this case proved or not?

FOREMAN OF THE JURY: Yes.

CLERK OF THE COURT: You say that the defendant is 'not guilty' and that is the verdict of you all?

FOREMAN OF THE JURY: Yes; and also that it was published for the public benefit.

CARSON: My lord, of course the costs of the defence will follow against Mr Wilde?

CLERK OF THE COURT: They follow as a matter of course.

JUDGE: They follow.

CARSON: Lord Queensberry may be discharged?

JUDGE: Oh, certainly.

The Court rises at about 11.15 a.m.

11. On 28 May 1895, three days after Wilde's conviction, Queensberry met his eldest son Percy in Piccadilly and a fight broke out. To his father's fury Percy had stood bail for Wilde after the second trial.

APPENDIX A

THE INDICTMENT AGAINST THE MARQUESS OF QUEENSBERRY
(PRO REF. CRIM 4/1118)

First Count

Central Criminal Court. To wit: The jurors for our Lady the Queen upon their oath present that John Sholto Douglas, Marquess of Queensberry contriving and maliciously intending to injure one Oscar Fingal O'fflahertie Wills Wilde and to deprive him of his good name fame credit and reputation and to provoke him the said Oscar Fingal O'fflahertie Wills Wilde and to excite him to commit a breach of the peace and to bring him into public contempt scandal and disgrace on the eighteenth day of February in the year of our Lord one thousand eight hundred and ninety-five and within the jurisdiction of the said Court unlawfully wickedly and maliciously did write and publish and cause to be written and published of him the said Oscar Fingal O'fflahertie Wills Wilde a false scandalous malicious and defamatory libel in the form of a card directed to the said Oscar Fingal O'fflahertie Wills Wilde containing divers false scandalous malicious and defamatory matters of and concerning the said Oscar Fingal O'fflahertie Wills Wilde according to the tenor and effect following that is to say 'For Oscar Wilde posing as somdomite' meaning thereby that the said Oscar Fingal O'fflahertie Wills Wilde had committed and was in the habit of committing the abominable crime of buggery with mankind to the great damage scandal and disgrace of the said Oscar Fingal O'fflahertie Wills Wilde to the evil example of all others in the like case offending and against the peace of our said Lady the Queen her Crown and dignity.

Second Count

And the jurors aforesaid upon their oath aforesaid do further present that the said John Sholto Douglas, Marquess of Queensberry contriving and maliciously intending to injure the said Oscar Fingal O'fflahertie Wills Wilde and to deprive him of his good name fame credit and reputation and to provoke him the said Oscar Fingal O'fflahertie Wills Wilde and to excite him to commit a breach of the peace and to bring him into public contempt scandal and disgrace on the said eighteenth day of February in the year of our Lord one thousand eight hundred and ninety-five and within the jurisdiction of the said Court unlawfully wickedly and maliciously did write and publish and did cause to be written and published of him the said Oscar Fingal O'fflahertie Wills Wilde a false scandalous malicious and defamatory libel in the form of a card directed to the said Oscar Fingal O'fflahertie Wills Wilde containing divers false scandalous malicious and defamatory matters of and concerning the said Oscar Fingal O'fflahertie Wills Wilde according to the tenor and effect following that is to say 'For Oscar Wilde posing as somdomite' to the great damage scandal and disgrace of the said Oscar Fingal O'fflahertie Wills Wilde to the evil example of all others in the like case offending and against the peace of our said Lady the Queen her Crown and dignity.*

PLEA OF JUSTIFICATION FILED BY THE DEFENDANT IN REGINA (WILDE) V. QUEENSBERRY (PRO REF. CRIM 4/1118)

Central Criminal Court. To wit: At the Sessions of Oyer and Terminer and General Gaol Delivery holden for the Central Criminal Court District at Justice Hall Old Bailey in the suburbs of the City of London on the twenty-fifth day of March in the year of our Lord one thousand

---

* There seems to be no clear reason for Wilde's lawyers putting two such similar counts into the Indictment, apart from covering all possible interpretations of the words on Queensberry's card. It is interesting to speculate whether it was the words of explanation used only in the first count – 'meaning thereby that ... was in the habit of committing the abominable crime of buggery', thus implying that Wilde was accused of being a sodomite rather than merely 'posing' as one – that prompted Charles Russell to search out the rent boys. If the second count had been used alone, Queensberry's plea of justification and defence of the accusation of 'posing' might have been quite different.

eight hundred and ninety-five comes into Court the said John Sholto Douglas Marquess of Queensberry in his own proper person and having heard the said Indictment read says that he is not guilty of the premises in the said Indictment above specified and charged upon him and of this he the said John Sholto Douglas Marquess of Queensberry puts himself upon the Country.

Second Plea

And for a further plea in this behalf to the Second Count of the said Indictment the said John Sholto Douglas Marquess of Queensberry says that our Lady the Queen ought not further to prosecute the said Second Count of the said Indictment against him because he says that the said alleged libel according to the natural meaning of the words thereof is true in substance and in fact in that the said Oscar Fingal O'fflahertie Wills Wilde between the month of February in the year of our Lord one thousand eight hundred and ninety-two and the month of May in the same year at the Albemarle Hotel in the County of London did solicit and incite one Edward Shelley to commit sodomy and other acts of gross indecency and immorality with him the said Oscar Fingal O'fflahertie Wills Wilde and that the said Oscar Fingal O'fflahertie Wills Wilde did then indecently assault and commit acts of gross indecency and immorality with the said Edward Shelley.

And that the said Oscar Fingal O'fflahertie Wills Wilde in the month of October in the year of our Lord one thousand eight hundred and ninety-two at the said Albemarle Hotel did solicit and incite one Sydney Mavor to commit sodomy and other acts of gross indecency and immorality and did then and there commit the said other acts of gross indecency and immorality with the said Sydney Mavor.

And that the said Oscar Fingal O'fflahertie Wills Wilde on the twentieth day of November in the year of our Lord one thousand eight hundred and ninety-two at a house situate at 29 boulevard des Capucines in Paris in the Republic of France did solicit and incite one Frederick Atkins to commit sodomy and other acts of gross indecency and immorality with him the said Oscar Fingal O'fflahertie Wills Wilde and did then and there commit the said other acts of gross indecency and immorality with the said Frederick Atkins.

And that the said Oscar Fingal O'fflahertie Wills Wilde on the twenty-second day of November in the year of our Lord one thousand eight hundred and ninety-two at the said house in Paris did solicit and incite one Maurice Salis Schwabe to commit sodomy and other acts of gross indecency and immorality with him the said Oscar Fingal O'fflahertie Wills Wilde and did then and there commit the said other acts of gross indecency and immorality with the said Maurice Salis Schwabe.

And that the said Oscar Fingal O'fflahertie Wills Wilde at the said house situate in Paris between the twenty-fifth day of January in the year of our Lord one thousand eight hundred and ninety-three and the fifth day of February in the said year did solicit and incite certain boys to the defendant unknown to commit sodomy and other acts of gross indecency and immorality with him the said Oscar Fingal O'fflahertie Wills Wilde and did then and there commit the said other acts of gross indecency and immorality with the said boys.

And that the said Oscar Fingal O'fflahertie Wills Wilde in the month of January in the year of our Lord one thousand eight hundred and ninety-three at the house situate at and being No. 16 Tite Street in the County of London did solicit and incite one Alfred Wood to commit sodomy and other acts of gross indecency and immorality with him the said Oscar Fingal O'fflahertie Wills Wilde and did then and there commit the said other acts of gross indecency and immorality with the said Alfred Wood.

And that the said Oscar Fingal O'fflahertie Wills Wilde about the seventh day of March in the year of our Lord one thousand eight hundred and ninety-three at the Savoy Hotel in the County of London did solicit and incite a certain boy to the defendant unknown to commit sodomy and other acts of gross indecency and immorality with him the said Oscar Fingal O'fflahertie Wills Wilde and did then and there commit the said other acts of gross indecency and immorality with the said boy unknown.

And that the said Oscar Fingal O'fflahertie Wills Wilde on or about the twentieth day of March in the year of our Lord one thousand eight hundred and ninety-three at the said Savoy Hotel did solicit and incite another boy to the defendant unknown to commit sodomy and other acts of gross indecency and immorality with the said Oscar Fingal O'fflahertie Wills Wilde and did there commit the said other acts of gross indecency with the said last mentioned boy.

And that the said Oscar Fingal O'fflahertie Wills Wilde in the said month of March in the year of our Lord one thousand eight hundred and ninety-three at the said Savoy Hotel and again in or about the month of April in the year of our Lord one thousand eight hundred and ninety-three at a house situate and being No. 7 Camera Square and again in or about the month of April in the year of our Lord one thousand eight hundred and ninety-three at a house situate at and being No. 50 Park Walk and again between the month of October in the year of our Lord one thousand eight hundred and ninety-three and the month of April in the year of our Lord one thousand eight hundred and ninety-four at a house situate and being No. 10 St James's Place all in the County of London did on each of the said occasions solicit and incite one Charles Parker to commit sodomy and other acts of gross indecency and immorality with him the said Oscar Fingal O'fflahertie Wills Wilde and did then and there commit the said other acts of gross indecency and immorality with the said Charles Parker.

And that the said Oscar Fingal O'fflahertie Wills Wilde between the month of October in the year of our Lord one thousand eight hundred and ninety-three and the month of April in the year of our Lord one thousand eight hundred and ninety-four at the said house No. 10 St James's Place did solicit and incite one Ernest Scarfe to commit sodomy and other acts of gross indecency and immorality with him the said Oscar Fingal O'fflahertie Wills Wilde and did then and there commit the said other acts of gross indecency and immorality with the said Ernest Scarfe.

And that the said Oscar Fingal O'fflahertie Wills Wilde in the said month of March in the year of our Lord one thousand eight hundred and ninety-three at the said Savoy Hotel did take indecent liberties with one Herbert Tankard.

And that the said Oscar Fingal O'fflahertie Wills Wilde on several occasions in the month of June in the year of our Lord one thousand eight hundred and ninety-three in the City of Oxford and also upon several occasions in the months of June July and August in the year of our Lord one thousand eight hundred and ninety-three at a house called 'The Cottage' at Goring in the County of Oxford did solicit and incite one Walter Grainger to commit sodomy and other acts of gross indecency and immorality with him the said Oscar Fingal O'fflahertie Wills Wilde and did then and there commit the said other acts of gross indecency and immorality with the said Walter Grainger.

And that the said Oscar Fingal O'fflahertie Wills Wilde upon several occasions in the months of August and September in the year of our Lord one thousand eight hundred and ninety-four at Worthing in the Country of Sussex and on or about the twenty-seventh day of September in the said year at the Albion Hotel Brighton in the same County did solicit and incite one Alfonso Harold Conway to commit sodomy and other acts of gross indecency and immorality with him the said Oscar Fingal O'fflahertie Wills Wilde.

And that the said Oscar Fingal O'fflahertie Wills Wilde did in fact at the said times and places commit the said other acts of gross indecency with the said Alfonso Harold Conway.

And that the said Oscar Fingal O'fflahertie Wills Wilde in the month of July in the year of our Lord one thousand eight hundred and ninety did write and publish and cause and procure to be printed and published with his name upon the title page thereof a certain immoral and obscene work in the form of a narrative entitled *The Picture of Dorian Gray* which said work was designed and intended by the said Oscar Fingal O'fflahertie Wills Wilde and was understood by the readers thereof to describe the relations intimacies and passions of certain persons of sodomitical and unnatural habits tastes and practices.

And that in the month of December in the year of our Lord one thousand eight hundred and ninety-four was published a certain other immoral and obscene work in the form of a magazine entitled *The Chameleon* which said work contained divers obscene matters and things relating to the practices and passions of persons of sodomitical and unnatural habits and tastes and that the said Oscar Fingal O'fflahertie Wills Wilde joined in procuring the publication of the said last mentioned obscene work that the said Oscar Fingal O'fflahertie Wills Wilde published his name on the contents sheet of the said magazine as its first and principal contributor and published in the said magazine certain immoral maxims as an introduction to the same under the title of 'Phrases and Philosophies for the Use of the Young'.

And the said John Sholto Douglas Marquess of Queensberry further says that at the time of the publishing of the said alleged libel in the Second Count charged and stated it was for the public benefit that the matters therein contained should be published because before and at the time of the publishing of the said alleged libel the said Oscar Fingal O'fflahertie Wills Wilde was a man of letters and a dramatist of prominence and notoriety and a person who exercised considerable influence over young men that the said Oscar Fingal O'fflahertie Wills Wilde claimed to be a fit and proper person to give advice and instruction to the young and had published the said maxims hereinbefore mentioned in the said magazine entitled *The Chameleon* for circulation amongst students of the University of Oxford and that the said works entitled *The Chameleon* and *The Picture of Dorian Gray* were calculated to subvert morality and to encourage unnatural vice and that the said Oscar Fingal O'fflahertie Wills Wilde had corrupted and debauched the morals of the said Charles Parker, Alfonso Harold Conway, Walter Grainger, Sydney Mavor, Frederick Atkins, Ernest Scarfe and Edward Shelley as aforesaid and that the said Oscar Fingal O'fflahertie Wills Wilde had committed the offences aforementioned and the said sodomitical practices for a long time with impunity and without detection.

Wherefore it was for the public benefit and interest that the matter contained in the said alleged libel should be published and that the true character and habits of the said Oscar Fingal O'fflahertie Wills Wilde should be known that the said Oscar Fingal O'fflahertie Wills Wilde might be prevented from further committing such offences and further corrupting and debauching the liege subjects of our said Lady the Queen and that such liege subjects being forewarned might avoid the corrupting influence of the said Oscar Fingal O'fflahertie Wills Wilde.

And this the said John Sholto Douglas Marquess of Queensberry is ready to verify wherefore he prays Judgement and that by the Court he may be discharged and dismissed from the said premises in the said Indictment above specified.

Dated and filed this thirtieth day of March, 1895, by Charles Russell, solicitor to the said Marquess of Queensberry.

[Signed]

CHARLES F. GILL.

THE JURY FOR THE QUEENSBERRY LIBEL CASE
(PRO REF. CRIM 4/1118 & CRIM 6/19)

Thomas More
    12 Firsby Road, Clapton, Gentleman
William Nicholson
    5 Burgholt Crescent, Clapton, Gentleman

William Charles Mantle
  41 Braydon Road, Clapton, Gentleman
Alfred Morrow
  27 Narford Road, Clapton, Gentleman
John James Minns
  36 Forburg Road, Clapton, Gentleman
Henry Haydon
  2 Drapers Gardens, Stockbroker
Aubrey May
  220 High Street, Stoke Newington, Butcher
Edmund Wordley
  91 Kelvin Road, Islington, Gentleman
Philip Frank Osborne
  26 Durley Road, Clapton, Gentleman
John William McDonald
  39 Upper Kyversdale Road, Clapton, Gentleman
Anthony Cole
  1 Howard Road, Willesden, Bank Messenger
John Edward Finch
  144 High Street, Stoke Newington, Bootmaker

Started Wednesday 3 April; ended Friday 5 April 1895.

Before Mr Justice Henn Collins.

On the first day Aldermen Sir Richard Hanson, Benjamin Faudel Phillips, Lieut.-Col. Horatio David Davies, Walter Vaughan Morgan and Alderman and Sheriff Marcus Samuel joined Collins, J. on the bench. The proceedings started at 10.30 a.m. and were adjourned at 4.45 p.m.

On the second day Alderman William Purdie Treloar joined Collins, J. on the bench. The proceedings started at 10.30 a.m. and were adjourned at 4.20 p.m.

On the third day Alderman James Thomson Ritchie joined Collins, J. on the bench. The proceedings started at 10.30 a.m. and were concluded at about 11.20 a.m.

THE FRENCHMAN AND THE PRIME MINISTER

The Grand Jury, which was sworn in at the Old Bailey on 25 March 1895 to consider whether the Regina (Wilde) v. Queensberry case should go forward, included a French journalist, Paul Villars, 11 Wellington Square, Chelsea, Gentleman, who was elected foreman and who signed the verso of the Queensberry Indictment 'True bill. P. Villars'.

A rumour, which seems to have been started either by Carson or his biographer Majoribanks in 1932 and repeated by Hyde in 1948 and others since, that Villars fed the whole proceedings of the Grand Jury hearing back to the French press in advance of the Old Bailey trial, which in turn made the English aware of the fact that the Prime Minister, Lord Rosebery's name had cropped up and that he was in some way implicated, appears to be unfounded.* Villars wrote for *Le Figaro* and nothing of these matters was reported in that paper before 6 April. However, he was also correspondent for the *Journal des débats* which, on 5 April, briefly reported the proceedings of the previous day by concentrating largely on the unflattering mention in the courtroom of Rosebery in one of Queensberry's letters. The conflation of these two facts seems to have led to the rumour. It was also most unlikely that the Grand Jury itself would have had any opportunity to consider Queensberry's letters as evidence, as they were at best peripheral to the Indictment, based as it was on the visiting card. On the other hand, by 5 April Lord Rosebery's name had been printed in connection with the libel trial in most of the main London newspapers, and whether this affected the authorities' decision to secure Wilde's final conviction at all costs, remains an open question.

---

* See Marjoribanks, *Carson*, pp. 203–4 and Hyde, *Trials*, pp. 41–2. Nancy Erber, in an otherwise admirable article on 'The French trials of Oscar Wilde' in the *Journal of the History of Sexuality*, 6 (1996), suggests that another journalist on *Le Figaro*, Jacques St.-Cere, was empanelled in the third trial, but an examination of the jurors' list in the Public Record Office (CRIM ref. 4/1120) shows that this, too, is without foundation.

APPENDIX B

THE OPINION OF CHARLES GILL, PROSECUTING COUNSEL IN REGINA V. WILDE, TO THE DIRECTOR OF PUBLIC PROSECUTIONS, HAMILTON CUFFE, AND CUFFE'S MEMO TO CHARLES STEWART MURDOCH C.B., ASSISTANT UNDER-SECRETARY AT THE HOME OFFICE STATING WHY LORD ALFRED DOUGLAS SHOULD NOT BE PROSECUTED.
(PRO REF. HO 45/245163)

Temple Gardens
19 April 1895

My dear Cuffe,

I have considered the question as to whether a prosecution ought to be instituted against Lord Alfred Douglas on account of his connection with the case of Oscar Wilde and Alfred Taylor, and in the result I have come to the conclusion that no proceedings should be taken on the evidence we have in the statements of the different witnesses.

Having regard to the fact that Douglas was an undergraduate at Oxford when Wilde made his acquaintance, the difference in their ages and the strong influence that Wilde has obviously exercised over Douglas since that time, I think that Douglas, if guilty, may fairly be regarded as one of Wilde's victims.

Apart altogether from that aspect of the case, although I am afraid there is little room for doubt that immoral relations existed between them, yet if an attempt were made to prove anything definite, it would be found, I think, that the evidence available only disclosed a case of grave suspicion. That is to say, that Wilde and Douglas were continually about together staying at all sorts of places, and that Wilde had written at least two remarkable letters to Douglas. Upon this sort of evidence it would not be possible to formulate any criminal charge and there is no proof of any act of indecency between them.

With reference to the evidence of the young men who have been called as witnesses against Wilde and Taylor, only two of them, Wood and Charles Parker, suggest misconduct on the part of Douglas with them. These witnesses would clearly require corroboration and although there is ample as against Wilde, even in his own cross-examination of his relations with them, as regards Douglas there appears to be no corroboration whatever.

Comments will no doubt be made as to Douglas not being prosecuted, but these comments are made by people who do not understand or appreciate the difficulties of proving such a case.

As a question of public policy, I think it would be most undesirable to start such a prosecution unless there was a strong probability that it would result in a conviction.

Yours sincerely,

CHAS F. GILL

20 April 1895

Dear Murdoch,

Wilde Case

With reference to our conversation yesterday, I send herewith a copy of a letter I have this morning received from Gill and a memorandum which I wrote last night. You will see that his and my views correspond.

Yours very truly,

H. CUFFE

[Annotated] Secretary of State to see.

In the course of the investigation of the charges against Wilde and Taylor, we have directed our attention to the question whether there was evidence sufficient to support any charge against Lord Alfred Douglas whose relations with Wilde have raised a strong suspicion (and perhaps it might be said leave little doubt) as to the real character of their intimacy.

Two of the young men who have given evidence here, under pressure made statements affecting Lord A. Douglas, each saying that on one occasion he was guilty of acts of indecency, but one of these young men is a person of the worst possible character, and there is no corroboration of their statements in this respect.

From the best information we can obtain as to Lord A. Douglas we believe that he is a person of weak character, that (assuming his guilt) Wilde obtained great influence over him when he was an undergraduate at Oxford, that he induced him to enter on these evil practices, Douglas being led away by admiration for Wilde's intellect and literary abilities, and that since that time Wilde has exercised almost absolute sway and control over this young man.

It is difficult to distinguish between the moral guilt of one person and that of another who indulge in these criminal practices, but in dealing with these young men whom we have called as witnesses we have thought we might safely and fairly distinguish between men like Taylor and Wilde who tempt others in a humbler position of life by offers of money and luxury and those who yield to the temptation and if our own view of the cause of Lord A. Douglas's fall is the true one I am disposed to think that morally his guilt is perhaps less in degree than those who have sold their virtue for money. We think he fell when a boy at Oxford and that since that time he has never had the force of will or character to emancipate himself from his degrading submission to Wilde whom, no doubt, he still regards with the utmost devotion and affection.

It may be hoped that if Wilde be convicted and Douglas be thus forcibly separated from him there may be a chance of his abandoning his present course of life and seeing its iniquity, and however this be, there is at present no evidence on which, in our opinion, we could properly ask for his conviction.

Irresponsible persons may say and very likely will say that he goes unprosecuted because of his position in life. I hope this will never be said with truth in respect of the action of any public Department, but equally I hope it may never be able to be said with truth that we have prosecuted a person *because* of his position in life who would otherwise not have been charged with any offence.

We think the evidence insufficient and if we are right it is specially incumbent on us to be careful, as in the present state of public opinion there would be a real danger of a conviction in such a case on unreliable evidence.

H. CUFFE

20 April 1895

12. The arrest of Oscar Wilde at the Cadogan Hotel from the *Illustrated Police Budget* 13 April 1895. 'The pet of London Society, one of our most successful playwriters and poets, arrested on a horrible charge.'

NOTES

For ease of reference Oscar Wilde's libel action against the Marquess of Queensberry is referred to as 'the Queensberry trial' and the two subsequent trials in which Wilde appeared as the defendant against the Crown on charges of gross indecency are referred to as 'the second trial' or 'the third trial'. Other abbreviated references are shown in full in the bibliography and list of manuscript sources. Hyde's *The Trials of Oscar Wilde* (1948), though little more than a revamp of Mason's *Oscar Wilde: Three Times Tried* (1912) and omitting the proceedings in the magistrates' court, is much more widely available and for this reason references to the second and third trials have been made to Hyde.

1 For a discussion of when this momentous meeting might have taken place see *Complete Letters*, p. 461.
2 Douglas, *Autobiography*, p. 64.
3 Douglas letter to Frank Harris, 20 March 1925 (MS Texas).
4 See note 45.
5 Constance Wilde letter to Oscar Wilde, 18 September 1892 (MS Clark).
6 Douglas, *Autobiography*, pp. 59–60.
7 Ibid., p. 99.
8 See *Complete Letters*, pp. 575 and 693–5.
9 Ibid., p. 634.
10 Ibid.
11 In his deposition for the Douglas v. Ransome et al. trial, 1912 (MS Clark) Ross maintains he positively discouraged Wilde from taking action.
12 Douglas, *Oscar Wilde*, p. 14.
13 *Complete Letters*, p. 703.
14 Hyde, *Trials*, p. 34.
15 Ibid., p. 201.

16 The MS of these witness statements is now in a private collection.

17 MS Hyde.

18 Alfred Douglas letter to Percy Douglas, 21 March 1895 (MS Hyde).

19 Sir Edward Clarke letter to Robert Sherard, 16 September 1929 (MS Reading University).

20 Harris, *Oscar Wilde*, pp. 192–201.

21 Pearson, *Oscar Wilde*, p. 288.

22 *Westminster Gazette*, 3 April 1895.

23 *Daily Chronicle*, 4 April 1895.

24 *Sun*, 5 April 1895. This statement was vigorously repudiated by his uncle the Revd Archibald Douglas in the paper the following day.

25 Douglas, *Autobiography*, p. 104.

26 *London Figaro*, 11 April 1895.

27 Holland, *Son of Oscar Wilde*, p. 61.

28 Marjoribanks, *Carson*, p. 240.

29 See note 128.

30 Gide, *In Memoriam*, p. 32.

31 *Complete Letters*, p. 709.

32 Ibid., p. 1044.

33 Ibid., p. 1019.

34 Harris, *Oscar Wilde*, p. 25.

35 See note 153.

36 C. H. Norman letter to the *Times Literary Supplement*, 27 September 1963. The subject of suborned witnesses is extensively discussed in Playfair, *Gentle Criticisms* and Douglas, *Oscar Wilde*. Both were written shortly after the trials in 1895, the first published and distributed very sparsely and the second remaining in MS form until its publication in 2002.

37 Mason, *Three Times Tried*, p. 322.

38 The jury lists are to be found in the Public Record Office ref. CRIM 4/ 1118, CRIM 4/1120 and CRIM 6/19.

39 The full proceedings at this brief hearing have not survived in transcript form and have been reconstructed from *Reynolds Newspaper*, 3 March 1895, *The Times*, 4 March 1895, Mason, *Three Times Tried* and from the depositions preserved in the Public Record Office ref. CRIM 1/41/6. Newton (1821–1900) was the magistrate at Great Marlborough Street from 1866 to 1897.

40 Charles Octavius Humphreys (1828–1902), recommended to him by his friend Robert Ross, was Wilde's solicitor throughout the three trials, but

not his first choice (see note 45). Humphreys's son, Travers Humphreys, appeared as a junior barrister alongside Sir Edward Clarke when the case came on at the Old Bailey (the Central Criminal Court) a month later. Wilde, from his later correspondence, had little rapport with the man who was supposed to be determining his future. In *De Profundis* he would write, 'What is loathsome to me is the memory of interminable visits paid by me to the solicitor Humphreys in your company, when in the ghastly glare of a bleak room you and I would sit with serious faces telling serious lies to a bald man, till I really groaned and yawned with *ennui*.' (*Complete Letters*, p. 759.)

41 Since the existence of the card in the Public Record Office became known, opinion has been divided over the correct reading of the Marquess's handwriting. Hyde's reading 'posing as a somdomite [*sic*]' cannot be correct. What Queensberry almost certainly wrote was 'posing somdomite' (see illustration, p. xiv). It is tempting to take the Marquess's own reading here in court as definitive, since he wrote it, but as Ellmann, *Oscar Wilde*, p. 412, explains, 'posing as somdomite' was easier to defend than simply 'posing somdomite', which is probably why Queensberry corrects the hall porter.

42 As it was spelled on the card, a variant which the Marquess seems to have preferred.

43 The warrant read, 'For that he did unlawfully and maliciously publish a certain defamatory libel of and concerning one Oscar Wilde at Albemarle Street on February 18, 1895 at the parish of St George's.'

44 Presumably the date of the libel itself. This exchange concerning the date is confirmed by the *Reynolds Newspaper* on 3 March 1895.

45 George Henry Lewis (1833–1911) an eminent and highly successful solicitor, much in demand by London society, who represented one side or the other in most of its *causes célèbres* over thirty-five years. Wilde had been friendly with him and his wife since his 1882 tour in America, when he corresponded quite extensively with both of them. He had used Lewis's services back in 1892 to pay off one of Douglas's blackmailers at Oxford, but when he tried to consult Lewis about Queensberry's threatening behaviour in July 1894, he discovered that Lewis was already acting for the Marquess. 'Although I cannot act against him, I should not act against you,' he wrote to Wilde. After this first appearance of Queensberry in court, Lewis passed the case onto Charles Russell. Wilde later wrote to Alfred Douglas in *De Profundis*, 'Through your using my

name as your friend with Sir George Lewis, I began to lose his esteem and friendship, a friendship of fifteen years' standing. When I was deprived of his advice and help and regard I was deprived of the one great safeguard of my life.' (*Complete Letters*, pp. 701–2.)

46 Mr William Tyser, aged fifty, who called himself a merchant. In the 1891 census he described himself as a 'shipowner' and was clearly a man of substance, living with his wife, two children and seven servants at 13 Gloucester Square, W. (At the time London was divided into eight postal districts: SW, SE, W, WC, NW, N, E, EC.) He was described by the *Star* at the second magistrates' court hearing on 9 March as 'a gentleman of military bearing with a fierce white moustache'. No connection has been established between him and Queensberry but he may well have been one of the Marquess's sporting cronies.

47 Wilde had been living at this address in Chelsea in London's South-West postal district since January 1885.

48 Mr J. R. Lyell, chief clerk at Marlborough Street magistrates' court.

49 The Café Royal was founded in 1865 by Daniel Thévenon at the bottom of Regent Street near Piccadilly Circus. With its excellent cuisine and wines, it attracted the expatriate French of London and by 1895 had become the finest restaurant in the metropolis. Aside from the gourmets and epicures, it also attracted the leading intellectuals, artists and writers of the time.

50 See note 82.

51 This and other letters from Lord Queensberry were later used by Sir Edward Clarke during the libel action. See pp. 214–18.

52 Edward Henry Carson (1854–1935) had been a contemporary of Wilde's at Trinity College, Dublin. By 1903 he had achieved the remarkable distinction of being a QC twice-over both in Dublin and in London, Solicitor-General for Ireland and MP for Dublin University. The Queensberry case made his reputation as an English advocate. On hearing that Carson was to appear against him, Wilde is said to have remarked, 'No doubt he will perform the task with all the added bitterness of an old friend.' Carson later had a very distinguished legal and political career in England, was knighted in 1900, made a Lord of Appeal in 1921 and remained a lifelong passionate Ulster Unionist.

53 By 'postcard' Carson clearly means Queensberry's visiting card.

54 The Vexatious Indictments Act of 1859, 22 & 23 Vict., c.17 was a statute intended to deter people from bringing malicious prosecutions.

55 Although the letters which were later read out during the libel action (see pp. 214–18) did not contain any direct statements about Lord Rosebery, Queensberry made certain implications concerning him which could have given rise to conjectures about his sexual leanings. See also note 238.

56 The Albemarle Club was a mixed club for men and women situated at 13 Albemarle Street off Piccadilly. It was next door to Carter's Hotel where Queensberry had been staying at the time he left his visiting card for Wilde at the Albemarle.

57 In January 1895 Wilde and Douglas travelled to Algiers where they arrived on the 17th; Wilde left for London on 31 January to attend the rehearsals of *The Importance of Being Earnest*, which was due to open on 14 February, but Douglas stayed on until the 18th.

58 The case was heard on 21 November 1879. See *Law Reports*, 1880, 5 QBD 1 (1879). Carson would have been well aware that establishing a defence at this stage in the magistrates' court along the lines of Queensberry intervening to save his son from the 'evil influence' of Wilde would not be permitted. His attempt to do so must be seen as a calculated move to raise the public profile of the case at a time when committal proceedings were less stringently controlled than they would be today.

59 The depositions of Wilde and Queensberry have been preserved in the Public Record Office in CRIM 1/4/6 together with those of Sidney Wright, the Albemarle Club hall porter and Detective-Inspector Greet. Mason, *Three Times Tried*, p. 6 reports that in reply to whether he should 'sign in full' the usher whispered 'Initials will do' but the document, nonetheless, has Wilde's full signature.

60 William Tyser, see note 46.

61 Edward George Clarke (1841–1931) was one of the foremost English barristers of his time. From humble origins, he made his way by dint of hard work and study to the top of his profession, becoming Solicitor-General from 1886 to 1892 and MP for Plymouth from 1880 to 1900. Clarke was a man of strong religious conviction and the author of several exegetical works on the Bible after his retirement in 1914. After the collapse of the Queensberry case he offered to defend Wilde without fee in his prosecution for gross indecency by the Crown.

62 Richard Henn Collins (1842–1911) was, like Wilde, an Irishman and had been a classical scholar at Trinity College. His reputation as a barrister was made in the field of common law, at which he excelled, especially where complicated business transactions were involved and in litigation

involving transport and the railways. He was appointed a judge of the High Court in 1891 and Master of the Rolls in 1901.

63 For the full text of Queensberry's plea of justification see Appendix A. It would appear that Sir Edward Clarke is splitting hairs over the actual wording.

64 Sir William Wilde (1815–76) was appointed medical adviser to the Irish Census of 1841 and Assistant Commissioner to those of 1851, 1861 and 1871. It was for this work that he was knighted in 1864. His medical work on the 1851 Census has been described as one of the greatest demographic studies ever conducted and has become a standard reference work on the Great Irish Famine.

65 Wilde gained a Royal Scholarship from Portora School to Trinity College, Dublin in 1871. He was elected a Queen's Scholar in the same year and made a Foundation Scholar in 1873. He crowned his achievements at Trinity by winning the Berkeley Gold Medal for Greek in 1874 and a Demyship (scholarship) to Magdalen College, Oxford.

66 For 'Ravenna' in 1878.

67 In fact in June 1881; Wilde himself later compounds the error by failing to correct Sir Edward.

68 This word is 'scientific' in the shorthand transcript but must be, as reported in *The Times* for 4 April, 'aesthetic'.

69 Lord Alfred Bruce 'Bosie' Douglas (1870–1945) was Queensberry's third son. He was educated at Winchester and Oxford where he attended Wilde's old college, Magdalen; but left without taking a degree in 1893. He and Wilde remained friendly, if not intimate, until Wilde's death in 1900. Douglas later married, converted to Catholicism and became a poet of some distinction, but the last half of his life was marred by incessant squabbles and litigation, largely against what he saw as unfair portrayals of his role in the Wilde affair and its aftermath.

70 Lionel Johnson (1867–1902), who had been at Winchester with Douglas. For an account of the meeting see Douglas, *Autobiography*, pp. 56–9.

71 Sybil Montgomery (1845–1935) married the Marquess of Queensberry in 1866 and divorced him in 1877, having borne him five children. His vile temper, his affairs and his attempt to bring his mistress to her house for Ascot week in 1886 finally drove her to break with him. For the details see Roberts, *The Mad Bad Line*, pp. 138–9.

72 Sybil Queensberry rented a house near Ascot from Lord Downshire called 'The Hut' and also 'St Ann's Gate' in the cathedral close at Salisbury.

73 For details see note 97.

74 Wilde rented Babbacombe Cliff near Torquay, the house of Lady Georgiana Mount-Temple, a distant cousin of his wife Constance, from mid-November 1892 to the beginning of March 1893. It was there that he wrote most of *A Woman of No Importance*.

75 Alfred Wood, a clerk, who had been out of employment since shortly before he met Wilde at the start of 1893. Estimates of his age vary between Wilde's twenty-three or twenty-four, given later under cross-examination, and the newspapers' 'about nineteen' at the magistrates' court hearing after Wilde's arrest. One thing is certain – he was a semi-professional blackmailer, who survived for lengthy periods without visible employment and who admitted in the second and third trials that he had extorted money from a man with the help of Parker and Allen. When making a statement to Charles Russell he gave his address as 50 Medina Road, London, N.

76 William Allen (alias Pea, aged twenty-seven in 1895) and Robert Henry Cliburn (alias Harris, Collins, Stephenson, Robertson and Carew, aged twenty-two in 1895) were notorious blackmailers and felons. Cliburn, at one time a telegraph boy for the Post Office, had a previous conviction for blackmail in 1890 and had served nine months. At the time of Wilde's action against Queensberry both men were in hiding at Broadstairs, where they were found by the agents of Charles Russell, Queensberry's solicitor, but they did not make any deposition. Allen was sentenced to eighteen months in 1897 and Cliburn to seven years in 1898, both for handling stolen goods and harbouring known offenders. In *De Profundis* Wilde later wrote, 'Clibborn [*sic*] and Atkins were wonderful in their infamous war against life. To entertain them was an astounding adventure.' (*Complete Letters*, p. 759.) George Ives's diary entry for 11 May 1912 (MS Texas) gives a good thumbnail sketch of Cliburn, describing him as 'one of the biggest blackmailers in London' and as having 'a beautiful but mad face, the face of a tiger though very handsome'.

77 Herbert Beerbohm Tree (1853–1917) actor-manager and half-brother of Max Beerbohm, author, caricaturist and critic. He was the manager and lessee of the Haymarket Theatre where *A Woman of No Importance* was in rehearsal at the beginning of April 1893 and opened on 19 April.

78 Fifteen numbers of *The Spirit Lamp* (see Mason, *Bibliography*, p. 209) were published between May 1892 and June 1893, the last eight of which

were edited by Alfred Douglas. Wilde published a poem and two prose poems in the magazine under Douglas's editorship.

79 Pierre Louÿs's translation reads:

> *Hyacinthe! Ô mon coeur! Jeune dieu doux et blond!*
> *Tes yeux sont la lumière de la mer! Ta bouche,*
> *Le sang rouge du soir où mon soleil se couche . . .*
> *Je t'aime, enfant câlin, cher aux bras d'Apollon.*
>
> *Tu chantais, et ma lyre est moins douce, le long*
> *Des rameaux suspendus que la brise effarouche*
> *A frémir, que ta voix à chanter, quand je touche*
> *Tes cheveux couronnés d'acanthe et de houblon.*
>
> *Mais tu pars! Tu me fuis pour les Portes d'Hercule;*
> *Va! Rafraîchis tes mains dans le clair crépuscule*
> *Des choses où descend l'âme antique. Et reviens,*
>
> *Haycinthe adoré! Hyacinthe! Hyacinthe!*
> *Car je veux voir toujours dans les bois syriens*
> *Ton beau corps étendu sur la rose et l'absinthe.*

See also p. 54.

80 The sonnet which Douglas sent him, 'In Sarum Close', contains the lines:

> I thought to cool my burning hands
> In this calm twilight of grey Gothic things

echoed below in Wilde's letter.

81 The original of the letter, written from Babbacombe Cliff around January 1893, has not survived. Most newspapers reported 'madness of kissing' rather than 'madness of kisses' as does Mason, *Three Times Tried*, p. 27, and Queensberry sent a telegram to his son Percy's wife on 21 May referring to 'madness of kissing' (MS Hyde). The transcript used at the trial, however, quotes 'madness of kisses' (MS British Library). See also pp. 104 and 267.

82 Douglas went to Cairo on 2 December 1893, returning about the beginning of March the next year. It was largely at the instigation of Wilde, who was finding Douglas's constant presence in his life both oppressive and disruptive, and who wrote to Sybil Queensberry in

November suggesting that she send her son to stay with her friend Lord Cromer, the Consul-General.

83 On 14 November 1882 Queensberry attended a performance of *The Promise of May* by Alfred Tennyson. As a Freethinker himself, he objected to Tennyson's portrayal of the agnostic villain of the piece, played by Hermann Vezin, rose to his feet in the middle of the performance and said so. After the first act he was forcibly ejected from the theatre. For a full account see Roberts, *The Mad Bad Line*, pp. 117–19.

84 During the recounting of this incident several newspapers (in particular the *Sun*, 3 April) recorded the fact that Sir Edward, by a slip of the tongue, substituted the name of the Prime Minister, Lord Rosebery, for that of Lord Queensberry. This occasioned much laughter in which Queensberry himself joined. Clarke realised his mistake a moment or two later and rebuked the public for its levity. It was the more ironic since 'the exalted personages' mentioned in Queensberry's letters include Rosebery. See pp. 216–17 and note 238.

85 See note 108.

86 A description of London after dark from R. L. Stevenson's *The Dynamiter.*

87 As a result of Wilde's legal action Gay and Bird placed a letter in the major newspapers attempting to disassociate themselves from the magazine and stating that they had stopped circulating the magazine of their own accord and not at the request of any contributor. By contrast the editor, J. F. Bloxam, had written to Charles Kains-Jackson on 19 November 1894, 'The next day I visited Gay and Bird. They were very enthusiastic about one contribution I had secured, which they described as "most powerfully written". To my amusement it turned out to be my own little story' (MS Clark). Jerome K. Jerome first drew public attention to the magazine on 29 December 1894 in his weekly journal *Today* and demanded its withdrawal from circulation. Wilde may have previously offended Jerome by saying that the author of *Three Men in a Boat* was 'vulgar without being funny'. A facsimile of *The Chameleon* with introductory matter was issued by the Eighteen Nineties Society in 1978.

88 John Francis Bloxam (1873–1928), an undergraduate at Exeter College, who was the author of 'The Priest and the Acolyte' although it was simply signed 'X'. He later became a Church of England priest, distinguished himself in the First World War earning an MC and bar (1917–19) and for the last five years of his life worked as a parish priest in Hoxton, one of the poorest areas of London. For a brief biography see

J. Z. Eglinton, 'The Later Career of John Francis Bloxam' in the *International Journal of Greek Love*, vol. 1 no. 2 (1966), pp. 40–2.

89 *The Picture of Dorian Gray* was first published in the July 1890 issue of *Lippincott's Magazine*. This American monthly periodical was published simultaneously on both sides of the Atlantic in slightly differing editions. Wilde later expanded the story and had it published in book form by the magazine's English distributors Ward, Lock & Co. in 1891. A second edition was printed shortly before Wilde's legal action but was only issued as a remainder in October 1895.

90 Clearly it is the 1891 book version to which Clarke is referring rather than *Lippincott's Magazine* of July 1890 which is implied in the plea of justification.

91 See note 65.

92 See note 67.

93 Wilde's American tour lasted from January to December 1882 during which he gave about 140 lectures in 260 days. For details see Beckson, *Encyclopædia*, pp. 190–1.

94 Wilde wrote *Salomé* in French in 1891 and while rehearsals were in progress with Sarah Bernhardt in the title role in summer 1892, it was banned by the Lord Chamberlain, the censor of plays. There is no evidence to suggest that a Paris production was in hand for 1895 and this may have been wishful thinking on Wilde's part to impress the Court. There is, however, a letter from Wilde to Robert Sherard dated 'Holloway Prison, 13 April 1895' explaining his dire fiancial predicament and asking him to try to sell the rights in the play to Bernhardt (*Complete Letters*, p. 643).

95 Wilde had completed two other plays: *Vera; or the Nihilists* and *The Duchess of Padua*. Neither had been staged in England, but both had more or less flopped on their respective productions in New York in 1883 and 1891. The only other plays he had written were still in fragmentary or scenario form: *A Florentine Tragedy*; *The Cardinal of Avignon*; and *La Sainte Courtisane*. For details of each see Beckson, *Encyclopædia*.

96 Cyril (1885–1915) and Vyvyan Wilde (1886–1967).

97 Wilde took a house, The Haven, 5 The Esplanade, Worthing, from the beginning of August to the end of September 1894. He stayed at Grove Farm, Felbrigg, near Cromer, Norfolk during the summer of 1892, probably for about a month in August–September. He rented The Cottage, Goring-on-Thames from June to October 1893. Theodore

Wratislaw's memories of a visit to Goring were published in 1979 by the Eighteen Nineties Society as *Oscar Wilde: A Memoir*. For Torquay see note 74.

98 Lionel Johnson. See note 70.

99 Lord Percy Sholto Douglas of Hawick (1868–1920), Queensberry's second son and later the ninth Marquess on his father's death in 1900, who, to his father's fury, went bail for Wilde on 7 May. He also told the *Sun* on 5 April at the end of the first trial that the whole Douglas family was behind Wilde against his father, which did nothing to improve relations between them. See Introduction p. xxx and illustration p. 284.

100 Lord Francis Archibald Douglas, Viscount Drumlanrig (1867–94), Queensberry's eldest son, who had been killed in a shooting accident the previous October. There were rumours that he may have committed suicide due to the imminent exposure of a homosexual affair he is supposed to have conducted the previous year with the then Foreign Secretary (and by this time Prime Minister) Lord Rosebery, when he had been Rosebery's private secretary. See Roberts, *The Mad Bad Line*, pp. 182–7 for a full account of the various conjectures on the subject as well as Trevor-Roper, *A Hidden Life*, p. 262 and Stokes, *Oscar Wilde*, p. 86.

101 At this time the relationship between Alfred Douglas and Constance, contrary to what has often been reported later, was cordial. See Douglas, *Autobiography*, p. 59. There also exists a letter from Constance to Oscar, 18 September 1892, offering to come up from Babbacombe and help nurse Douglas when the two men were staying at Cromer and Douglas was ill (MS Clark).

102 An account of Douglas's stay at Torquay was published in *The Letters of Oscar Wilde*, p. 867 (1962) as a letter to Lionel Johnson from Campbell Dodgson, who was acting as Douglas's Greek tutor at the time. See also Wilde's letter to Campbell Dodgson, 23 February 1893 in *Complete Letters*, p. 555.

103 Alfred Waterhouse Somerset Taylor (1862–??) was brought up in a good middle-class family who derived their wealth from cocoa manufacture. His father died in 1875 and he was educated briefly at Marlborough College (1877–8), but not being very academic he was superannuated. He then entered the militia with a view to obtaining a commission, but resigned in 1883 when, on coming of age, he inherited £45,000. This fortune he dissipated over the next ten years and went bankrupt in 1894. He was arrested the day after Wilde, tried on the

same charges and sentenced to the same prison term. He later
emigrated to Canada and the USA, being paid by his family to stay out
of the country. In 1901, when Alfred Douglas was staying in an
American hotel, he rang for room service and to his astonishment
Alfred Taylor appeared (Hyde, *Douglas*, p. 140).

104 A 'leading question' is one that suggests the answer to the person being
interrogated. Such questions are generally permitted only in
cross-examination.

105 Pierre Louÿs (1870–1925), whom Wilde had met during a visit to Paris
in 1891 and to whom he had dedicated the French edition of *Salomé*
because Louÿs had helped him to polish the language. Louÿs had been
in town for the first night of *A Woman of No Importance* on 19 April. He
disapproved of Wilde's homosexual behaviour and they later quarrelled
as a result. He sat next to Edward Shelley during a performance of
Lady Windermere's Fan in July 1892. For a full account of their
friendship see H. P. Clive, 'Pierre Louÿs & Oscar Wilde' in *Revue de
littérature comparée*, 43 (1969), pp. 353–84.

106 Queensberry's letter of 1 April 1894. See p. 214.

107 Wilde wrote extensively on the subject of Douglas's relationship with
his father in *De Profundis* and especially on his feelings about being
caught in the crossfire: 'In your hideous game of hate together, you had
both thrown dice for my soul, and you happened to have lost. That was
all.' See *Complete Letters* pp. 705–9.

108 Wilde received a letter from C. O. Humphreys, written by some terrible
irony on the very day he received Queensberry's card, to say that
George Alexander and the staff of the theatre were not prepared to give
evidence. For the full text of the letter see Introduction p. xx.

109 But see Wilde's letter to Ada Leverson of early December 1894 in
which he says, 'Your aphorisms must appear in the second number of
The Chameleon: they are exquisite. "The Priest and the Acolyte" is not
by Dorian: though you were right in discerning by internal evidence
that the author has a profile. He is an undergraduate of strange beauty.
The story is, to my ears, too direct: there is no nuance: it profanes a
little by revelation: God and other artists are always a little obscure.
Still, it has interesting qualities, and is at moments poisonous: which is
something. Ever yours, Oscar.'

110 When the story appeared in book form Wilde had, in fact, added six
new chapters, divided the original last chapter in two and added a

preface consisting of twenty-five aphorisms as well as toning down some of the overtly homoerotic passages.

111 Sir Edward's line of questioning betrays the fact that he was probably unaware of the nature of what Edward Carson would later refer to as the 'purged passages' and he is attempting to interpret Queensberry's plea of justification as referring only to the book form. See the exchange between Clarke and Carson on p. 82–3.

112 For a detailed discussion of the press criticism of both editions of *Dorian Gray*, see Mason, *Art and Morality*, and *Complete Letters*, pp. 428–49.

113 This is inaccurate and glosses over the storm of critical protest engendered by the first publication in *Lippincott's Magazine*. Ward, Lock & Co., the English distributors of *Lippincott's*, wrote to Wilde on 10 July 1890 saying, 'We have received an intimation from Messrs W. H. Smith & Son this morning to the effect that your story, having been characterised by the press as a filthy one, they are obliged to withdraw *Lippincott's Magazine* from their bookstalls.' (PRO ref. CRIM 1/41/6.)

114 No such letter has survived. Carson is most probably confusing it with the letter of 3 April written by Queensberry to Alfred Douglas and later read out in court by Sir Edward Clarke. See p. 215.

115 There does not appear to have been a farm by this name near Cromer and in Torquay Wilde stayed at Babbacombe Cliff. It was most probably the shorthand writer's rendering of Felbrigg.

116 The Albemarle Hotel was at 1 Albemarle Street and the Avondale at 68a Piccadilly on the corner of Dover Street.

117 Wilde and Douglas left London for Monte Carlo on 12 March 1895 and returned about 20 March. For Wilde's comments on the madness of such a trip when he should have been preparing for his impending court case, see *Complete Letters*, p. 690.

118 In October 1894, when Wilde's family returned to London after their family holiday at Worthing, he moved into the Hotel Metropole in Brighton with Alfred Douglas, although in *De Profundis* he mistakenly calls it the Grand, which was another hotel. They stayed there from 4 to 7 October and then moved into lodgings from 8 to 18 October. The hotel bill was still outstanding at the time of Wilde's arrest and is now in the Public Record Office with the bankruptcy papers (B 4/429). The address of the lodgings has occasionally been misreported as

No. 20 but on the MS of *The Importance of Being Earnest* (New York Public Library) Wilde himself has given the address as No. 26. For an account of their tempestuous stay in Brighton, see *Complete Letters*, pp. 696–700.

119 The second half of the epigram read: 'Science is the record of dead religions.'

120 Cf Wilde's essay 'The Rise of Historical Criticism' in which he writes, 'Religions may be absorbed, but they are never disproved.' (*Complete Works*, p. 1202.)

121 Cf. Jack in the last scene of *The Importance of Being Earnest*: 'It is a terrible thing for a man to find out suddenly that all his life he has been speaking nothing but the truth.'

122 From *An Ideal Husband*, end of Act One, Lord Goring to his father the Earl of Caversham.

123 Within two years, Wilde was writing to Douglas from Reading Gaol, to say that he now realised that true self-realisation could only be achieved through suffering. See *De Profundis* in *Complete Letters*, especially pp. 728–53.

124 The second half of the aphorism reads 'The aim of perfection is youth.' Neither the shorthand transcript nor the newspapers record it, but given Wilde's reply, Carson probably completed it.

125 David Hunter-Blair (1853–1939) later recorded his Oxford reminiscences of Wilde 'Oscar Wilde as I Knew Him' in the *Dublin Review*, July 1938, in which he remembers Oscar replying to a question about his future: 'Perhaps I'll lead the βίος ἀπολαυστικός [life of enjoyment] for a time, and then – who knows – rest and do nothing. What does Plato say is the highest end man can attain here below καθεύδειν καὶ ὁρᾶν τὸ ἀγαθόν – to sit down and contemplate the good. Perhaps that will be the end of me too.'

126 Cf. Lady Bracknell's remarks on Cecily Cardew in the last act of *The Importance of Being Earnest*. 'There are distinct social possibilities in your profile. The two weak points in our age are its want of principle and its want of profile.'

127 See note 112.

128 The reference to 'outlawed noblemen and perverted telegraph boys' was as near to an accusation of homosexuality as the paper could allow itself. It was an oblique reference to the so-called Cleveland Street scandal of August 1889 in which a house had been raided where

telegraph boys from the General Post Office nearby were found to be offering their services to aristocratic customers. It was rumoured that a number of high-ranking politicians had also been involved, but the government brought pressure to bear on the police not to make arrests until the influential clients of the establishment had been able to cover their tracks. For a full account of the incident and its repercussions, see Hyde, *The Cleveland Street Scandal.*

129   The unsigned review was long thought to have been written by the editor, W. E. Henley (1849–1903) but was, in fact, by his henchman Charles Whibley (1860–1930). There was a certain amount of self-congratulatory correspondence that passed between them after the collapse of Wilde's case, which Henley felt vindicated their original attack on *Dorian Gray.* It was partly reproduced in John Connell, *W. E. Henley* (1949).

130   See Lawler, *Dorian Gray* for a detailed comparison of the two editions.

131   Most probably the passage which Carson highlights later (see p. 87). Walter Pater (1839–94) refused to review the version in *Lippincott's Magazine* as being 'too dangerous', but he later reviewed the book with praise in the *Bookman* for November 1891. In echoes of the novel given by Lord Henry to Dorian Gray (see p. 94), when Wilde was in prison he would refer to Pater's *Studies in the History of the Renaissance* as 'that book which has had such a strange influence over my life'. See also illustration p. 88.

132   See note 110.

133   Sir Edward had been given a copy of the American printing as the English one did not contain 'The Powers of the Air'. In fact, Carson might have done better to use Ward, Lock & Co.'s English printing where 'Oscar Wilde' is in larger type. *Lippincott's Magazine,* although paper-covered, certainly had Wilde's name prominently displayed on the outer wrapper.

134   There is no date on the ordinary first edition; only the signed 'large-paper' version carries the publication date.

135   The section 'My father . . . a painter' was omitted in the 1891 version; but so, more significantly, was the sentence starting 'I knew that if I spoke to Dorian . . .'

136   Wilde's essay, 'The Portrait of Mr W. H.', was published in *Blackwood's Magazine* for July 1889. He later expanded it and gave it more homosexual overtones, and was due to have it published by Elkin

Mathews when he and John Lane had dissolved their partnership, but Mathews then declined to publish it 'at any price'. See *Complete Letters*, pp. 604–13. The manuscript of the expanded version finally resurfaced in America and was published in 1921.

137 Wilde was widely read on the subject of Shakespeare as a study of the sheriff's enforcement sale of his effects at Tite Street shows (*Catalogue of the Library . . . April 24th 1895*; see illustration p. 326); however, Hallam was not among the books listed. The passage to which Wilde took objection is in chapter 5 of volume III of Henry Hallam's *Introduction to the Literature of Europe in the 15th, 16th and 17th Centuries*: 'We find a more ardent tone of affection in the language of friendship than has since been usual . . . and it is impossible not to wish that Shakespeare had never written them [the sonnets].'

138 *À Rebours* was published in 1883 and in an interview which he gave to the *Morning News* (20 June 1884) while on his honeymoon he declared, 'This last book of Huysmans is one of the best I have ever seen.'

139 Wilde changed '*Décadents*' to '*Symbolistes*' and 'evil' to 'subtle' in the 1891 version.

140 In the MS of *Dorian Gray* (Morgan Library) Wilde had originally called the book *Le Secret de Raoul* by Catulle Sarrazin. Both author and work are fictional, though the author may have been a conflation of Catulle Mendès and Gabrielle Sarrazin with both of whom Wilde was acquainted, and the book an oblique reference to Raoule de Vénérande in the scandalous novel by Rachilde (Marguerite Vallette), *Monsieur Vénus* (1889).

141 The passage from *À Rebours* which Carson might well have selected occurs at the end of chapter 9 when Des Esseintes encounters a young man by chance in the street and takes up with him: 'From this chance meeting sprang a mistrustful friendship that nevertheless was prolonged for months. To this day, Des Esseintes could not think of it without a shudder; never had he experienced a more alluring liaison or one that laid a more imperious spell on his senses; never had he run such risks nor had he ever been so well content with such a grievous sort of satisfaction.'

142 In the 1891 version, Wilde inserted another paragraph here with Dorian explaining the rumours surrounding the people mentioned by Basil Hallward, none of which imply sodomy, and launching into a diatribe against English hypocrisy. See p. 223.

143 See note 81.

144 The words that Carson could not read were 'I had sooner *be rented* all day'.

145 Mrs Ellen Grant, the landlady of 13 Little College Street, testified at the second trial that Taylor had lived at that address from January 1892 to August 1893, paying £3 per month. He then moved to 3 Chapel Street where he stayed from August to December 1893. When he moved from Chapel Street he left behind a box of papers which the landlady, Mrs Sophia Gray, later handed over to Charles Russell and which were instrumental in helping Queensberry build his case.

146 The Florence Hotel and Restaurant, owned by Luigi Azario was at 57–8 Rupert Street in Soho.

147 Most probably Maurice Salis Schwabe, whose name is again concealed later (see pp. 183–95). Schwabe (1872–1916) was the eldest son of Colonel George Schwabe, a respected army officer who had commanded the 16th Lancers, and who later became a major-general and the Lieutenant-Governor of the Royal Hospital in Chelsea. The family was well-to-do, had interests in the fabric printing industry and when in England tended to live in Mayfair with a full complement of servants. Maurice's aunt Julia Schwabe had married Sir Frank Lockwood in 1874, who, as the Solicitor-General, would conduct the Crown prosecution of Wilde in the third trial. Maurice's involvement in the Wilde affair would therefore have been doubly embarrassing. Alfred Douglas maintained contact with Schwabe after Wilde's death and related that he had been killed in the First World War by a party of Germans who had just surrendered and who had mistaken him for a traitor on account of his name and his perfect German (Lemonnier, *Oscar Wilde*, p. 121).

148 In Wood's deposition with Charles Russell, Queensberry's solicitor, he stated that he and Wilde had met regularly over the course of a week late at night on the corner of Tite Street. Wilde had then taken him back to his house and committed indecencies with him. He also stated that there was a young man of seventeen called Ginger employed in the house at that time.

149 Conventions of the time regarding social address were subtle and precise, depending on the degree of intimacy between individuals and their social status. Broadly speaking, both in written communication and conversation, one would have started with 'Sir', progressed to 'Mr Wilde', thence to 'Wilde' on its own when a fair degree of familiarity

had been established, and only to 'Oscar' to reflect a close friendship. Hence Carson's line of questioning at this flouting of convention.

150 There would appear to be a slight discrepancy here as *A Woman of No Importance* had already opened on 19 April.

151 Wilde was in the habit of staying in the West End before and after the opening nights of his plays. This is confirmed both by his correspondence and the evidence of the proprietor of the Albemarle in the second trial. In this case it was for *Lady Windermere's Fan*, which opened on 20 February 1892.

152 Charles Elkin Mathews (1851–1921) and John Lane (1854–1925) together founded the Bodley Head publishing house in 1887. They published an author's edition of Wilde's *Poems* in 1892, *Salomé* in 1893, *Lady Windermere's Fan* in 1893, *The Sphinx* in 1894 and *A Woman of No Importance* in 1894. They terminated their partnership in September 1894 and Wilde stayed with Lane as his publisher. However, as soon as Wilde's libel action started both men hurried to disassociate themselves from him entirely and Lane withdrew his books from sale. See also note 220.

153 Edward Shelley (1874–1951) was the second son of a blacksmith living in Fulham, London. He started work at the Bodley Head in 1890 and left in 1893. Although used by the prosecution in the second trial and said by the judge to be the only credible witness, in the third trial he was shown, like his elder brother, to be mentally unstable. Whatever else Wilde may have done with Shelley, he was considerate and concerned for his welfare, even offering him £100 to continue his studies (see Hyde, *Trials*, p. 298), so Shelley's readiness to give evidence against Wilde may have been motivated as much by the £20 (more than half a year's salary) he was paid for two days' attendance at the Queensberry trial (see Mason, *Three Times Tried*, p. 167 and Playfair, *Gentle Criticisms*) as by the threat of prosecution himself if he did not co-operate. He joined the Grenadier Guards in July 1895, fought in the Boer War and was discharged in March 1903. For an admirable brief biography see Mallon, *In Fact*, pp. 213–27.

154 This sounds far grander than it was. Wilde published his *Poems* in 1881 in 750 copies, which he divided equally into a first, second and third edition. In 1882 he reprinted 500 and called them the fourth and fifth. Most of the fifth remained unsold and he got Mathews and Lane to reissue it with a Charles Ricketts title page as a signed 'Author's Edition' in 1892.

155 Bernard Quaritch (1819–99), a bookseller and bibliophile whose shop was at 15 Piccadilly. Wilde knew him personally and attended some of the meetings of the bibliophile dining club, the Sette of Odd Volumes, of which Quaritch was a founding member.

156 In fact, Shelley's letter of 21 February 1892. See p. 230. Hyde incorrectly says this is Maurice Schwabe, but it must be the Mr B—— mentioned in Shelley's letter. See note 223.

157 In Shelley's deposition to Charles Russell he states quite clearly that they dined in the public room at the Albemarle Hotel.

158 The Lyric Club was situated in the Prince of Wales Buildings in Coventry Street, off Piccadilly Circus. It was not a conventional gentleman's club but one at which readings, concerts and other performances were staged for the members.

159 Kettner's, owned by Giovanni Sangiorgio, was at 28–31 Church Street, off Shaftesbury Avenue. It still occupies the same premises, although the street name was changed to Romilly Street in 1937.

160 The Hogarth Club was at 36 Dover Street, off Piccadilly.

161 Given that monetary values today are about seventy times those of the 1890s, this seems excessively expensive and would have been equivalent to half a month's salary for a domestic servant and about £140 at today's prices. However, rail fares were fixed at the statutory tariff of a penny per mile and as Cromer was 200 miles from London the fare is about correct. The National Railway Museum has calculated that 1900 was, in real terms, the most expensive time ever to travel by rail.

162 The book was a lightweight romance, *The Sinner's Comedy* (1892), by John Oliver Hobbes, the pseudonym of Pearl Mary-Teresa Craigie, who once claimed that her witticisms equalled those of Wilde. Certainly such gems as 'She was a very amiable, intelligent woman, who played Schumann with a weak wrist and was noted for her cookery recipes' show the marked influence of *Dorian Gray*.

163 Alfonso Harold Conway gave his address to Charles Russell as 1 Bath Place, Worthing.

164 As an example of Mason's somewhat haphazard editing, copied by Hyde, he includes here in Carson's cross-examination of Wilde about Wood, exactly the same quip that Wilde makes to Sir Edward Clarke under re-examination on the following day: 'I never heard . . . that he had any connection with literature.'

165 *The Wreck of the Grosvenor* by W. Clark Russell (1891). Some time after

the Second World War, the granddaughter of Inspector Brockwell, who arrested Wilde at the Cadogan Hotel on 5 April, was going through her grandfather's books and came across a copy of R. L. Stevenson's *Treasure Island* inscribed on the title page 'Alfonso Conway from his friend Oscar Wilde. Worthing, Sept. 1894' and with 'Conway, 5 Buckingham Road, Shoreham' in another hand on the verso. She tore the page out as a memento and threw the book away (MS Magdalen P155/C2/5). The surviving page is now in the Hyde Collection.

166 Mason, *Three Times Tried*, p. 61 says that besides the cigarette case and the book, a silver-mounted, crook-handled grape-vine stick was produced at this juncture.

167 Although the shorthand reports state that the ribbon was 'red and black', several newspapers record the colours as 'red and blue', as does Mason, and Conway himself confirms this in his deposition to Charles Russell. The Corps whose colours they were was the Royal Engineers.

168 The Albion Hotel, owned by Thomas Gadd, was at 35 Queen's Road, Brighton.

169 *The Importance of Being Earnest.*

170 The perfuming of rooms was common practice at this time in certain artistic circles, where it was intended to create a strange, exotic, even decadent atmosphere. In Osbert Sitwell's *Noble Essences*, p. 137, he describes how Ada Leverson arrives early for a party at Aubrey Beardsley's house to find him perfuming the flowers. See also *The Picture of Dorian Gray* (*Complete Works*, p. 101) and *À Rebours*, chapter 10.

171 Sydney Arthur 'Jenny' Mavor (1866–1952), son of a veterinary surgeon, was one of the 'respectable' middle-class young men to be involved in the Wilde scandal. He was questioned by Charles Russell, but claimed he had never made a statement (see Mason, *Three Times Tried*, p. 156) and when summoned as a witness for the Crown in the second trial, he denied that any improprieties had taken place between him and Wilde. Alfred Douglas later maintained that Mavor's *volte face* was at his instigation (see Douglas, *Autobiography*, p. 119). According to Peter King, former head of History at Hurstpierpoint College, Sussex, Mavor had taught English at the school between 1917 and 1925, a fact corroborated by J. E. Kite who was one of his pupils (MSS Magdalen P155/C2/5). Reginald Turner (1869–1938), an alumnus of the College and intimate friend of Wilde's in the 1890s, may well have recommended Mavor to

the school. When Hyde's *Trials* was published in 1948, Mavor wrote to him, and Hyde passed the letter on to John Betjeman, who planned to visit Mavor with Siegfried Sassoon. In the event Cecil Beaton, an old friend of Betjeman's, did make the trip, only to find that Mavor had died some weeks before. See John Betjeman, *Letters*, vol. II, pp. 24–30.

172 The Solferino, owned by Peter Lözerich, was at 7–8 Rupert Street in Soho. The building has since been replaced.

173 Frederick Atkins (aged twenty in 1895) had been variously a billiard marker, a bookmaker's clerk and a music hall comedian, working in the latter profession under the name of Fred Denny, Dennis or St Denis. He lived for some years with James Dennis Burton, aged fifty, a bookmaker whose occasional clerk he became when Burton went to the racecourses. Burton ran a lucrative sideline in blackmail through youths like Atkins and Parker who would persuade men to go home with them. By arrangement 'Uncle Burton' would then turn up and blackmail the victim for committing indecencies with his 'nephews'. Atkins's testimony was utterly discredited in the second trial when he was discovered to have been lying under oath about one of these escapades. See Hyde, *Trials*, p. 217.

174 See p. 180.

175 Charles Oliver Parker (1876–?) had been a gentleman's valet and was out of employment when he and his brother William met Alfred Taylor at the St James's Restaurant (see note 181) in 1893. Taylor subsequently introduced them to Wilde. In his deposition to Charles Russell, Parker stated that indecent acts took place between him and Wilde, and he later became the chief witness for the prosecution in the second trial. He admitted to being acquainted with Allen and Cliburn (see note 76) and was almost certainly involved in blackmailing activities himself. He was also associated with Burton (see note 173 and Hyde, *Trials*, p. 198). In October 1894 he enlisted with the Royal Artillery, but was discharged in June 1895, significantly only days after the end of the third trial, 'his services being no longer required' (PRO ref. WO 97/3612). Sir Shane Leslie met him in about 1907, down and out in the rain on the Dundalk–Dublin road and gave him a florin, which elicited a confession about his part in the trials (Hyde letter to Croft-Cooke, 1962, MS Texas).

176 Taylor's birthday was on 8 March, but the dinner took place on 10 March. See Hyde, *Trials*, p. 263.

177 Most newspapers reported this last word as 'original'.

178 Near Windsor in Berkshire.

179 Some reports include '. . . and his groom' – as does Mason – and add that Sir Edward Clarke also protested at Carson's remark.

180 Carson's whole line of cross-questioning over Wilde's relationship with Charles Parker is based on the deposition that Parker made to Charles Russell in which he says that Wilde took him back to the Savoy Hotel after Taylor's birthday dinner and invited him to dinner in his room there a week later.

181 St James's Restaurant at 24–6 Piccadilly, the London Pavilion, a music hall in Piccadilly Circus and the Knightsbridge Skating Rink were, according to Rupert Croft-Cooke, *Feasting with Panthers*, p. 268, notorious as meeting places for young men wanting to be picked up.

182 A 'street Arab' in the sense of a homeless urchin. See also Wilde's letter to Phoebe Allen on the subject in *Complete Letters*, p. 306.

183 Camera Square no longer exists. In its place is now Chelsea Park Gardens off Beaufort Street in Chelsea.

184 See note 181.

185 The Crystal Palace, so called because of the 300,000 hand-blown panes of glass used in its structure, was the Hyde Park venue for the Great Exhibition of 1851. After the exhibition closed it was moved to Sydenham where it was destroyed by fire in 1937.

186 See note 175.

187 With the exception of Walter Gilworth, who should be Walter Pilsworth, and Arthur Marling, who should be Arthur Marley, the shorthand clerk has spelled the names correctly. The miscreants' ages and addresses are given in the police court report in the *Daily Telegraph* of 14 August 1894.

188 See note 128.

189 A brief account of the raid is also give in Mason, *Three Times Tried*, pp. 99–100. Marling/Marley was a female impersonator who appeared in court 'wearing a capacious yellow dress, profusely trimmed with lace, with a low neck and short sleeves, and a long train. A fan, suspended by a cord, was carried in his hand.' He was bound over to keep the peace for three months.

190 The Agence Dalziel was a press and information agency operating in Paris at the time.

191 Club trains were originally conceived as a form of exclusive travel for wealthy industrialists in the Midlands and the north of England. The closest approximation to them in living memory are probably the Pullman trains of the *Brighton Belle* type.

192 He was going to see the Librairie de l'Art Indépendant about the first edition of *Salomé*, which was to be published in French.

193 As with the other young men who appear in Queensberry's plea of justification (see Appendix A) Carson's precise questions are based on Atkins's deposition to Charles Russell in which he mentions the name of Maurice Schwabe.

194 On 11 April in the Bow Street magistrates' court at the second hearing after Wilde's arrest Atkins said that he 'wrote something about *A Woman of No Importance*'.

195 The Café Julien was at 3 boulevard des Capucines.

196 The Grand Hotel was at 12 boulevard des Capucines.

197 Carson's pronunciation of the famous Paris night spot was the occasion of some amusement in court in which Wilde himself also joined. Having at first said 'Moolong Roojie', a junior counsel whispered something to him, at which he apologised: 'I beg your lordship's pardon. I believe I should have said "Moolang Rooj".' See *Star*, 4 April and *Daily Chronicle*, 5 April.

198 Atkins supplied it himself in the second trial: 124 Tachbrook Street, Pimlico.

199 In fact it was 28 Osnaburgh Street, as testified by Mary Applegate, the housekeeper, in the second trial.

200 Fred Atkins contracted smallpox about this time and asked Wilde to visit him (Hyde, *Trials*, p. 207). Wilde did so and the day after Atkins was transferred to the 'hospital ship', where those with contagious diseases were quarantined and cared for.

201 Harry Barford, according to the evidence in the second trial (Hyde, *Trials*, p. 207). There is no record of his career as an actor and he may well have been on the music hall stage like Atkins.

202 Cf. his own mother's remark in reply to a friend who wanted to bring a 'respectable' guest to one of her Dublin 'At Homes': 'You must never employ that description in this house; only trades people are *respectable*.'

203 Ernest Edward Scarfe (1873–?) was from a modest background; his mother appears to have been a domestic servant in London and his father a butler. Despite giving a statement to Charles Russell, he was not used as a witness by the prosecution in the later trials.

204 See note 181.

205 Scarfe revealed the name of his employer in his deposition to Charles Russell: it was Hitchcock & Williams.

206 At the time of his bankruptcy some months later, Wilde still owed Lewis's £43 7s 3d and Thornhill's £43 1s 3d, so the latter would have little compunction in disclosing confidential details to Queensberry's solicitors (PRO ref. B 4/429). George Frederick Claridge gave evidence for the prosecution about this cigarette case in the second trial.

207 The following information was doubtless provided by Aloys Vogel, the owner of the hotel, who gave evidence against Wilde in the second trial. He had initially believed the young men that Wilde had been bringing to his establishment had been connected to the theatre, but later became suspicious. In order to discourage Wilde's custom, he pressed through his solicitors for a small unpaid bill in 1894, but to his annoyance discovered that Wilde had been staying for more than two weeks around the time that *An Ideal Husband* opened on 3 January 1895 (Hyde, *Trials*, p. 218). As Oscar said in 'Phrases and Philosophies', 'It is only by not paying one's bills that one can hope to live in the memory of the commercial classes.'

208 This was at the time from November 1892 to March 1893 when Wilde was mostly at Babbacombe Cliff. See note 74.

209 Walter Grainger, born in 1876, was the son of a general labourer and a laundress living in Oxford. At the time he gave a statement to Charles Russell he was living at 129 Bullingdon Road, Cowley, Oxford.

210 They were at No. 34 High Street above the Loders Club.

211 Viscount Encombe (1870–1900) was one of Douglas's closest friends at Winchester and Oxford. He made a short career in the army after leaving Oxford. To his credit he bothered to send a letter of support to Douglas who was living in France after Wilde's conviction.

212 Several newspaper reports indicate that he added, 'I did not say that.'

213 Grainger stated in his deposition to Charles Russell that he had gone into Wilde's bedroom, where he had been seen by the butler. Charles Russell did not manage to get any testimony from the butler to corroborate the fact. According to Wilde, when Constance was considering divorce, her solicitors intended to use Grainger as a principal witness. See *Complete Letters*, p. 704.

214 Antonio Migge who gave evidence at the second trial.

215 He was there to oversee the final corrections and the printing of *Salomé*.

216 In his deposition to Charles Russell, Atkins stated that the waiter at the hotel had seen them in bed together.

217 See p. 243 and illustration.

218 According to the *Sun* on 4 April: 'Throughout the reading of these letters the scene in court was one of the most painful and astounding character. Sir Edward read on imperturbably, just in the tone he would have read a bill of costs. But the Marquis of Queensberry stood up, gazing alternately at Mr Wilde in one corner, and at his son at the opposite end of the court. Every now and then he turned to the man in the witness-box and ground his teeth together and shook his head at the witness in the most violent manner. Then when the more pathetic parts of the letters came, the poor old nobleman had the greatest difficulty in restraining the tears which welled into his eyes, and forced him to bite his lips to keep them back.'

219 For the *St James's Gazette*'s coverage of the trial, see Introduction p. xxxii.

220 John Lane cabled from New York, where he was at the time of the trial, to state explicitly that he had never 'introduced' Shelley to Wilde (Hyde, *Trials*, p. 159). Wilde, for his part, has immortalised Lane as Algy's butler in *The Importance of Being Earnest*.

221 In the third trial Shelley stated that the inscription which Wilde had written in *Dorian Gray* was 'To Edward Shelley, poet and friend, from Oscar Wilde, poet and friend'.

222 Marguerite, Countess of Blessington (1789–1849) published *A Journal of Conversations with Lord Byron* (1842), which recorded in lively detail her encounters with Byron in Italy.

223 Quite possibly Sydney Barraclough, with whom Wilde was friendly about this time. Barraclough (1871–1930) had come to London in 1886 to try to make a name for himself as an actor and vocalist. Wilde was anxious that he should play the part of Gerald in *A Woman of No Importance* but could not persuade Tree to engage him.

224 Charles Ricketts (1866–1931) had a hand in the designing or illustrating of almost all Wilde's books from 1891 onwards. Ricketts was paid £75 for his designs for *The Sphinx*.

225 The French edition of *Salomé* was published on 22 February 1893. The number of copies for Lane is almost certainly exaggerated as there were only 600 printed. See *Complete Letters*, pp. 545–9 and Guy and Small, *Oscar Wilde's Profession*, pp. 156–62.

226 Probably the taunts from other employees at the Bodley Head, who

called Shelley 'Miss Oscar' or 'Mrs Wilde', which he described in the second trial. See Hyde, *Trials*, p. 215.

227 In his deposition to Charles Russell, Shelley stated that he was working for Robert Bullock & Co., tea merchants, at 1 Dunster Court, Mincing Lane.

228 In a letter to Alfred Douglas about this time Wilde wrote, 'I had a frantic telegram from Edward Shelley, of all people! asking me to see him. When he came he was of course in trouble for money. As he betrayed me grossly I, of course, gave him money and was kind to him. I find that forgiving one's enemies is a most curious morbid pleasure; perhaps I should check it.' (*Complete Letters*, p. 590.)

229 John Lane, Shelley's previous employer. Shelley was obliged to reveal the name in the second and third trials. In a self-serving letter to Lane two days after Wilde's arrest, Shelley wrote, 'You will have doubtless learnt from the newspapers the result of the Wilde case long before this note reaches you, so that I need not refer to that subject beyond expressing my sense of loathing and regret at being mentioned in connection with Wilde.' (MS Texas.)

230 The *Daily News* article appeared on 11 June 1894 and was not as vitriolic as Shelley is making out, though the critic at one point writes that 'Considerations of space, and, we are reluctantly compelled to admit, of decency, forbid us to tell etc. . . .'

231 Charles Edward Denniger Hinxman (1874–94), son of a civil servant and himself a clerk at the Colonial Office, was born a few streets away from Shelley in Fulham, London, and had clearly been a childhood friend. He had died of tuberculosis on 27 July.

232 From Wilde's poem 'The Burden of Itys'.

233 The *Athenæum* reviewed *The Sphinx* on 25 August 1894, pointing out its decadent motif and language but praising 'the skilfulness with which the metre is handled and the easy flow and sonorousness of the lines'.

234 He had been to see George Alexander about *The Importance of Being Earnest*. For this and the trip to Dieppe, see *Complete Letters*, p. 607.

235 From the local records apparently a Miss Lord, but there is no obvious connection with Constance Wilde.

236 This refers to George Wyndham, Alfred Douglas's cousin. Wyndham (1863–1913) was the Conservative MP for Dover and had been Arthur Balfour's private secretary from 1887 to 1892. Douglas approached him shortly before Wilde's arrest to see if a warrant had already been issued

and possibly to see, if it had not, whether Wyndham could intervene with Balfour. Fortunately for Wyndham's integrity, the machinery of the law was already in motion.

237 The revolver once went off accidentally when Douglas was brandishing it in the Berkeley Hotel in Piccadilly. See *Complete Letters*, pp. 699 and 708.

238 A letter from Queensberry to his father-in-law, Alfred Montgomery, of 1 November 1894, just after Drumlanrig's death, was not produced at the trial but makes Queensberry's view on certain 'exalted personages' quite clear. 'Now that the first flush of this catastrophe and grief is passed, I write to tell you that it is a judgement on the whole lot of you. Montgomerys, the snob queers like Rosebery and certainly Christian hypocrite Gladstone – the whole lot of you.' Quoted in Ellmann, *Oscar Wilde*, p. 402. The MS is now at the University of Tulsa.

239 The rooms (E4 Albany) were those of his friend, George Ives who records the visit of Bloxam and Wilde in his diary entry for 13 November 1894 (MS Texas). This visit is also referred to in Bloxam's letter of 19 November 1894 (see note 87), in which he says, 'We discussed the paper fully,' so, contrary to what he testified in court, Wilde may well have had prior knowledge of 'The Priest and the Acolyte'. In another diary entry for 10 December 1894 Ives claims that he was responsible for suggesting *The Chameleon* as a name.

240 See note 122.

241 According to several newspaper reports Wilde left the court at this point (2.55 p.m.) and did not return until well into Carson's opening speech.

242 Frank Harris in his *Oscar Wilde*, p. 199, gives an account of meeting Wilde in the Café Royal with Bernard Shaw shortly before the trial began and saying to him, '"No jury would give a verdict against a father, however mistaken he might be. The only thing for you to do, therefore, is to go abroad" . . . I appealed to Shaw, and Shaw said he thought I was right: the case would very likely go against Oscar, a jury would hardly give a verdict against a father trying to protect his son.'

243 In this instance Carson is using the 1891 book version of the story for which, in this passage, Wilde only made three minor stylistic changes from the 1890 magazine version.

244 It was said that a news-stand in the Strand, which normally sold a few

copies of *Lippincott's* a week, sold eighty in a single day on its first appearance. See also note 113.

245 The question of whether Douglas was more a victim than an accomplice was much discussed behind closed doors at the time. Charles Gill gave his opinion to the Director of Public Prosecutions, Hamilton Cuffe, who in turn wrote to the Home Secretary about whether Douglas should be prosecuted or not. These documents are reproduced in Appendix B. Douglas himself later wrote to W. T. Stead at *The Review of Reviews* on 15 November 1895, 'Perhaps if I were in prison myself I should be infinitely happier. What makes me more unhappy than anything else is the feeling that my friend is bearing nearly all the burden and I so comparatively little. People look upon me as the victim of his superior age and wisdom and therefore an object of pity, while they reserve their execration for him. All this is so utterly wide of the real truth. So far from his leading me astray it was I that (unwittingly) pushed him over the precipice.' (Sotheby's Sale Catalogue, 19 July 1994, lot 150.)

246 Tree was still on his first American tour, which had started at the end of January. News of the first day's proceedings had reached America by wire and Tree reacted by telling the *New York Times* (4 April), 'I know nothing more about the matter than is stated in the dispatch, but I always treat an anonymous letter with contempt' and declined to discuss the matter further.

247 See note 79.

248 See note 144.

249 Compare Wilde's own account in *De Profundis* (*Complete Letters*, p. 995).

250 Sir Edward Clarke and his junior, Willie Mathews, returned to the Court at this point, having been absent for about ten minutes. Clarke was then seen to pluck Carson by the gown.

A.D. 1895.   No. 6907

16, Tite Street, Chelsea.

Catalogue of the Library of

Valuable Books,

Pictures, Portraits of Celebrities, Arundel Society Prints,

HOUSEHOLD FURNITURE

CARLYLE'S WRITING TABLE,

Chippendale and Italian Chairs, Old Persian Carpets
and Rugs, Brass Fenders,

Moorish and Oriental Curiosities,

Embroideries, Silver and Plated Articles,

OLD BLUE AND WHITE CHINA,

Moorish Pottery, Handsome Ormolu Clock,
and numerous Effects :

Which will be Sold by Auction,

By Mr. BULLOCK,

ON THE PREMISES,

On Wednesday, April 24th, 1895,

AT ONE O'CLOCK.

13. While on remand, the complete contents of Wilde's Tite Street
house were auctioned by the sheriff's men to pay his ever-mounting
debts. The whole sale made a mere £285.

BIBLIOGRAPHY AND
MANUSCRIPT SOURCES

Printed Books and Periodicals

Beckson, Karl, *The Oscar Wilde Encyclopædia* (New York: AMS Press, 1998)

Betjeman, John, *Letters Vol. II*, edited by Candida Lycett Green (London: Minerva Books, 1996)

The Chameleon (London: Gay and Bird, 1894)

Clarke, Sir Edward, *The Story of My Life* (London: John Murray, 1918)

Cohen, Ed, *Talk on the Wilde Side* (London: Routledge, 1993)

(Croft-Cooke, Rupert, *Bosie* (London: W. H. Allen, 1963)

—————— *Feasting with Panthers* (London: W. H. Allen, 1967)

—————— *The Unrecorded Life of Oscar Wilde* (London: W. H. Allen, 1972)

Douglas, Lord Alfred, *Autobiography* (London: Martin Secker, 1929)

—————— *Without Apology* (London: Martin Secker, 1938)

—————— *Oscar Wilde: A Summing-Up* (London: Duckworth, 1940)

—————— *Oscar Wilde: A Plea and a Reminiscence*, ed. Caspar Wintermans (Woubrugge: Avalon Press, 2002)

Ellmann, Richard, *Oscar Wilde* (London: Hamish Hamilton, 1987)

Foldy, Michael S., *The Trials of Oscar Wilde* (New Haven: Yale University Press, 1997)

Gide, André, *In Memoriam* (Paris: Mercure de France, 1910)

Guy, Josephine and Ian Small, *Oscar Wilde's Profession* (Oxford University Press, 2000)

Harris, Frank, *Oscar Wilde His Life and Confessions* (New York: published by the author, 1916)

Healy, T. M., *Letters and Leaders of My Day* (London: Thornton, Butterworth, 1928)

Holland, Vyvyan, *Son of Oscar Wilde* (London: Rupert Hart-Davis, 1954)

Hyde, H. Montgomery, *The Trials of Oscar Wilde* (London: William Hodge, 1948)

―――― *Carson* (London: Heinemann, 1953)

―――― *The Cleveland Street Scandal* (London: W. H. Allen, 1976)

―――― *Lord Alfred Douglas* (London: Methuen, 1984)

Lemonnier, Léon, *La Vie d'Oscar Wilde* (Paris: Nouvelle Revue Critique, 1931)

Mallon, Thomas, *In Fact: Essays on Writers and Writing* (New York: Pantheon Books, 2001)

Marjoribanks, Edward and Ian Colvin, *Life of Lord Carson*, 3 vols (London: Gollancz, 1932–6)

Mason, Stuart [pseud. of Christopher Millard], *The Priest and the Acolyte* (London: Lotus Press, 1907)

―――― *Oscar Wilde: Three Times Tried* (London: Ferrestone Press, 1912)

―――― *Oscar Wilde: Art and Morality*, second enlarged edition (London: Frank Palmer, 1912)

―――― *Bibliography of Oscar Wilde* (London: T. Werner Laurie, 1914)

Murray, Douglas, *Bosie* (London: Hodder & Stoughton, 2000)

Playfair, I. [pseud. J. H. Wilson], *Gentle Criticisms on British Justice* (Newcastle upon Tyne: privately printed, 1895)

Public Record Office, *Oscar Wilde: Trial and Punishment 1895–97* (London: PRO Publications, 1997)

Queensberry, Marquess of and Percy Colson, *Oscar Wilde and the Black Douglas*, (London: Hutchinson, 1949)

Raffalovich, Marc-André, *Uranisme et Unisexualité* (Lyons and Paris: Storck et Masson, 1896)

Roberts, Brian, *The Mad Bad Line* (London: Hamish Hamilton, 1981)

Schroeder, Horst, *Additions and Corrections to Richard Ellmann's Oscar Wilde* (Braunschweig: privately printed, 2002)

Sitwell, Osbert, *Noble Essences* (London: Macmillan, 1950)

Smith, Derek with Sir Edward Clarke *The Life of Sir Edward Clarke* (London: Thornton, Butterworth, 1939)

Stokes, John *Oscar Wilde: Myths, Miracles, and Imitations* (Cambridge University Press, 1996)

The Spirit Lamp (Oxford: James Thornton, 1892–3)

Trevor-Roper, Hugh, *A Hidden Life* (London: Macmillan, 1976)

Wilde, Oscar, *The Letters of Oscar Wilde*, edited by Rupert Hart-Davis (London: Rupert Hart-Davis, 1962)

―――― *The Picture of Dorian Gray*, edited by Donald Lawler (New York: Norton Critical Editions, 1988)

―――― *Complete Works*, Centenary Edition (London and Glasgow: HarperCollins, 2000)

―――― *The Complete Letters of Oscar Wilde*, edited by Rupert Hart-Davis and Merlin Holland (London: Fourth Estate, 2000)

Newspapers with Accounts of the Trial

LONDON
Le Courier de Londres
Daily Chronicle
Daily Graphic
Daily News
Daily Telegraph
Echo
Evening News
Evening Standard
Globe
Illustrated Police Budget
Illustrated Police News
London Figaro
Morning
Morning Leader
Morning Post
News of the World
Observer
Pall Mall Gazette
People
Reynolds Newspaper
St James's Gazette
Standard
Star
Sun
Sunday Times
The Times
Weekly Dispatch
Westminster Gazette

PARIS
L'Écho de Paris
Le Figaro
Galignani's Messenger
Le Gaulois
Le Journal
Le Journal des débats
La Lanterne
La Plume
Le Temps
NEW YORK
Evening Post
Independent
New York Herald
New York Times
New York Tribune
The World

Principal Manuscript Sources Consulted

British Library, London: the transcribed verbatim shorthand reports of the magistrates' court proceedings for 9 March 1895 and of the Central Criminal Court (Old Bailey) proceedings for 3, 4 and 5 April 1895, as well as various documents and letters used at the trial.

Public Record Office, Kew: the official legal records of the case – indictments, pleas, jury books and depositions, as well as interdepartmental files on the case, and Wilde's bankruptcy files.

William Andrews Clark Memorial Library, Los Angeles: many letters to Wilde and correspondence between members of Wilde's circle relevant to the trial and the events leading up to it.

The Hyde Collection, New Jersey: a large part of the Lord Alfred Douglas archive and other Queensberry papers, especially Douglas's letters to his brother Percy.

New York Public Library, New York: part of the MS and the TS of *The Importance of Being Earnest*.

Magdalen College, Oxford: the working papers of Harford Montgomery Hyde for his biographies of Wilde and Douglas, and a part of the Lord Alfred Douglas archive including Sybil Queensberry's letters to her son.

Harry Ransom Humanities Research Center, Austin, Texas: the working papers of Rupert Croft-Cooke and those of Harford Montgomery Hyde for his 1948 edition of the trials, as well as a part of the John Lane–Bodley Head archive; also the voluminous diaries of the early homosexual campaigner George Ives (1867–1950).

Pierpont Morgan Library, New York: the complete MS of *The Picture of Dorian Gray* in its 1890 *Lippincott's Magazine* form.

Private Collection: the witness depositions taken down by Charles Russell and his agents in preparing the case for the defence and filing the plea of justification.

ACKNOWLEDGEMENTS

Background research into this first-ever publication of the unabridged proceedings of Oscar Wilde's libel action has taken me down some curious Victorian byways, from railways through restaurants to rent boys. However, it would have been impossible to complete it without the generous help of those whose specialised knowledge, especially of the 1890s, has proved invaluable.

Terry Rogers, archivist at Marlborough School, provided details of Alfred Taylor's schooldays; Martin Williams, archivist at Hurstpierpoint College, gave me much useful material on Sydney Mavor's career there as a teacher; Robin Darwall-Smith, archivist at Magdalen College, Oxford, alerted me to the existence of letters in H. Montgomery Hyde's papers which enabled me to trace the later activities of some of the young men involved in the trial; Timothy d'Arch Smith's unrivalled knowledge of the Victorian homosexual sub-culture has been especially helpful; Neil McKenna shared his research into Wilde's 'feasting with panthers' and provided some important background details for the footnotes; Peter Vernier's searching of the Census records saved me much valuable time; Sally Brown facilitated access to the trial transcript and with the practised eye of manuscript curator interpreted some of its less legible squiggles; Philip Atkins at the Railway Museum had near-instant answers to questions which might otherwise have taken days to research, as did the most efficient staff at the Worthing Reference Library on precise details of the town and its inhabitants when Wilde stayed there in 1894; Caspar Wintermans's knowledge of Lord Alfred Douglas's life is second to none and my ruthless exploitation of it has merely strengthened a close friendship; Barbara Hewson, lawyer by profession, Wildean by inclination, allowed me what seemed limitless access to her expertise and clarified many legal and procedural points in the text. I am indebted also to Gabriel Austin, Charlotte Gere, Mark Lasner, Ulick O'Connor,

Horst Schroeder and Charles Tattersall, as well as to Guy Holborn at Lincoln's Inn Library and Carole Read at the Old Bailey for their help and advice. John Rubinstein and John Stratford, Lord Alfred Douglas's literary executors kindly granted me permission to use the extract from Douglas's poem 'Two Loves' as well as the text of his 'illegible' postcard to his father. June Radford and Anthony Barrington-Brown most generously provided a previously unpublished photograph of their great uncle, Sydney Mavor. Marion Rea's sharp eye for inconsistencies as, quick-fingered through the night, she transcribed from my tapes, was an unexpected bonus. My sincere thanks go to them all.

I have dedicated this volume to a man who has contributed more than anyone to my understanding of my grandfather's social and sexual behaviour. For some people Wilde's sexuality is distasteful; for others it is a stick with which to beat right-wing homophobia; for John Thomas, a curator of rare books at the University of Texas, it merely adds to the richness of Wilde's complex character, another avenue down which to explore his contribution to the *fin de siècle*. He made me aware that what was Wilde's public disgrace has become our privileged insight into a private and vital part of his life. If the deadlines for publishing this trial transcript been twice as long, and had John and I not been some six thousand miles apart, I should have been proud to share the title page with him. As it is, I take this opportunity to express my profound thanks to him for his tireless research into the manuscript collections of the Harry Ransom Center at Austin on my behalf, his comparative analysis of the printed sources of the trial and above all for a valuable friendship.

INDEX

Where there is a footnote giving a person's main particulars it will be found
on the first page reference after that person's name.

W=Wilde; Q=Queensberry; AD=Alfred Douglas; C=Carson.